The Master Musicians Series

BIZET

Series edited by Stanley Sadie

VOLUMES IN THE MASTER MUSICIANS SERIES

Bach *E. & S. Grew*
Bartók *Lajos Lesznai*
Beethoven *Marion M. Scott*
Bellini *Leslie Orrey*
Berlioz *J. H. Elliot*
Bizet *Winton Dean*
Brahms *Peter Latham*
Bruckner *Derek Watson*
Chopin *Arthur Hedley*
Debussy *Edward Lockspeiser*
Delius *Alan Jefferson*
Dvořák *Alec Robertson*
Elgar *Ian Parrott*
Franck *Laurence Davies*
Grieg *John Horton*
Handel *Percy M. Young*
Haydn *Rosemary Hughes*
Mahler *Michael Kennedy*
Mendelssohn *Philip Radcliffe*
Monteverdi *Denis Arnold*
Mozart *Eric Blom*
Mussorgsky *M. D. Calvocoressi*
Purcell *Sir Jack Westrup*
Rakhmaninov *Geoffrey Norris*
Ravel *Roger Nichols*
Schoenberg *Malcolm MacDonald*
Schubert *Arthur Hutchings*
Schumann *Joan Chissell*
Sibelius *Robert Layton*
Smetana *John Clapham*
Richard Strauss *Michael Kennedy*
Stravinsky *Francis Routh*
Tchaikovsky *Edward Garden*
Vaughan Williams *James Day*
Verdi *Dyneley Hussey*
Vivaldi *Michael Talbot*
Wagner *Robert L. Jacobs*

IN PREPARATION

Britten *Michael Kennedy*
Liszt *Derek Watson*
Prokofiev *Rita McAllister*
Rameau *Neal Zaslaw*
Puccini *Mosco Carner*
Shostakovich *Geoffrey Norris*

THE MASTER MUSICIANS SERIES

BIZET

by

Winton Dean

With eight pages of plates
and music examples in the text

J. M. DENT & SONS LTD
London, Melbourne and Toronto

Printed in Great Britain
by
Biddles Ltd · Guildford · Surrey
and bound at the
Aldine Press · Letchworth · Herts
for
J. M. DENT & SONS LTD
Aldine House · Albemarle Street · London

First published 1948
Revised 1965, 1975
Paperback edition 1977
Last reprinted 1978

Hardback ISBN: 0 460 03163 5
Paperback ISBN: 0 460 02170 2

TO

PHILIP RADCLIFFE

In the hope that I have not already killed his enthusiasm for Bizet

PREFACE TO THE THIRD EDITION

WHEN the first edition of this book appeared in 1948, no adequate biography of Bizet and no thorough study of his music existed. There was no catalogue even of his published works. He was not considered a worthy subject for research or a composer of much consequence. Even *Carmen* was regarded as something of a fluke. In France, Pigot's semi-official life, discreet, uncritical, and suppressing many important facts, had been followed by a series of superficial, inaccurate and generally hostile studies. Historians still cited the tendentious volume issued under the name of H. Gauthier-Villars. We now know, from Bernard Gavoty's preface to Émile Vuillermoz's *Gabriel Fauré* (Paris, 1960), that Colette's feckless husband, for reasons of his own, put his name to Vuillermoz's work. It is difficult to decide which of the two emerges from this episode with the greater discredit.

While I was able to fill gaps and correct errors, chiefly by examining autograph manuscripts, many of them of unpublished works, the biographical situation was subsequently transformed by the appearance in 1958 of Mina Curtiss's *Bizet and his World*, based on her discovery of the Halévy-Bizet papers and on much additional research. This material threw a new and unexpected light on Bizet's character and many circumstances of his life. My second edition, published outside the Master Musicians series in 1965, had as a result to be largely rewritten. After it went to press a new score of *Carmen*, edited by Fritz Oeser, was published in Bärenreiter's Alkor Edition. Unfortunately, despite the best intentions and the use of previously unknown material, this proved to be a musicological blunder of the first magnitude; instead of clarifying the text, it hopelessly corrupted it. I have gone into this fully elsewhere; but it has been necessary to recast my chapter on *Carmen* and to issue warnings, since the Oeser edition, by performances in several countries, has acquired a currency that in the long run can only injure Bizet's reputation.

Preface

A few further facts have come to light, some of which affect the chronology of Bizet's work. Recently a number of musical autographs and more than a hundred letters, formerly in the collection of Captain Rudolf Nydahl, passed into the possession of the Stiftelsen Musikkulturens Främjande, Stockholm. This foundation in 1972 issued a catalogue compiled by the curator, Mr Gunnar Holst, to whom I am indebted for his patient courtesy in answering questions and supplying photographs. In the last few years several of Bizet's works have been published for the first time; but the major operas are still available only in untrustworthy texts, and there has been no sign of what is most urgently required, a complete scholarly edition of the music of one of France's most gifted composers.

I am happy to acknowledge once more the debt I owe to the work and assistance of others, especially Mrs Mina Curtiss, Mr Philip Radcliffe and M. Michel Poupet, who has continued to unearth fresh nuggets of information from Paris newspapers and archives.

W. D.

1974.

Note on the 1978 reprint

I have incorporated, chiefly in Appendix B, a few corrections and modifications, most of them suggested by M. Michel Poupet and Miss Lesley Wright, to whom I am grateful. One work has been removed from the canon and five added. The opera on a Caucasian subject (pp. 79–80) was never planned by Bizet. Of the additions the most interesting is a third piano piece belonging to the Verlaine set (p. 149). The others, all very early and of little consequence, are the fragmentary opening of a cantata for solo voice (*c.* 1850) and three keyboard pieces published as supplements to the *Magasin des Familles* about 1852: *Méditation religieuse* for organ, harmonium or piano, *Romance sans paroles* and *Casilda, polka-mazurka* for piano. All three are in C major; the *Romance sans paroles* is distinct from No. 46 (p. 264). The Yorloff motive in *Ivan IV* (p. 168) first occurs in fragmentary form at Yorloff's entry in Act II, in a passage suppressed by Busser. Marie's Act I air (p. 169), though uncancelled in the autograph, appears to have been rejected by Bizet in favour of the duet for Marie and the Young Bulgarian, which does not feature in the original pagination.

W. D.

CONTENTS

ILLUSTRATIONS

Between pages 118 and 119

CHAPTER I

CHILDHOOD AND TRAINING (1838–57)

On 25th October 1838, at 26 Rue de la Tour d'Auvergne,[1] Paris, a son was born to the wife of one Adolphe Amand [*sic*] Bizet, a worthy but humble musician, and registered under the formidable designation Alexandre César Léopold. It seems that the operative name was intended to be César, for one of his Conservatoire compositions is signed 'César Georges Bizet, known as Potin' (Gossip).[2] But the imperial *praenomen* was too much for the child's godfather, who at once called him Georges; as Georges he was baptized on 16th March 1840 at the church of Notre-Dame-de-Lorette; and as Georges he was always known, first to his family and friends and later to the world. His godparents were Philippe Louis Brulley de la Brunière and Hippolyte Sidonie Daspres. The Rue de la Tour d'Auvergne runs almost due east and west about half way between the Gares de l'Est and Saint-Lazare on the southern slopes of Montmartre. By 1840 the family had moved two doors along to No. 22, and Bizet continued to live in the district for the whole of his Paris life.

Adolphe Bizet (born 16th August 1810, died 20th December 1886), who like Schubert's father survived his famous son by some years, came of artisan stock in Rouen. He was the posthumous son of a linen-weaver presumed killed in the Napoleonic wars. In October 1837 he was working in Paris as a hairdresser and wig-maker, but by the time of his marriage on 26th December that year he had become a teacher of singing. He seems to have been an industrious man without any notable talent. His wife's family, who disapproved of her marriage to a man without money or prospects, thought more of his character than of his intelligence and refused to dignify him with the

[1] Not the existing house, which dates from about 1850, but its predecessor, 'une maisonnette avec jardin', built towards the end of the eighteenth century.

[2] The autographs of his entries for the Conservatoire fugue competitions in 1854–5 are signed 'A. C. L. Georges Bizet'.

title of artist. His favourite pupil, Hector Gruyer, whose stage name was Guardi, was cast to create the part of Faust in Gounod's opera, but, as Gounod tells us, 'despite a charming voice and a very agreeable presence he could not sustain the burden of this important role', and had to be replaced.[1] This was a great blow to the Bizets, and caused a temporary estrangement between Georges and Gounod. Adolphe Bizet also composed on a small scale: a bundle of his manuscripts, mostly dedicated to his son and Gruyer, is at the Bibliothèque Nationale. They include a cantata *Imogine*, a string Quartet (dated 1st February 1853), songs, fugues, piano works and two fantasies for military band on themes from Halévy's *La Reine de Chypre*. At least one of his songs was published in 1854. In his later years he developed a passion for gardening, and meal-time conversation at his house at Le Vésinet was divided between music and vegetables. A photograph shows him as a sturdy old man with a white spade-shaped beard.

Bizet's mother (born 22nd December 1815, died 8th September 1861) was Aimée Marie Louise Léopoldine Joséphine Delsarte (the name is sometimes spelt del Sarte, and even Delzart, in which form it appears in the church register at Georges's baptism), and came of a musical family with a strong vein of eccentricity. Her father, Nicolas Delsarte, combined an unsuccessful career as a lawyer and later as wine merchant and café proprietor at Solesmes and Cambrai with a bent for scientific experiment. His inventions included an improved steam-engine and a miner's lamp, but his defective business sense impoverished his family, and his wife and four children left him. The eldest of these, François Alexandre Nicolas Chéri Delsarte (1811–71), moved to Paris, where he became a well-known teacher of singing with many successful and fashionable pupils, one of whom in 1859 published a treatise on his method. He studied physiology, anatomy and psychology, and applied their principles to his work. He abandoned a job at the Théâtre des Variétés to become a Saint-Simonian and later studied for the Church. At his concerts he was

[1] He sang the part only four times in the middle of the run, having missed the earlier performances through illness. He subsequently appeared in Italian opera-houses and died at an advanced age, a chevalier of the Legion of Honour, in January 1908.

instrumental in reviving the works of Lully, Rameau and Gluck, and he edited a volume, *Les Archives du chant*, in so scrupulous a manner that he not only refused to put a personal gloss on this old music but even reproduced misprints (or what the nineteenth century took to be misprints) in the original editions. He finally abjured the world and gave himself up to speculation on philosophy and aesthetics. Bizet received lessons from his uncle (who presented him with a page purloined from the autograph score of Hérold's opera *Le Pré aux clercs*) and also from his aunt, a cultivated woman and protégée of Cherubini; but he does not seem to have been intimate with them. Indeed his passionate anticlericalism and equally fierce resolve to maintain financial independence may have been stimulated by the atmosphere of mysticism and cultivated poverty in which the Delsartes lived.

Aimée Bizet was herself a talented pianist, and according to Ludovic Halévy a woman of the highest intelligence. From her son's letters she emerges as a homely, affectionate person, troubled by chronic ill health and a great capacity for worrying over the welfare of her nearest and dearest. She had continually to be reassured that her son was running no needless risk in Italy. There is no truth in the statement, sometimes heard, that Bizet had Jewish blood, but a member of the Delsarte family has claimed [1] that there was a Spanish strain, deriving from a surgeon in the army of Charles V who settled in Flanders.

Georges, an only child, had the advantage of growing up in a musical home. At the age of four he learned his notes from his mother at the same time as his letters. He soon formed the habit of listening to his father's lessons through the door. When at the age of eight he was called in and given a piece to sing at sight, he astonished his father by singing it correctly without looking at the music. Thus early did he show signs of that prodigious musical memory which served him so well in later years, but in one sense served the world so ill: for he took to the grave at least one opera he had completely composed but not bothered to write out in full. From the first Adolphe Bizet intended his son to be a composer.

[1] *Revue de Musicologie,* November 1938.

Perhaps through having made a late start himself, he was determined to lose no time, and now set about teaching him the piano and the rudiments of harmony. This enthusiasm for long-term planning nearly miscarried, for Georges was at first more attracted to literature than to music, and his parents had to hide his books to prevent his reading when he should have been working at his music. Bizet never lost his love of literature and at his death left a large and varied library.[1] The notion fostered by certain French critics that he had no general culture outside music is ludicrously wide of the mark. He had considerable feeling for the visual arts and was one of the liveliest letter-writers among leading composers. His friends included Alexandre Dumas *fils*, Edmond About and the painter Eugène Isabey.

At the age of nine he had learned all his father could impart, which was doubtless little enough. Steps were then taken to send him to the Conservatoire. He was not old enough to enter, but, hoping for a special dispensation in view of his precocity, Adolphe Bizet enlisted the support of a friend at the Opéra, and together they went to see Meifred, a famous horn virtuoso and a member of the Committee of Studies at the Conservatoire. An interview was arranged and began inauspiciously. Meifred was contemptuous: 'Your child is very young.' 'True,' replied the proud father, 'but if he is small in stature he is big in knowledge.' 'Really? And what can he do?' 'Sit down at the piano, strike some chords, and he will name them without a mistake.' Meifred did as suggested, and the boy, with his back to the piano, not only named the most recondite chords that Meifred could play, but elaborated in detail all their functions. Meifred was enthusiastic: 'You, my boy—you will go straight to the Institut!' The Conservatoire classes were already full; so, until a regular place was available, he was sent to Marmontel's piano class on the introduction of his uncle Delsarte. At this time he was able to play Mozart's piano sonatas with taste and without affectation. On 9th October 1848, just before the completion of his tenth year, he was officially admitted to the Conservatoire in the splendour of his full Christian names.

[1] It has since been dispersed; *see* Appendix G, p. 292.

Precocity

Something must be said on the question of his precocity. The Meifred anecdote, of course, proves nothing beyond a good memory and a quick ear; it implies no artistic ability (who but a fool would look for this in a boy of nine?). Adolphe Bizet's not unnatural pride, together with the over-adulatory tone of Bizet's first biographer, Charles Pigot, provoked some later French writers to dismiss his precocity as a legend and allow him nothing but a textbook competence, an attitude easily extended to a depreciation of his whole career. These critics pointed to the lack of evidence behind the legend; they failed to observe the equal lack of evidence against it, and were duly confounded by the discovery of the Symphony in C major, written at the age of barely seventeen, which reveals not only sure technical ability but signs of a natural genius perhaps never exceeded by a composer of Bizet's years, Mozart, Schubert and Mendelssohn not excepted. There can be no doubt that Bizet as a child showed quite exceptional gifts, both of assimilation and, as time went on, of creation also. His teachers were aware of this: when he was sixteen Halévy said of him: 'There is a great musician.' Marmontel was struck by the individuality of his views and preferences, which he sensibly encouraged, as well as by his perseverance. He described him in youth as fair and pink, with a plump but alert face. As he grew up his features strengthened and took on that appearance of energy and sincerity, not untouched by irony, that can be seen in his portraits. He was very short-sighted and habitually wore spectacles. His most prominent feature was a mass of fair curly hair, later supplemented by an ample beard.

Six months after his admission Bizet won the first prize for solfeggio. He was then introduced to Zimmerman, at the latter's request. Pierre Joseph Guillaume Zimmerman was an old man and had recently retired from his post as chief professor of the piano; but he loved teaching and still took private pupils for composition. He was so impressed by Bizet that he offered to teach him counterpoint and fugue.[1] Zimmerman had been a pupil of Cherubini, who was regarded as the leading contrapuntist of his period and, by Beethoven

[1] This admiration was not shared by his family, who 'were always reproaching him for wasting his time on a little idiot who would never amount to anything' (Bizet to Hector Gruyer, 31st December 1858).

among others, as one of its greatest composers. It was this tradition that young Bizet imbibed. When Zimmerman was ill, which was often, his place was taken by Charles Gounod, who in June 1852 became his son-in-law by marrying his daughter Anna. Gounod took an immediate liking to the boy, who in return conceived an admiration for Gounod, both as man and artist, which, though modified in later years, left a permanent mark on his style. This influence was not altogether healthy. Gounod's character was a strange mixture; drawn with equal passion to the Church and the theatre, he combined an almost feminine charm with extreme emotionalism and instability. He was subject to frequent nervous breakdowns. For two years before the 1848 Revolution he had called himself an abbé and signed his name with a cross; in 1851 the actor Edmond Got described him as a philandering monk, exuberant and shamelessly pushing, with a propensity for kissing everyone he met of either sex on the slightest provocation. Many references to him in Bizet's correspondence, suppressed until recently, reveal an acute mixture of attraction and repulsion. Of Gounod's early kindness there is no doubt. Among other things he obtained for Bizet the chance to earn money by transcribing many of his works, beginning with the choruses of *Ulysse* (1852), the vocal score of *La Nonne sanglante* and a piano duet arrangement of his first Symphony (both 1855). The last was the model of Bizet's own Symphony in the same year.

In 1851, the first time he competed, Bizet won the second prize in Marmontel's piano class; in the following year he shared the first prize with one Savary. Of his skill as a pianist there were no two opinions. Marmontel, himself a brilliant performer and a very successful trainer of others, paid ample tribute to his gifts; so did Berlioz, Liszt and indeed everyone who heard him. In his Conservatoire days he had not developed that delicacy and mellow touch that characterized his playing later, but he was already a brilliant virtuoso. At all times he showed extraordinary skill at playing from full scores. From Marmontel he passed to Benoist's organ class. Benoist,[1] according to Saint-Saëns, was a very ordinary organist but an

[1] He was organ professor at the Conservatoire for more than half a century. Both he and Marmontel outlived Bizet.

admirable teacher and was much loved by his pupils. He was employed by the Opéra for writing ballets, which he used to score in his class while his pupils played the organ (it is said that this in no way interfered with his teaching), and for putting life into the scoring of other people's works: his clarinet parts to Sacchini's *Œedipe à Colone* earned warm praise from Berlioz for the Italian composer. Again Bizet was quick to learn: in 1854 he won second prizes for organ and fugue, in the following year first prizes for both.

Meanwhile on Zimmerman's death in 1853 he had entered Halévy's composition class. Jacques François Fromental Élie Halévy was an important figure in French music and in Bizet's life. A Jew (his real name was Lévy, but like Meyerbeer and Reyer he preferred the fashionable course of lengthening it), he was a prolific composer of operas in various styles. As a composer he had (like his master Cherubini) little lyrical gift, but on occasion a powerful sense of the stage, and it is not surprising that in his serious operas he fell more and more under the influence of Meyerbeer. As a teacher he seems to have been indulgent to a fault. He was often so absorbed in his work that he forgot to turn up for his classes, when his pupils took it upon themselves to give each other instruction far less indulgent than their master's. As a man he was indolent, good-natured and charming; hence he was continually bothered by self-seekers, impossible tenors and would-be artists of every description. It was doubtless this pliancy that led Bizet to describe him, in a letter to his mother from Rome, as 'such a slippery gentleman that you don't know how to handle him'. His brother, Léon Halévy, archaeologist and dramatist, and Léon's better-known son Ludovic, were both among Bizet's librettists, and in later years he was to enter more closely into the family circle by marrying Fromental Halévy's daughter. His father-in-law's influence on his musical style cannot be compared with that of Gounod, a much more individual composer; but Halévy's intellectual curiosity and wide range of interests may have left their mark on his mind.

A number of Bizet's student compositions survive in manuscript at the Bibliothèque Nationale. These consist mostly of piano works and fragments of cantatas set as exercises for earlier Prix de Rome competitions. The earliest, two Songs without Words for soprano voices, date from the boy's twelfth year. Rather more ambitious efforts followed: *Grande Valse de Concert* (Op. 1), a brilliant piece in the superficial manner of contemporary *salon* music with one theme that remotely anticipates the trio of the Minuet in *L'Arlésienne*, and *Premier Nocturne en fa majeur* (Op. 2), both for piano, and dating from September 1854;[1] *Première Ouverture pour orchestre*, more solidly constructed and showing strong Italian influence; and, in 1855, *Première Symphonie*. This last is the delightful work in C major, first performed under Weingartner in 1935. We know nothing of the circumstances of its composition, except that it was begun on 29th October 1855, four days after his seventeenth birthday, and finished before the end of the following month: Bizet was already an expeditious worker. Octave Séré's statement, taken from Jules Martin's *Nos Auteurs et compositeurs dramatiques* (Paris, 1897), that a one-act operetta by Bizet called *La Prêtresse* with libretto by Philippe Gille was produced at Baden in 1854 presents a puzzle. No evidence can be found for such a performance. Yet Bizet did at some time write (or begin) a work with this title: the voice part of a single air, a cavatina for soprano in G flat, exists in his autograph.

Exactly a month before Bizet began his Symphony, Halévy recommended him to the director of the Opéra-Comique as 'a young composer, pianist and accompanist'. Perhaps he served the Opéra-Comique in some humble capacity at this time (if so, it is his first known connection with the theatre). At any rate, he was already marked out for future success. As early as 1853 Halévy had declared him fit to compete for the Prix de Rome, the highest honour that France could confer on her young artists. But Bizet prudently abstained till 1856. The principal set piece for the Prix de Rome was a cantata on some edifying subject drawn from the Bible, ancient history or the age of chivalry (a fugue and a short chorus with piano accompaniment were also required). The text for 1856 was *David*, by Mlle de Montréal, who wrote under the pseudonym Gaston d'Albano. Gounod, taking a very fatherly tone, advised Bizet not to be in too much of a hurry, not to seize the first idea that came into his head under the

[1] Some of these early unpublished works, and others of later date, were performed at a meeting of the Société Française de Musicologie on 27th October 1938, in honour of the centenary of Bizet's birth.

impression that it would be the only one, to be self-critical and not to work at night, since night work usually had to be done over again in the morning. The judges deliberated for a long time. Eventually they decided to give no first prize, but awarded Bizet a second prize, which did not entitle him to the Rome subsidy. It did, however, provide him with free tickets for the Paris lyric theatres. He may have been kept back because of his youth (the same fate would have befallen Paladilhe a few years later, had not Berlioz pointed out with tart logic that the prize was given for talent, not age).

Between his first and second attempts at the Prix de Rome Bizet wrote his first stage work.[1] Offenbach, in whom the fashionable Paris of the Second Empire already liked to see its glittering reflection, offered a prize (1,200 francs and a gold medal worth another 300) for a one-act operetta, the winning work to be produced at the Bouffes-Parisiens theatre. His declared object, announced in *Le Figaro* of 17th July 1856 and prefaced by a none too accurate excursion into musical history, was to restore *opéra-comique* to its pristine French gaiety and elegance. More probably he wished to make an honest woman of operetta; to which end he acquired a formidable jury headed by Auber, Halévy, Scribe and Gounod. The libretto was *Le Docteur Miracle* by Léon Battu and Ludovic Halévy; the latter was one day to collaborate with Bizet in a work of very different calibre. Bizet, perhaps glad of a change from fugues and cantatas, wrote his score very rapidly, and the prize (for which there were seventy-eight[2] candidates) was divided between him and Charles Lecocq, his colleague in Halévy's class but his senior by several years. Lecocq, whose name appears in the printed libretto as 'Jules Lecoq', continued in the same vein, and spent the rest of his long life turning out a stream of operettas, of which only one, *La Fille de Madame Angot*, achieved lasting popularity.

It was considered impossible or inadvisable to mount both operettas

[1] Not counting the very early one-act *opéra-comique*, *La Maison du docteur*, probably written for private performance among his colleagues at the Conservatoire.

[2] Reduced by a preliminary contest to twelve, of whom six were given the libretto. Their entries had to be in by 15th December 1856.

in the same programme, and so they were produced (with the same cast) on succeeding nights; Lecocq's on 8th April 1857, Bizet's on the 9th. The order was decided by lot after Lecocq had protested against Bizet taking priority. Each work was played eleven times. The affair received little attention, which is not surprising: serious musicians regarded operetta as a very debased form. Bizet's 'omelette quartet', however, was praised (it was encored on the first night), and other promises of talent were detected here and there. Jouvin in *Le Figaro* (16th April) found signs of learning but sought in vain for melody; this absurd criticism was to become the standard reaction of much of the Paris press to all Bizet's music. Many years later Lecocq, who felt slighted at having to share the prize, wrote a highly disingenuous account of the episode, containing faint praise of Bizet's music ('not bad, but rather heavy') and feline aspersions on Halévy, whom he accused of improperly influencing the jury in Bizet's favour, and Offenbach.[1]

Bizet was now invited to Offenbach's popular Friday night parties, where he once accompanied a parody of *Il Trovatore*, written by Edmond About, at a fancy-dress ball. He also made the acquaintance of Rossini. The old man, described at this time by Paladilhe's father as 'no more than a noble ruin in whom intellectual life seems almost extinct', received Bizet kindly, presented him with a signed photograph, and on his departure for Rome gave him cordial letters of introduction to the librettist Felice Romani and Francesco Florimo, librarian of the Naples Conservatory.

Two prizes were offered by the Prix de Rome committee for 1857. The winner, the laureate of the year, would get the full five years' pension; the runner-up, to whom would go the previous year's prize, would have only the four years' pension that remained, a nice economy being thus exercised in favour of the State. The cantata set was *Clovis et Clotilde* by one Amédée Burion; it concerns the Frankish King Clovis's conversion to Christianity at the hands of his wife and father-in-law. The text so charmed Gounod that he told

[1] *Le Docteur Miracle* nearly achieved the distinction of being the first work by Bizet to be heard in London. Both operettas were announced during Offenbach's season at the St James's Theatre in May and June 1857 but not performed.

Bizet he would like to have entered himself. Again the judges found difficulty in making their award. On 3rd July the jury, drawn from the musical section of the Académie des Beaux-Arts, among whom Berlioz figured for the first time, after several ballots gave the first prize to Charles Colin (later oboe professor at the Conservatoire; died 1881), the second to an obscure pupil of Carafa;[1] Bizet was unplaced. Next day the full Academy on the first ballot awarded Bizet the first prize, Colin the second.

Thanks to the suffrage of painters, sculptors and architects Bizet had reached his first major goal, having experienced scarcely a check. After a brilliant Conservatoire career he had won the highest academic honour open to a young musician. But it was no more than the first step. It entitled him to few advantages after his five years' pension was over; it was of little help, as many former winners had found to their cost, in getting his works performed; still less did it guarantee a favourable reception from the public. As Gounod wrote in his letter of congratulation (5th July 1857): 'Now your real artistic life is going to begin—a serious and severe life.' No doubt at the time Bizet enjoyed his triumph to the full and thought little of future obstacles. His cantata was performed (for the first and last time) at the Institut on 3rd October, in accordance with long-hallowed tradition. It was a festive occasion, with a specially invited audience of garlanded academicians, relatives and friends. The work had a great success and was long and loudly applauded. The auguries for the future were good.

[1] *See* p. 18.

CHAPTER II

ROME (1857–60)

THE winners of the various Prix de Rome (there were prizes for painting, sculpture, architecture and engraving as well as music) received a pension from the State for five years. In return for this they had to submit a work or works every year, on which the relevant section of the Académie des Beaux-Arts in Paris made a report—or rather two reports, one for publication and another, of a more confidential nature, that was sent to the artist personally. These works submitted were known as *envois*. There were certain regulations as to their nature: the first *envoi* of a musician, for instance, had to be a mass or other sacred work on a large scale. Other regulations, which differed at various periods, governed the residence of the pensioners. In Bizet's time the painters, sculptors and engravers spent the full five years in Rome, the architects three years in Rome and two in Athens, and the musicians two in Rome, one in Germany and two in Paris. In most respects these stipulations seem reasonable enough; but during the middle and later years of the last century there was great debate about the value to a musician of two years in Rome. When the prize was opened to musicians in 1805 the rule could be justified: French music was at a transitional stage and Italy still retained some of her ascendancy of the previous centuries. But by 1850 French musicians regarded Italy (not without some reason) as musically decadent and calculated to debase rather than enhance an artist. At that time it was scarcely possible to hear the German classics without going to Germany, and there was something to be said for spending more than a year in that country. Gounod, who won the prize in 1839, spent well over a year there. On the other hand Italy did offer opportunities, by no means negligible to provincial young Frenchmen, of coming in contact with a wider culture. If Rome's present was artistically inglorious, there was still her past, and even to a musician art should mean something more than minims and crotchets. This point was strongly argued by Gounod in an article written in 1882 replying to the detractors of the French Academy at Rome; and Bizet, with his temperamental love (physical and spiritual) of the Mediterranean sun, and his insistence on the need of literary and wide artistic culture in a musician, wholeheartedly agreed with him.[1] But perhaps the greatest value of all to a young artist lay in the opportunities it gave him to find himself in beautiful and congenial surroundings and free from the preoccupation of earning his daily bread. To all too many of them, Bizet included, it was the first and last such opportunity that life afforded.

The French Academy in Rome was housed in the Villa Medici. This noble palace, built in 1540 for Cardinal Ricci and reconstructed with the assistance of Michelangelo by Cardinal Alessandro de' Medici (later Pope Leo XI), had been acquired by France in 1803. Standing amid its own gardens on Monte Pincio, it commands a magnificent view over Rome, with the Sabine mountains in the distance. Here the pensioners lived a communal life under a director, usually a distinguished artist, appointed for a six-year period by the French State. When Gounod went out the director had been the painter Ingres, who was succeeded after a year by another painter, Victor Schnetz. Schnetz was again in office when Bizet arrived, and no doubt was able to smooth his path. A gruff, genial and conspicuously hirsute man, he was deservedly popular with the students. He held the post for three periods, eighteen years in all (1840–6, 1852–64).

Bizet and his four fellow pensioners left Paris on 21st December 1857 and travelled by Lyons, Vienne, Valence, Orange, Avignon, Nîmes, Arles, Marseilles, Toulon, Nice, Genoa, Leghorn, Pisa, Lucca and Florence. This was probably his first journey of more than a few miles, and his letters are full of delighted comments. In view of later circumstances his impressions of the Rhône valley are interesting (except for a hurried and anxious return journey he never visited it again). It was 'magnificent country', the weather was like spring, as hot and sunny as Paris in July. The ancient buildings, the mountain scenery, above all the sea, made a tremendous impression: 'The

[1] 'I sincerely pity those who have not won the prize, or those who get it before attaining the necessary maturity.'—Letter of 17th August 1860.

spectacle of nature is something so unknown to me that I find it impossible to analyse my impressions. . . . An artist ought to profit by it, be he painter or musician, sculptor or architect.' Bizet and his companions were indefatigable tourists: no climb was too rough for them if it promised a fine view or interesting ruins. Within a week he had grown noticeably thinner and worn out two pairs of shoes: he is careful to point out to his parents that the mountains are made of rock, not of clay 'like our bourgeois Montmartre'. At Toulon they went round the harbour in a boat and looked over two battleships.

Early in the New Year they reached Italy, and Bizet was thankful for the Italian lessons he had taken in Paris; he was the only one who had a smattering of the language. This was fortunate, for he had from the first been appointed treasurer of the party, and some care had to be taken if the treasure was not to disappear. Despite the joy of picking roses and oranges at the roadside, his first impressions of Italy, like Gounod's eighteen years before, were not very favourable. He admired the scenery, especially the *corniche* road between Nice and Genoa, but was disgusted with much of the architecture—'churches painted like monuments in cardboard'—and with the people, who seemed to be all priests and beggars (and Bizet found himself making less and less distinction between the two). 'The Piedmontese have several ways of begging—humbly by day, and with a blunderbuss by night.' The travellers were in Florence by 12th January, and Bizet went to see Verdi's *I Lombardi*, but found the performance very bad. The Tuscans too showed a remarkable propensity for extracting money from travellers, and this is one of his complaints all over Italy. They stayed eight days at Florence, where Bizet's enthusiasm for the art treasures knew no bounds. He was particularly impressed by Raphael and Andrea del Sarto, a painter apparently unknown in Paris. Yet paradise as it was (*féerique* is Bizet's word), Florence had no living art whatever, not a single musician, poet or painter of talent. This again he was to find all over Italy, and he put it down to the fact that political decadence is always followed by decadence in art.

On 27th January, four days before the latest date allowed by the regulations, the party arrived in Rome, which apart from occasional journeys was to be Bizet's home for the best part of three years. He settled down at once. Within a month he was a social success: he had a triumph as a pianist at Schnetz's house, went to a masked ball dressed as a baby, dined often with the Russian ambassador, whose cuisine was reputed to be the best in Rome and far superior to that of the Villa Medici, and was up to the ears in invitations. But, he is quick to point out, he accepts few of them: 'I am not here to amuse myself.' And he set to work composing a *Te Deum* for the Rodrigues prize, worth 1,500 francs and restricted to the Rome pensioners. Here already we see two characteristic sides of the man, an easy assurance in personal relations and an intense capacity for hard work. He was not spoiled by social success; impetuous as he was, he could soon take a detached view of his actions. After mentioning his ovation as a pianist, he adds: 'It is only fair to say that there are no pianists in Italy, and if you can only play the scale of C with both hands you pass for a great artist.'

Bizet's years in Rome were probably the happiest of his life. He embraced Gounod's good advice to open his heart like a child to all that Rome offered 'in her incomparable and inexhaustible abundance' and to admire as much as possible, for 'admiration broadens the soul'. Despite his contempt for the Italians, both as a nation and as individuals, he soon came to love the city—and not its more obvious beauties alone. Every street, even the dirtiest, had its character, and he would not have it different: 'I should cry murder if a single pile of dirt were removed.' He loved the museums and art galleries, the second-hand bookshops and in particular the climate and the surrounding countryside. Living in the Villa Medici with fellow countrymen and fellow artists, at the expense of the French Government, he was having the best of two worlds. At that time the French, owing to the imperialistic tendencies of Napoleon III, were not trusted in Italy, being hailed alternately as liberators and traitors in proportion as they saved the Italians the trouble of fighting for their independence. They did not mix in society (with the exception of Schnetz, who according to Bizet was Italian at heart and had 'espoused Italian interests and customs to the extent of never washing his hands'), but they were both feared and courted. The students at the Villa Medici made themselves free of the country, untroubled by political considerations and treating the Italians as an inferior race.

Bizet enjoyed the communal life, found it so easy to work that he dreamed of one day returning to Rome to compose, revelled in the sunrises and sunsets, and made periodic excursions into the country. In the early summer of 1858 he spent a fortnight in the Alban Hills, playing on various organs and finding them all barbarous. On his return he visited the chief organ-builder in Rome, who looked surprised at his inquiries and told him that he had no organs, nor even a case or the wood to make one; but if Bizet wanted one built, let him pay in advance, and he would go and buy the necessary tools. The man had taken over his father's business ten years before, and never had occasion to build an organ; he lived by his other professions, which were those of flautist, tobacconist, cab-hirer and national guard.

Bizet's relations with his fellow pensioners caused his mother some anxiety. A few of them were jealous of his social success and his popularity with Schnetz, which was not based on artistic affinity. Schnetz was quite unmusical (in 1860 Bizet advised Paladilhe, if he had to play any music in the director's presence, to say it was Verdi, even if in fact it was Beethoven, Bach or Chopin), though he greatly enjoyed Bizet's Clapisson parody [1] when the students gave a party to celebrate his appointment as Commander of the Legion of Honour. A certain lack of tact may well have antagonized some of Bizet's colleagues, including the humourless Colin. 'I have succeeded in living very peaceably with fifteen of them,' he told his father in May; 'the other five are utterly ridiculous, as I keep telling them to their considerable irritation.' He was called an opportunist because he enjoyed society, yet expressed contempt for it. This cynical veneer was probably encouraged by About, who saw a lot of Bizet at this time and whose satirical tongue gave more pleasure to him than to the French Government. He was writing bitter articles on the priesthood for a Paris paper, and was presently recalled for imperilling international relations.

Nevertheless Bizet had a real gift for friendship. He demanded, and gave, complete frankness and loyalty. Though his temper was quick, he was equally swift to withdraw a harsh remark or unfair

[1] *See* p. 45.

judgment. The one thing he could not tolerate was deception or intrigue. Samuel David, Prix de Rome winner of 1858, whom at first he liked, earned his permanent hostility because he ran with the hare and hunted with the hounds. He also found David's musical tastes irritating. He is 'pretentious and boring', he told Marmontel. 'He talks to me of Verdi, Donizetti, Fesca, and I reply with Mozart, Mendelssohn, Gounod. We don't understand one another. He is constantly telling me that my music is not sufficiently lowbrow [*canaille*]; I find his lacking in distinction. You couldn't find two natures more opposed and antipathetic than ours'.[1] (This was after Bizet had abjured *Don Procopio*.) Until Guiraud's arrival he found the musicians among his colleagues less congenial than the other artists. At one stage he was giving a course of musical instruction to a painter and a sculptor, making them sing portions of Mozart operas; but, he told Marmontel in a long and delightfully exuberant letter (11th January 1859), he was too much of an egoist to be a good teacher.

In the summer of 1859 Bizet went for a prolonged holiday. Leaving Rome on 15th May with two companions and a dog (of whom he liked the latter not least), he spent some days at Anzio, where there was a convict settlement. He described the 250 convicts as the happiest and most esteemed part of the population, without a thief among them. He paid a visit to Cape Circe, went on to Terracina and then turned inland through magnificent mountain scenery, visiting among other places Frosinone, Anagni and Rietri, and returning to Rome on 14th July. He sent Marmontel an amusing account of the tour:

> What a country, and what travelling companions—Cicero at Astura, at Cape Circe Homer and his Ulysses, at Terracina Fra Diavolo. This is pure Scribe, and it amuses me to think that only three leagues divide Scribe from Homer. I leave tomorrow for Naples and am going to pass some hours with Tiberius and Nero. That is rather a come-down, as you see, but Virgil and Horace will console me for the tyrants.

Despite the discomforts of travel, including bugs and lack of sleep, he enjoyed every moment. He rose at four in the morning, made progress with riding and Italian, and proposed to learn Latin. The

[1] Letter of 17th January 1860, unpublished portion.

travellers had not been incommoded by the war in northern Italy, culminating in the battle of Magenta. In fact Bizet found the Italians little interested in fighting for their national unity: 'They know how to shout and form provisional governments, and that's all.' Garibaldi's inability to raise ten thousand men from the whole of Italy he called a disgrace. He was kept at Rome by a touch of rheumatism resulting from a cold bath, but on 4th August left for Naples, where (and at Pompeii) he remained till late in October. Although the bay was wonderful, and Pompeii set his imagination on fire, he was disappointed with the town of Naples. Soon one of his companions was threatened with typhoid. At the first alarm five of the eight who composed the party rapidly decamped, leaving Bizet and one other—a friend of a fortnight's standing, himself badly afflicted with boils [1] —to nurse the sick. Before returning to Rome Bizet too was stricken with illness, a heavy cold bringing on an attack of the throat complaint and rheumatism from which he suffered all his life and which were eventually to kill him.

An amusing incident happened about this time. Before leaving Paris, Bizet had been given a letter of introduction to Mercadante from one of the professors at the Conservatoire, an ancient Neapolitan nonentity named Carafa.[2] He had intended to use this on his visit to Naples, where Mercadante lived, but whether through neglect or preoccupation with the sick-bed, he had not done so. On his return to Rome, overcome by curiosity, he opened the letter. It read as follows: 'The young man who will bring you this letter has had great success with his studies. He has won the chief prizes at our

[1] This was Paul Dubois, the sculptor who in 1875 made the bust for Bizet's tomb.

[2] Michele Enrico Francesco Vincente Paolo Carafa di Colobrano (1787–1872) was one of those curious figures thrown up by the Napoleonic wars. Originally a rich man and a soldier (he fought both for and against Napoleon, and was decorated for his part in the Moscow expedition), he was compelled in 1814 to take up music for a living, wrote innumerable operas and piano pieces after the manner of Rossini and died a member of the French Academy. Among his operas, very popular in their day, were *La Fiancée de Lammermoor* and *Masaniello* (produced two months before Auber's work on the same theme).

Conservatoire. But, in my humble opinion, he will never be a dramatic composer as he has not a groat's worth of enthusiasm.' Bizet was much amused. 'You old scoundrel!' he broke out in a letter to his mother. 'One day, father Carafa, I promise to write your biography and give this letter in facsimile.' On his return to Paris he met Carafa, who asked him if he had used the letter. Bizet's reply was characteristic: 'Monsieur Carafa, when one has the good luck to possess the autograph of a man like you, one keeps it.'

In November, with the approval of Schnetz, Bizet applied for permission to spend the third year of his pension in Italy instead of Germany.[1] He gave as reason that he had begun an important work, which he would be unable to finish before July. 'In leaving Italy without having finished my work, I should be afraid of finding myself unready by the time the *envois* are due and, on the other hand, of not being able to profit as I desire by my stay in Germany.' Schnetz in his letter of recommendation said that the 'beautiful Italian climate' should have a happy influence on Bizet's work, and we may well agree. The 'important work' can only have been the abortive Symphony (mentioned below) which was very soon destroyed. But on 9th December the authorities granted the request. Another source of encouragement was the arrival early in 1860 of Ernest Guiraud, winner of the 1859 prize, whom Bizet knew well in Paris and who was to be his close friend for life. In June 1860 he made another short tour in the mountains. In July his portrait (which he describes as 'ravishing') was painted by his friend Giacomotti.[2] In the same month, his mind full of plans for his future life in Paris, he said farewell to Rome.

[1] This seems to have worried Gounod, who a year later was still advising him to go to Germany: he must work hard in order to fertilize the germs he had brought from Rome, which would otherwise remain sterile. But Bizet never stayed long in Germany, though he paid at least one visit to Baden. He told Marmontel in January 1860 that he proposed to visit the country later at his leisure.

[2] There is also an unfinished portrait painted during his first year in Rome by a fellow pensioner, Sellier. This shows Bizet without beard or spectacles. He first grew his beard in the spring of 1858, despite the opposition of Schnetz, who thought his face the wrong shape for it.

Of the many compositions projected by Bizet in Italy few reached completion. The *Te Deum* submitted for the Rodrigues prize was begun in February 1858 and the scoring finished in May. Bizet, who had no feeling for sacred music and very little for established religion, found it an effort and wanted it out of the way so that he could tackle an Italian opera libretto which greatly pleased him. This was *Parisina*, already set by Donizetti; Bizet intended it as his first *envoi*. But he seems never to have begun it, nor did an *opéra-comique* in one act with words by Edmond About progress much further. Bizet, who treated it less seriously than About, found the libretto 'charming, but a little too comic for the Opéra-Comique'. His comments on the *Te Deum* are those he nearly always passed on a recently completed work:

> I don't know what to think of it. Sometimes I find it good, sometimes detestable. What is certain is that I'm not cut out to write religious music. So I shall refrain from writing a mass. I shall send an Italian opera in three acts, I like that better.

Here common sense and his artistic conscience spoke together, but, as we shall see, there was another voice as well.

In June he found that his chosen poem, presumably *Parisina*, was no good; but after a long search, during which he went through 'all the libraries of Rome and read two hundred pieces', he found what he wanted in a second-hand bookstall in a back street. It was 'an Italian farce after the manner of *Don Pasquale*. . . . I am decidedly built for *la musique bouffe*, and I lose myself in it completely.' This libretto, accurately described by Bizet, was *Don Procopio* by one Carlo Cambiaggio. It was not a new work: it had been set by Vincenzo Fioravanti and others in 1844, and was even then only a reduced version of Prividali's *I pretendenti delusi*, set by Mosca [1] and produced at Milan in 1811. Bizet set happily to work, aware that the authorities would censure his choice of subject, but hoping for a good report on the music.

[1] In this work Mosca claimed, somewhat barrenly, to have anticipated Rossini in the use of the orchestral *crescendo*. It had for some time been common in Italian and French opera.

In September he heard that the only other competitor had won the Rodrigues prize. His immediate reaction was: 'That's most upsetting!!! But still, I shan't die of it.' A few days later he gave three reasons for not being downhearted: he was not in Paris whereas Barthe, the winner, was; he had neither the ability nor the knowledge to compose church music; and Barthe was in the fifth year of his pension and, being unable to compete again, was probably, and not unjustly, rewarded by the judges for a good string of *envois*. 'For all these reasons I have not had to console myself for a defeat which is no defeat and which has no publicity.' Whatever may be thought of Bizet's reasons (and the second at least was on the mark), the significant thing is that he should have had to give them at all: this is one of the first signs of that inner lack of confidence that so long dogged this apparently spontaneous and ebullient composer. It was this, and no mere love of money or flattery, that made some measure of worldly success so important to him. In the misfortune that deprived him of this success in his lifetime, rather than in the mere fact of early death, lay his tragedy.

Meanwhile *Don Procopio* continued to go well. He was aware that his music was Italian (he likened it to Cimarosa rejuvenated): 'On Italian words one must write Italian music; I have not tried to cast off this influence.'[1] But he intended to aim higher. 'I feel certain dramatic tendencies developing in me, as a result of which next year I shall try a grand opera.' His second *envoi* was to be an opera on Victor Hugo, *Esmeralda*, his third a symphony: for if he was drawn more and more to the stage, he never lost the ambition to shine in absolute music. At this period we see manifest for the first time that division of aim which is discussed in Chapter XII. To which of the two types of genius—natural genius or rational genius—did his own talent conform? Should he interpret by instinct, or hunt for an 'idea' and cudgel his brains working it into shape? Should he follow Mozart and Rossini on the one hand, or Beethoven and Meyerbeer on the other? If pressed too hard the distinction

[1] These words were printed at the head of the vocal score when *Don Procopio* was published in 1905. The autograph was lost for many years and only came to light in 1894, among Auber's posthumous papers. The first performance took place at Monte Carlo in 1906.

becomes unreal, for both processes obviously coexist; but that it represented a parting of the ways for Bizet there can be no doubt. So far, in the Symphony and *Don Procopio*, he had followed the instinctive way, composing fluently and with little revision, allowing his imagination to work without much conscious interference. Now he began to have doubts. He became self-conscious. In a letter to Gounod in September he compared himself to a bad swimmer in deep water: 'I flounder a lot and progress little. . . . I have always been very much the student; it is not easy to become one's *self*.' His letters in the winter of 1858–9 are full of confessions like this:

> I mistrust my facility: I have around me ten intelligent fellows who will never be more than mediocre artists, and all because of the fatal confidence with which they abandon themselves to their great cleverness. Cleverness in art is almost indispensable, but it only ceases to be dangerous the moment the man and the artist find themselves. I want to do nothing *chic*, I want to have *ideas* before beginning a piece, and that is not how I worked in Paris. It results in a certain paralysis which I shall only completely surmount in a year or two.

Bizet seems to have been confusing cleverness with spontaneity; at any rate, a kind of paralysis did set in, and its effects are apparent for a good deal longer than two years.

The immediate result of the struggle was a determination to compose 'German music'. This term must not be taken literally. In the years that followed Bizet did fall under the influence of German composers, particularly Schumann, Weber and Mendelssohn, but by German music he meant the other type of genius, the rational as opposed to the natural. And (strange as it seems today) this included the music of Gounod, in which the Schumann influence was strong and which sounded positively Teutonic to ears attuned to the Italian vivacity of Rossini, much of Meyerbeer and the reigning school of Auber. It is ironical that Bizet was particularly pleased to find *Don Procopio* free from the influence of Gounod; for he was about to abandon the method of *Don Procopio*. 'Next year I shall write something tragic and purely German. I shall finish perhaps by pleasing everyone or, rather, by pleasing no one.' As if to emphasize the irony in the last words, his next letter contains this comment on the early death of a fellow composer: 'Worry yourself sick to get the Prix de

Rome, struggle to make a good position on your return, and it will all end perhaps in death at thirty-eight.' Bizet died at thirty-six: he almost literally finished by pleasing no one.

The summer of 1859 saw many projects taken up and abandoned. No progress was made with *Esmeralda* (years later he gave it to Galabert to set as an exercise and improvised a couple of scenes at the piano). The visit to Cape Circe and its grotto suggested an ode-symphony [1] to be entitled *Ulysse et Circé.*

> There are some charming things to be done on this subject—the chorus of Ulysses' companions, the scene of Circe's spells, the drunkenness scene. There will be four purely symphonic pieces and five or six with voices and chorus.

Nor was this all.

> Convinced that an intelligent musician should find the idea for his poems for himself, I am very busy. Get the *Tales of Hoffmann* from the library and read *Le Tonnelier de Nuremberg*. I want to do three acts on this delicious poem. Tell me what you think of it in your next letter. The singing contest will be a very original and undoubtedly effective scene. There are also some things in Voltaire's tales that please me very much.

He urged his mother on no account to mention the *Tonnelier* idea, or he would find it already on the stage when he returned to Paris. But his mother's reaction was cool. In July he wrote:

> I am annoyed that the success of this story seems less sure to you than to me. The scenes of the portrait, the singing contest, the games and the workshop are nevertheless certain in their effect; and then it's so attractive, so German! Read it again and you'll discover that touch of sentiment that only Germans can find, and that is so popular with us.

(France was just falling under the spell of Schumann.) Here, probably because of his mother's attitude, Bizet dropped the idea. Perhaps it was as well. For the three acts on this delicious poem were to be the work of a very different composer: the seed of *Die Meistersinger* had already lodged in Wagner's brain, although neither poem nor music was yet begun.

[1] This form achieved a brief popularity in France about the middle of the century; its prototype was Félicien David's *Le Désert.*

At the same time *Ulysse et Circé* was discarded. 'Old Homer is obstinate about being arranged or rather disarranged. I should like to do something new. I'm looking for it. Shall I find it?' In August his ideas were still more ambitious. 'I have my head full of Shakespeare: Hamlet! Macbeth! But a librettist?' This search for that operatic rarity, a satisfactory libretto, was to bother Bizet all his life. About the end of September he put his second *envoi* aside (deciding to wait for the report on his first) and began a symphony. Yet he wrote in October:

> For some time I have been cherishing the idea of a tragi-comic-heroic *Don Quixote*, and I read in a paper that Gounod is working at it. It seems that my ideas are not too bad. One of these days someone will do my *Tonnelier*.

It is significant of his lack of self-confidence that, while one promising plan was dropped, probably on account of his mother's coolness, the prospect of rivalry with Gounod killed another.

Meanwhile the first (public) report on *Don Procopio* had arrived. Bizet had been awaiting it in mingled confidence and defiance. ('Whatever they say won't change my opinion in the least, for good or ill.') The report was entirely favourable and made no mention of his breaking the regulations. The judges found a notable advance on his earlier work and, after commending nearly every item in the score, especially the first finale, the serenade and the trio for three basses, summed up as follows:

> In short, this work is distinguished by an easy and brilliant touch, a youthful and bold style, precious qualities for the *genre* of comedy, towards which the composer shows a marked propensity. These qualities open the way to novel effects, and M. Bizet will not forget the obligation he has undertaken as much towards himself as towards us.

Bizet was much encouraged: 'I feel more confident than ever, though I don't conceal from myself the immense progress that remains to be achieved before I get anywhere, but I have good hopes.'

The symphony was now to be his second *envoi*, but early in December, after two months' work on it, he found he had taken a wrong turning and began afresh. He noted that he had become very hard to please; *Don Procopio* he now found 'extremely feeble'. Yet he was still sufficiently in the mood to dream of beginning his Paris career at the Théâtre Italien—a new idea, as he said, but, considering the low repute of that theatre, a questionable tactic. Towards the end of the month the second symphony went the way of the first—into the fire; but Bizet had found a librettist, one Louis Delâtre, whom he described with justifiable irony as 'a very learned man, who knows and speaks twenty-five languages but writes his own in a not very intelligent manner'.[1] To him Bizet entrusted a scenario based on the *Lusiad* of Camoens. *Vasco de Gama*, which became his second *envoi*, was an ode-symphony avowedly after the manner of David's *Le Désert* and *Christophe Colomb*. The music came easily enough, but Bizet had trouble with Delâtre's verses, some of which he had to rewrite. He was still pursued by ideas for a symphony: by the middle of January 1860 he had 'almost got as far as putting a finale on its feet', and he hoped to get his third *envoi* well ahead while writing his second. He was pleased with his progress. 'I revise very easily and I know the value of what I am writing: two good symptoms. . . . The very good is so difficult that a whole lifetime is not enough to approach it.'

Other projects still crowded his brain. Disgusted with Delâtre, he decided to be his own librettist. 'I have an enormous longing to write something in the comic vein, such a longing that I am rhyming for myself an *opéra-comique* on a piece by Molière, *L'Amour peintre*.' For some time he worked on this and *Vasco de Gama* together. But the second report on *Don Procopio* arrived in the middle of March and instantly put a stop to *L'Amour peintre*. This document, signed by Ambroise Thomas, duly censured Bizet for writing a comic opera instead of a mass, and proceeded: 'We will recall to him that the liveliest natures find in meditation and the interpretation of the sublime a style that is indispensable even in light compositions and without which a work will have no lasting qualities.' This egregious nonsense (might it be held to justify the sacred works of Sir Arthur

[1] This did not prevent him from publishing a treatise on the conjugation of French verbs (1851), besides poetry and books on classical antiquities in French and Italian. He was much older than Bizet, who in another letter wrote him down 'an ass, very learned but without intelligence or taste'.

Sullivan?) could not have surprised Bizet, and certainly should not have dismayed him; yet his self-reliance was so weak that he instantly succumbed.

The most simple thing would be to complete my *envoi* with a Credo. This portion of the Mass includes drama and action besides religious sentiment. The Resurrexit, Et ascendit, etc., would allow me to abandon Christian sentiment a little and substitute action, drama. But that would be repugnant to my ideas: I don't want to write a mass before being in a state to do it well, that is a Christian state. I have therefore taken a singular course to reconcile my ideas with the exigences of Academy rules. They ask for something religious: very well, I shall do something religious, but of the pagan religion. Horace's marvellous *Carmen saeculare* has been tempting me for a long time. . . . It is more beautiful than the Mass from a literary and poetic point of view; it is Latin poetry instead of prose, and so much more measured, more rhythmical, and as a consequence more musical. Then, to tell the truth, I am more pagan than Christian. I have always read the ancients with infinite pleasure, while in the Christians I have found only system, egoism, intolerance and a complete absence of artistic taste. It goes without saying that I except the works of St Paul and St John.[1]

He considered writing to Thomas, developing these ideas, but seems to have thought better of it. Instead he indulged in an outburst of petulance (to his mother) on the musical section of the Academy and the slapdash manner in which they judged the *envois*.

The work is played as it comes, and only once, then the areopagus sits in judgment on a young man who is the equal, if not the superior, of most of his judges (this applies not only to me but to everyone). . . . What can one expect from those animals? Reber is dumb, Berlioz absent, Auber asleep, Carafa and Clapisson listen (alas!). There remains only Thomas, but he is so lazy!

Perhaps provoked by this state of affairs, he thought of trying his hand at musical criticism. 'I'm not much more of an ass than many others who don't write too badly: why shouldn't I also try to say what I

[1] Giacomotti recalled Bizet declaring that 'during Holy Week, when I listen to the simple children in the choir of the poorest village church singing the splendid prose that shines with the aura of Christianity, of penitence and remorse, I emerge with the illusion that I am a Christian. When I hear a Mass by Cherubini, I come out feeling like a dilettante.'

think of our art and our artists?' He could hardly have found a less adequate reason for embarking on a critic's career.

The *Carmen saeculare* was never finished; Thomas and his committee never received from Bizet a religious *envoi* of any sort. The sole result of the incident was the abandonment of a promising light opera. But Bizet's mood of self-distrust was followed, as if in compensation, by a bout of extreme assurance. Looking through *Vasco de Gama* [1] before sending it to Paris, he found it much better than he expected.

Whatever the gentlemen of the Academy say, my opinion is formed, and it is good, very good even. I tell you this in secret, altogether confidentially: if I compare my *Vasco de Gama* with the great things of art I remain well below them, that goes without saying, but if I want to compete with our good contemporary work—I mean Thomas, Verdi, Halévy—I believe I have, if not the advantage, at least the right to dispute it.

He goes on to assess the position he believes he has reached.

I can declare at last that I am a musician, a thing I have long doubted. Whether I arrive in two, four or ten years does not matter. I am young enough not to lose the hope of enjoying my successes. Then hope, hope —that means certainty. For the rest, the moment is propitious: Gounod alone is a man; behind him is nothing. Verdi they say will write no more, and even if he does I doubt if he will often recapture those flashes of genius that appear in *Trovatore*, *Traviata* and the fourth act of *Rigoletto*. His is a fine artistic nature ruined by negligence and cheap success. . . . I like *La Juive* better than *Il Trovatore* musically; but I reverse my opinion in the matter of emotional content. When it comes to feeling, neither of them has any. . . . Ah! one needs a lot of strength to create art. It is hard, very hard, especially at Rome. The sirocco has a terrible effect on my nerves. You know me, and you know that I am not of a very nervous disposition: well, in the days of the sirocco I can't touch *Don Giovanni* or *Figaro* or *Così fan tutte*; Mozart's music has too strong an effect on me, and that makes me really very ill. Certain things of Rossini's, too, produce the same result. It's surprising, but Beethoven and Meyerbeer never go as far as that. As for Haydn, he has long sent me to sleep, likewise old Grétry. I don't mention Boieldieu, Nicolo,[2] etc., who no longer exist for me.

This confession reveals very clearly where his true affinities lay.

[1] It was intended to have a sequel: at the bottom of the autograph score Bizet wrote the words 'Fin de la Iière Partie'.

[2] Isouard.

Bizet held the lowest opinion of the musical state of Italy. Within a month of his arrival in Rome he was writing: 'Italy is poisoned by bad taste. It is a country completely lost to art. Rossini, Mozart, Weber, Paer, Cimarosa are here unknown, misunderstood or forgotten.' He told Gounod in September 1858 that nine months without hearing a note of good music had left him unable to judge his own work. The great religious ceremonies he described as unworthy farces from the musical point of view; this had also been Gounod's opinion twenty years earlier. The one composer whom he found it difficult to place—and this held good all his life—was Verdi. He was susceptible to his genius, but, perhaps because of the Gounod element in him, refused to surrender to it. 'Verdi is a man of great talent,' he wrote in February 1859,

> who lacks the one quality that is essential for making great masters—style. But he has wonderful bursts of passion. His passion is brutal, it is true, but that is better than having no passion at all. His music exasperates sometimes, but it never bores. In short, I don't understand the enthusiasts or the detractors he has roused; he deserves, it seems to me, neither the one nor the other.

Like many others, Bizet did not understand the development then taking place in Verdi's style that was to lead to the two great operas composed years after his own death. He found *Un ballo in maschera* 'noisome', contrasting it with Gluck's *Orfeo*, in which certain people affected to find no melody. His great hero among the living, of course, was Gounod, 'an essentially original composer; imitating him, you remain a pupil'. But although the letters are full of praises of Gounod the musician, they contain some biting comments on the man.[1] Bizet's intense interest in *Faust*, which he hailed as a masterpiece before he heard it (no doubt Gounod had shown him the unfinished manuscript in Paris), was linked with his hopes for his father's pupil Hector Gruyer, who was to sing the title role. When Gruyer twice failed to make the grade, first at the dress rehearsal in March 1859, again at the revival of the opera in September, Bizet was bitterly

[1] Including the assertion that Gounod had repaid a friend's kindness in Rome by having a love affair with his wife—a misdemeanour that Bizet himself was to commit later, if we can believe Céleste Mogador.

resentful and took the misfortune as a personal affront. His enmity extended to Gounod's family, especially his wife, who he was convinced was prejudiced against Gruyer. He congratulated his father on snubbing her: 'She is a good woman, but she loves her husband in a *stupid* way. She does him great harm and is a disastrous influence.' Gounod 'is the weakest man in the world where friendship is concerned. . . . A man has only a certain number of virtues, and all of Gounod's are concentrated on his art.' Despite frequent outbursts of spleen Bizet could not fight off his subjection to Gounod's personality or deny his genius. 'He is the most remarkable musician we now have (except Rossini and Meyerbeer), and that proves again that to be a great artist it is not necessary to be an honourable man.' And the letter in which he warned Gruyer against the weakness of Gounod's judgment contains his most enthusiastic tribute: 'What a sympathetic nature! How willingly one submits to the influence of that warm imagination! For him art is a priesthood: he has said so himself. I add that he is the only man among our modern musicians who truly loves his art.'

Whether Bizet wrote and remonstrated with Gounod is not clear; it must have been difficult to quarrel with a man who, when he left for Rome, explicitly assumed Zimmerman's 'very warm paternal interest' in his career. In the spring and summer of 1859 he more than once declared that he would not be the first to resume the correspondence, adding: 'If I wish to know *Faust*, it is more as a musician than as a *friend* of Gounod's.' Yet in January 1860 he was complaining that Gounod had not written, 'which is all the more absurd since when he sees me again he will weep with emotion. And indeed so will I, for there is nothing so contagious as friendship, feigned or real. I find great joy in seeing even the externals of friendship; it is so seductive and so rare!' Here again his basic insecurity stands revealed. When Gounod did write in August, it was in the old affectionate terms, though he added that Gruyer had been a personal as well as an artistic disappointment.

Bizet was a devoted son, taking continual pains to reassure his parents of his safety and good behaviour, and always wishing them at hand so that he could profit by their advice. He made elaborate plans for his future in Paris. He preferred to have separate lodgings in the same house as his parents (then living in the Rue de Laval), but if he lived at home he must have his own key.

I do not want you to have to open the door to people whom I'm going to put out five minutes later—that's for directors, singers, etc. Besides, I'm very capricious in my way of life: sometimes I go for walks by moonlight till impossible hours. My liberty of action would be cramped by the fear of displeasing you: that is what we must avoid.

Like Verdi, but unlike an artist of the popular conception, he had a vein of shrewd common sense, especially in money matters. He declared that living within one's means was 'the motto of every honest man and every philosopher', and proceeded, as a young man will, to count his future chickens at the Opéra and Opéra-Comique. When he has made 100,000 francs

papa will give no more lessons, nor I either. We shall begin the life of a *rentier* . . . 100,000 francs is nothing—two little successes with *opéra-comique*. A success like *Le Prophète* brings in almost a million. So this is not a castle in Spain.

At times he seems to know a little too well on which side his bread is buttered. There is something self-righteous in his comment on a colleague aged twenty-eight who had little experience of the seductions of Paris life. He adds coolly: 'I know that disease, but I will have none of it. I will take my share of the cake like anyone else, and it is sometimes a little bitter; I will take it without gluttony and in such a manner as not to have indigestion.' On another occasion, while admitting that gambling amuses him, he says he has become very severe in regard to the passions.

As regards the fair sex I am less and less the French cavalier. I see nothing in that beyond the satisfaction of self-esteem. I would willingly risk my life for a friend, but would think myself an idiot if I lost a hair of my head on account of a woman. I say such things only to you, for if they became known they would prejudice my future success. . . . I dine every week with Kisseleff,[1] which pleasantly flatters what remains of my sensual greed. I say 'what remains'. For there also I've changed. I no longer love cakes or ices or sweets (except *marrons glacés*). I have become a little perfection. Only

[1] The Russian ambassador.

my natural quarrelsomeness remains: an elbowing in the street, a gaze too long fixed on me, and brrrrrr—off I go! I do all I can to improve myself, but it's difficult, very difficult.... Time is a great teacher, he'll manage to perfect me—if it's possible.

This is not the only evidence of his immature attitude to women and marriage, which persisted long after his return to Paris. In April 1858 he expressed profound contempt for one of his Delsarte cousins who had jilted his fiancée in order to marry a servant girl he had got with child. Bizet regarded it as 'cowardly to renounce his position in order to wallow in miserable poverty' and condemned the 'unpardonable weakness' of his uncle in not banishing the boy for ever from the paternal roof. Two years later, in connection with the marriage of another Delsarte cousin, he 'deplores, without understanding them, all the transports of the thing called love'.

There was certainly a vein of shallow thinking and egotism in the young Bizet. Abjuring the need for settled principles, he set out to conquer the world under the guidance of his own star.[1] His judgments of men and politics were superficial and erratic (he went through a phase of jingoistic chauvinism when Napoleon III was trying to win military glory in Italy). He sent a message to Gruyer: 'If I could give him a little of my assurance [*aplomb*], how things would go! . . . Assurance—in a word, character—and he is certain of success.' But, as he soon found, assurance is not enough. Beneath his apparent detachment and self-confidence there grew up a profound and gnawing self-distrust, rooted in fear. He had not thought out the deeper things in life. 'The older I grow', he wrote on hearing of the death of a child, 'the more the idea of death terrifies me. That does little credit to my philosophy, but it is a feeling of which I am not master.' He had a superstitious belief, which he was half ashamed to confess to his father, that his friendship brought bad luck. His hatred of priests and organized religion is also symptomatic.[2] As early as 1859 he viewed certain aspects of his future career with alarm: 'I

[1] Witness the repeated references in his letters to 'ma chance'.

[2] 'It is odd that the more I am strengthened in my Christian beliefs, the more I detest those who are charged with teaching them to us. Happily one can love God without loving the priests.'

already detest that whole breed of directors and performers whom I am going to have the pleasure of frequenting. Failure is a thing those people never forgive.' Whatever truth there might be in that last sentence, Bizet did not yet know it from personal experience.[1] He had to learn that ability is not an infallible or immediate passport to worldly success, and like other men of genius he had to learn it the painful way, by failure. Needing some tangible encouragement, he was to fix his eyes a little too much on the world's applause; he longed for it, expected it, and was all the more resentful when it was withheld.

But it is essential to remember that we are dealing with a very young man. A number of passages in the Rome letters have been used by unscrupulous critics and biographers, especially in France, to denigrate Bizet's character throughout life. It is not very difficult, and not very creditable, to select sentences from the naïve letters of an ambitious and impetuous young man, written rapidly[2] and in confidence to his parents, rearrange them, treat them as considered judgments and so present a wholly false picture. Some of these passages have been misunderstood. For instance, when Bizet wrote, immediately after the failure of Gounod's opera *Le Médecin malgré lui*: 'I shall probably have much less talent and less settled convictions than Gounod: as things are, this is a chance of success,' the irony in the last words is scarcely veiled.[3] Vuillermoz goes so far as to state that it would have been better for Bizet had these letters never been published. But it is obvious that the conception of Bizet as a bourgeois careerist, calculating his chances of success in terms of hard cash and only making artistic progress by mistake and when aiming at something quite different, is a travesty. He had not, indeed, the reckless abandonment of Berlioz, the inward concentration of Beethoven or the dogged capacity for long-term planning of Wagner. But that is not to say that he loved his art any less than they did. The

[1] He was undoubtedly thinking of Gruyer's rejection from *Faust.*

[2] Bizet asked his mother to forgive the confusion in his letters, as he never re-read them.

[3] He added, in a passage suppressed by the editor of the letters: 'Don't repeat this to anyone. People are already too disposed to treat me as a man without convictions.'

trouble springs largely from the romantic view of the artist as a starving visionary in a garret, indifferent to daily bread and common sense, his mind suffused with the rosy haze of infinite aspiration. Bizet, like Mozart and most other eighteenth-century composers (not to mention Verdi), did not forget that music was his livelihood as well as his vocation; and if he occasionally sinned in offering the public what he thought they liked instead of what his inner nature knew to be good, it was not through prostituting his art to serve his purse. There is no evidence that money at any time held an excessive place in his ambitions; in later life he more than once refused all payment from pupils over whom he took endless trouble. He was a man in some degree divided against himself, and the attitude of his better (and predominant) half towards the artist who consciously abuses his heritage is stated clearly in a letter he wrote to Marmontel just before leaving Rome:

> To the devil with all those who have seen in our sublime art nothing but an innocent tickling of the ear. Silliness will always have numerous admirers; but still I don't complain, and I assure you I shall always take pleasure in being appreciated only by men of genuine understanding. I have little use for this popularity to which people nowadays sacrifice honour, genius and fortune.

At the end of July 1860 Bizet finally left Rome, intending to reach Paris in December after a leisurely tour of northern Italy with Guiraud. They were a nicely contrasted pair, Bizet with his quick temper and abounding vitality, Guiraud already notorious for the good-humoured indolence that caused him to postpone the task of recording his reminiscences of his friend, till one day he fell asleep in his office chair at the Conservatoire and omitted to wake up. Bizet had a wonderful send-off from the Academy. People he never much cared about shook his hand with tears in their eyes, and he himself, like Gounod on a similar occasion years before, was overcome with emotion. 'I had a frightful attack of nerves; I wept for six hours straight off. I realized I was liked at the Academy, and that was very moving.'

For the first six weeks of his journey home Bizet kept a diary. This curious document, wholly extrovert in temper, contains little about music, except that he played the organ at a few churches, or about people—other than prostitutes, for whom he had an insatiable appetite (he had just parted regretfully from a mistress in Rome). One of them, whom he found a bit skinny, inspired the mysterious comment: 'Oh, Berlioz, *que n'étais-tu là?*' The main themes of the diary are architecture, painting and sculpture. Much of it is the routine catalogue of the bourgeois doing the sights, but by no means all. Apart from a lively interest in the pictorial arts, Bizet had definite preferences, a feeling for history, some taste and perhaps a little knowledge. He often made stylistic comparisons and remarks on pictorial composition. His inclination was towards the primitives and illuminated manuscripts; he was particularly impressed by the Giottos at Assisi and Padua. There are also comments on his reading, which included Musset, Mérimée (*Les Mécontents*, which he found charming) and Alfred de Vigny; he was severe on the latter's *Chatterton* and criticized the versification of his translations of *Othello* and *The Merchant of Venice*. We have other evidence of his reading, probably at Rome, in the form of manuscript notes on many volumes of Greek and Latin classics in translation, the complete works of Beaumarchais (who, he remarked of the preface to *Le Barbier de Séville*, 'should have had *Wagner* for a collaborator'), books by Lamartine and Chateaubriand (in whom he found 'cold gaiety—Catholic gaiety'), and the seventeen volumes of Baron Grimm's *Correspondence*.

Bizet and Guiraud travelled by Viterbo, Orvieto, Perugia, Assisi, Rimini, Ravenna, Bologna, Ferrara and Padua to Venice, where they arrived by train on 4th September. At Rimini Bizet found his usual delight in sea-bathing and tried without much success to teach Guiraud to swim. He also conceived the plan for a work that was to occupy him on and off for most of his life.

> I have in mind a symphony which I should like to call *Rome, Venice, Florence and Naples*. That works out wonderfully: Venice will be my andante, Rome my first movement, Florence my scherzo and Naples my finale. It's a new idea, I think.

This was the germ of *Roma*. He told his mother that he was following Auber's advice and had already taken down a lot of music in a notebook.

He found Guiraud's company very congenial, despite the difficulty of waking him up in the mornings, and they sang Mozart all day long. But Bizet himself felt a renewed restlessness.

> I have become excitable [*nerveux*] beyond measure, that is to say the opposite of what I was in Paris. I cannot stay where I am; after seven hours of sleep bed becomes intolerable to me, and I notice that for some time I have been growing insensible to the pleasures of the table. I feel a kind of continual irritation, a need, a desire that I cannot define.

It was in this condition that he reached Venice, to find a letter from his mother written from hospital. He had for some time been worried by reports of her health, and the sight of the word 'hospital' produced an extreme neurotic reaction.[1] After a quarter of an hour of dumb fury he picked a quarrel with a gondolier and rushed at him with the firm intention of strangling him. Guiraud pulled him back, mildly observing that he had better read the rest of the letter first. This revealed that things were not quite as bad as he had feared, but he decided to cut short his tour and return to Paris. Two days later he made the last entry in his diary. The illness of a companion delayed him for a day or two in Nice. As he passed anxiously through Provence another of his fellow travellers, Gaston Planté, made a sketch of him in the coach.

[1] This was characteristic. In October 1858 a disquieting letter had inspired a quarrel with two of his colleagues at the Villa Medici. His illness in the autumn of 1859 (p. 18) seems to have been precipitated by rage over Gruyer's second failure in *Faust*.

CHAPTER III

FIRST STEPS IN PARIS (1860–3)

IN ORDER to follow the vicissitudes of Bizet's career after his return to Paris, it is important to understand the background to French musical life under the Second Empire. Virtually the only road open to the young composer of serious ambitions and without private means was the stage. In 1860 there seemed to be no future for a French composer of symphonies and no market for his wares. The only organization that gave regular orchestral concerts was the Société des Concerts du Conservatoire, founded by Habeneck in 1828. It had a small hall, with a limited audience who mostly took tickets by the season, and it concentrated on the accepted classics, making no attempt to cultivate native talent. Not till 1868 were its doors opened to Gouvy, who for twenty years had been regarded as France's most promising symphonist. The Société Sainte-Cécile, founded by Reber and the violinist Seghers in 1848, had introduced Mendelssohn's 'Italian' Symphony and some works of Gounod's early symphonic period, but its career had closed in financial failure in 1854. The composer who wanted to hear his orchestral works had to hire an orchestra and a hall, a procedure which, as Berlioz and others found, was both uncomfortable and unprofitable. The first sign of advance was the foundation in 1861 of Pasdeloup's Concerts Populaires de Musique Classique, which while mainly devoted to Beethoven and other classics did give many young native composers, including Bizet, their first chance; but it was not till after the Franco-Prussian War that the way was cleared for the flourishing French school of orchestral music of the last years of the century. With the foundation of the Société Nationale (1871) and Colonne's concert organization (1873) the one-sidedness of French musical life came to an end; but by then Bizet's days were numbered.

Chamber music was in no better case. There were the fashionable *salons*, where pianist-composers like Thalberg and Stephen Heller (and occasionally Liszt) amazed their listeners with cascades of virtuosity, and titled ladies accompanied themselves on the harp in a succession of banal romances. But, failing another genius like Chopin, this was hardly the nursery of a virile and enduring art. Serious chamber music, such as Beethoven's quartets, was played only in select circles, and would probably have been incomprehensible to the general public and the bevies of dilettanti that made up a large part of musical Paris. There was no hope for ambitious young Frenchmen, and composers like Lalo and Franck, who were both years older than Bizet, had to wait for the Société Nationale to give French chamber music a new lease of life.

With church music in full decadence, there remained only the stage. Here at first glance the situation seems more promising. Opera and ballet (which the French liked to combine in a single spectacle) had originally been aristocratic forms, and at the premier national theatre, the Opéra [1] in the Rue Lepelletier, they continued to be so regarded; but the musical heirs of the French Revolution and First Empire, in particular Auber, Boieldieu and Hérold, had brought them within the comprehension of the middle classes. Thus the old Opéra-Comique, which had originated over a century earlier as a parody of the tragic stage, now took up residence in the Salle Favart as a kind of bourgeois younger brother of the Opéra. But though there were two permanent opera-houses in Paris, they were not in a healthy state of growth. Each had its own narrow conventions and its equally narrow public, and the latter made sure that the former were never relaxed. The Opéra was the more hidebound of the two. By the middle of the century it had become little more than a *salon* for snobs, to a greater extent even than the Covent Garden of pre-war seasons. The audiences were more interested in themselves than in the performances, which combined the lowest level of taste with the highest rate of public expenditure. The repertory consisted mostly of old music revived, and music by foreigners at that; for France was going through a period of intense snobbery towards her own composers of serious music. It is a curious fact that the leaders of the French stage have so often been foreigners: Lully triumphed in the

[1] Its full title was (and is) Académie Nationale de Musique.

seventeenth century, Gluck and Piccinni in the eighteenth, and in the forty years following 1825 the twin stars were Rossini and Meyer-beer, whose rivalry entertained the fashionable world and barred the way to native talent.[1] Even with the death of these two champions the position did not improve: between 1852 and 1870 the only new French work of the smallest merit (and it had little enough) produced at the Opéra was Ambroise Thomas's *Hamlet*, and during the whole of Bizet's working life in Paris (1861–75) fewer than a dozen new operas were introduced.

The Opéra-Comique, though it produced more native work, was equally hidebound. Under the guidance of Auber it had evolved a form of its own, of which the epithet 'comique' gives a misleading impression. The term is not synonymous with our 'comic opera'; it did (until *Carmen*) imply a happy ending, but its most distinctive characteristic was that recitative was replaced by spoken dialogue, as in the German *Singspiel*. The Paris bourgeoisie liked its music broken up into small self-contained units set in a framework of ordinary speech, and successful *opéra-comique* composers—Auber, Adam, Boieldieu and the rest—having found an idiom that satisfied the public of 1830, ossified it and reproduced it for the next forty years. They avoided all complications, whether psychological or technical ('learned music' was a term of reproach more feared than 'highbrow' is today), all profundity, all enthusiasm and all experi-ment. Their music was clear, elegant, polished, often charming, essentially middle-class and sometimes dreadfully vulgar. Some of their earlier operas have a glitter that has still not worn off; but they never advanced, and never stretched their audiences' imagination. Auber was still writing for the Opéra-Comique in 1869 at the age of nearly ninety, and works like Boieldieu's *La Dame Blanche* and Hérold's *Le Pré aux clercs* remained popular favourites till the end of

[1] Meyerbeer is said to have paid people to go to sleep ostentatiously during his rival's operas. Rossini retired from operatic composition in 1830, but his figure continued to loom large at the Opéra and throughout French musical life. Many other foreigners set up business in Paris, including Spontini, Donizetti and Bellini; even Wagner and Verdi came to try their fortunes. But the Opéra audience's stomach for foreign music proved notoriously unable to digest *Tannhäuser*.

the century. In the sixties the great new success at the Opéra-Comique, as at the Opéra, was a work by Thomas—*Mignon*; and this at the time when Wagner was finishing *Die Meistersinger*.

Outside the two State theatres there were the Théâtre-Italien, a decadent and peripatetic institution that satisfied the craze for Italian opera of the second rank, and the operetta theatres, where from the middle fifties Offenbach was king. His easy, tuneful, well-turned but essentially trivial muse suited the tastes of the Second Empire, and he worked under ducal patronage. 'Between the Conservatoire, which is a school,' said a Minister of Public Instruction, 'and the Opéra, which is a museum, a single intermediary—the Opéra-Comique—is not enough.' From time to time between 1847 and 1870 there were attempts to operate a second intermediary, known as the Théâtre-Lyrique (this was the name of the company, not of the building, which was more than once changed). The directors, who were men of some vision, avoided the cliques and the conventions (including obligatory spoken dialogue and the preference for foreigners) that beset one or other of the regular theatres, and tried to give enterprising programmes and build up an enterprising public. Unfortunately, though receiving a certain amount of support from the State and private patrons, the scheme was hardly ever solvent and several times had to close down before the war of 1870 gave it its death-blow. It was the Théâtre-Lyrique that produced Berlioz's *Les Troyens à Carthage*, most of Gounod's best work, including *Faust* (which the Opéra refused to touch till it had ten years' success behind it), and the early operas of Reyer, Guiraud, Bizet and Delibes.

There were other difficulties under which a young composer of original leanings had to labour. This was still the age of the prima donna, whose passions and predilections exercised a strong control over composers and directors alike (the wife of Carvalho, director of the Théâtre-Lyrique, was one of the leading singers of the day). Not only was the voice exalted at the expense of the orchestra, and the individual number at the expense of dramatic unity and psychological consistency; the composer was expected to subordinate his style to particular singers (Meyerbeer's scores are full of details which appear only because such and such a soprano or bass could outreach his or her colleagues). It is easy for critics of another age with different standards to reproach Bizet for his concessions to Christine Nilsson in *La Jolie Fille de Perth*; but this was the general practice of the time, and the composer who refused to conform was apt to find himself in the gutter. The attitude of most directors was frankly financial. They regarded an operatic score not as an artistic whole, but as so much material that could be chopped about and presented in the most appetizing manner. Meyerbeer with his board-room attitude to opera did not create a fashion; he merely fitted the supply to the demand, and the young composer was expected to do the same without receiving the deference due to an established reputation. He was regarded as very small fry indeed: he was the servant, not only of the director, but of the stage-manager, the ballet-master and even the librettist. Cuts were frequently made against his wishes, and if he wanted anything extra, such as musicians in the wings, he had to pay for it out of his own pocket. Bizet had to fight most of these restrictions as late as the production of *Carmen.*

Another handicap was the deplorable level of musical criticism. With a few notable exceptions, such as Berlioz and Reyer, the prejudice and conservatism of the regular critics was exceeded only by their ignorance of the technique and the history of music.[1] This fact may be connected with the ill-disguised contempt with which leading French literary circles of the middle of the century regarded the art of music and its practitioners.[2] It is not surprising to find that Théophile Gautier, who confessed that he preferred silence to music, was among other things a music critic. Saint-Saëns in his memoirs quotes 'one of the most brilliant of the reviews' of 1864:

Our real duty—and it is a true kindness—is not to encourage them [young

---

[1] Musical history and aesthetics were not taught at the Conservatoire (or anywhere else in France) until 1871.

[2] One result of this divorce, of course, was that few good writers condescended to collaborate with a musician (*L'Arlésienne* was a striking exception). Consequently a race of hacks arose whose job was to turn out libretti to order. It is not surprising that French libretti of the middle of the century are almost incredibly bad. Even Scribe, with his seventy-six volumes of published libretti, all conforming more or less exactly to one of two types (the *opéra* and the *opéra-comique*), was a sizable artist compared with most of his successors.

composers] but to discourage them. In art vocation is everything, and a vocation needs no one, for God aids. What use is it to encourage them and their efforts when the public obstinately refuses to pay any attention to them? If an act is ordered from one of them, it fails to go. Two or three years later the same thing is tried again with the same result.

So the theatres are justified in falling back on established favourites. That is a mild presentation of the method used by the bulk of the French musical press during Bizet's lifetime; and it is interesting to see how Gounod, the one composer before Bizet who attempted to develop French opera, fared at their hands. He was denied the gift of melody; he was variously called the disciple of Handel, Gluck, Spontini, Schumann and Wagner, acclaimed as the reviver of the style of Palestrina and reproached (by the pontifical Scudo in 1862) with his taste for the late Beethoven quartets, 'the polluted source from which have sprung the evil musicians of modern Germany, the Liszts, Wagners, Schumanns, not to mention Mendelssohn in certain equivocal details of his style'. His first opera, *Sapho* (1851), was too modern even for Berlioz, who considered that its attempts at dramatic realism transcended what was permissible in music. If Berlioz thought this of *Sapho*, is it surprising that nearly every music critic in Paris should have burnt his fingers over *Carmen*?

Such was the musical background of Paris when Bizet returned from Rome. He seems at first to have thought of applying for a teaching post at the Conservatoire. This was the comfortable course, and that taken by Guiraud and the majority of Prix de Rome winners; but though it provided financial security, it also imposed fetters, and the composer was apt to become submerged in the pedagogue. Whether for this reason or another, Bizet did not pursue the matter. He still had nearly two years of his Rome pension to run and could afford to look about him, though aware that a hard struggle lay ahead. He was exceedingly ambitious and at the same time afraid; he already classed the tribes of directors, singers and critics as his potential enemies. Moreover he was throughout his life the victim of constant ill health. From the age of fourteen he had suffered from quinsy (*angine*), which attacked him regularly in the spring or early summer. He was also subject to articular rheumatism, possibly the product of rheumatic fever. At Rome during March 1858 he had difficulty in swallowing and lost a great deal of weight; everyone advised him to have his tonsils out. On other occasions his letters report ulceration of the throat and similar complaints. Yet there is no self-pity. He more than once declares that illness has done him a world of good: 'This monotony of good fortune and health was growing tedious.' It is difficult to estimate the seriousness of these attacks, which were often very painful; but they must have impaired his resistance, both physical and mental, and made the hackwork he subsequently had to perform for a living and his repeated failure to win worldly success peculiarly hard to bear.

The first year after his return to Paris was darkened by the lingering illness of his mother, who died on 8th September 1861. Thus at the outset of his career, when his mercurial nature most needed guidance, he was deprived of that being whom he believed most fitted to give it. Psychologists may find significance in a dream which he subsequently related to Galabert. 'At night I would feel a terrible agony. I would be forced to throw myself down in an armchair, and then I would think I saw my mother coming into the room. She would cross and stand beside me and put her hand on my heart. Then the agony would increase. I would suffocate, and it seemed to me that her hand, weighing on me so heavily, was the true cause of my suffering.' Shortly before his mother's death he told Gounod that he was conducting two love affairs at once. One of them, with his parents' maid Marie Reiter, resulted in the birth of a son, Jean, in June 1862—exactly nine months after his mother's death. Marie remained in the service of Adolphe and later Geneviève Bizet until her death in 1913. She nursed Bizet during his last illness. Jean, who was brought up in the household as a sort of cousin, became director of the press of *Le Temps* and an officer of the Legion of Honour and died in 1939, leaving a wife and family.

Bizet's third *envoi*[1] was finished in the late summer or autumn of 1861, a year late. There has been some confusion over this, but the following facts are clear. Bizet informed the authorities that he intended to submit a symphony, almost certainly the one entitled

[1] A letter of Gounod's (19th August 1861) mentioning a symphony and an overture on which Bizet was then working must refer to this.

Rome, Venice, Florence and Naples, which he had projected in the previous summer. However, the illness and death of his mother interrupted his work, and he sent in only two movements, a scherzo and a funeral march, supplementing them with an overture, *La Chasse d'Ossian.* The scherzo, which subsequently found a place in *Roma,* may have been the movement originally intended to depict Florence, but it seems unlikely that he would have chosen a funeral march for Venice. The inference is that this piece was written on the death of his mother and tacked on to the scherzo because it was the only thing he had ready for submission.[1] Of *La Chasse d'Ossian* we know nothing except its mention in the Academy's report, though Bizet's habit of using up the material of discarded works may later have laid it under contribution.

The reports of the Academy were reasonably encouraging. In *Vasco de Gama* authority (in the person of Halévy) had discovered 'elevation of style, spaciousness of form, fine harmonic effects, and rich and colourful orchestration'. They predicted a brilliant future for the composer, but warned him 'to beware of certain harmonic audacities which can sometimes be qualified as harshness'. The third *envoi* met with nothing but praise. The Academy noted, as well it might, the grace and skill with which the chief motive of the scherzo was handled and praised the overture in much the same terms as *Vasco de Gama.* It found the talent shown in his earlier exercises amply fulfilled, and this time took no exception to his harmony.

There are few letters dated from this period, but one or two incidents throw light on Bizet's powers and temperament. On 26th May 1861, after a dinner-party at Halévy's, Liszt favoured the company by playing one of his latest works. It was full of appalling (and no doubt spectacular) difficulties, and at the end all crowded round to congratulate the master on the work and its apparently effortless performance. 'Yes,' replied Liszt, 'it is a difficult piece, horribly difficult, and I only know two pianists in Europe capable of playing

[1] The fact that he used its main theme in *Les Pêcheurs de perles* a year or two later tends to confirm that it was not a part of the Italian symphony, a project he never abandoned. It has no connection with the published Funeral March for orchestra, written in 1868 as the prelude to the opera *La Coupe du Roi de Thulé.*

it as it is written and at the speed I desire: Hans von Bülow and myself.' Halévy, standing by the piano, suddenly remembered Bizet and his memory. 'Did you notice this passage?' he said, striking a few chords in approximation to what Liszt had played. Bizet sat down and played the passage from memory. Liszt, much impressed, thereupon produced the manuscript, and Bizet astonished the company by playing the piece right through without mistake or hesitation. Liszt seized him by the hand and declared: 'My young friend, I thought there were only two men able to surmount the difficulties with which it was my pleasure to adorn this piece. I was wrong: there are three, and in justice I should add that the youngest of the three is perhaps the boldest and most brilliant.'

The story may have been touched up (a young man who was present wrote of Bizet's 'ordinary talent which contrasts so markedly with Liszt's and is much more agreeable'), but there are many testimonies to Bizet's skill. Berlioz ranked him as a score-reader with Liszt and Mendelssohn, and others paid tribute to his beautiful touch, subtle gradation of tone and ability to suggest each instrument of the orchestra. His performances of original keyboard music, especially Bach's Preludes and Fugues,[1] Beethoven's 32 Variations in C minor and works by Mendelssohn and Chopin, were equally admired. There is no doubt that he could have become one of the leading concert pianists of the age. According to Pigot he did receive many tempting offers, but always refused to play in public, though he appeared at musical parties and occasionally at charity concerts reported in the press. The reason is clear: he did not wish to compromise his career as a composer. The French public liked to keep musicians in separate compartments: if a performer composed a piece it was given the damning label 'musique de pianiste'. Bizet went so far to avoid this danger that he composed regrettably little for the instrument of which he was such a master and never wrote the concerto he planned.

Another anecdote, dating from an earlier period, shows his powers put at the service of parody. Among the most successful operatic composers of the day was one Clapisson, a pretentious nonentity,

[1] Bizet's enthusiasm for Bach was unbounded. In an undated letter to a publisher he offered to arrange excerpts from the first twenty volumes of the complete edition in vocal score, to be issued in annual instalments.

who after a great success at the Opéra-Comique with a work called *La Fanchonnette* was in 1854 elected to the Academy in preference to Berlioz. This impelled Bizet [1] to improvise at the piano, with a vivid imitation of Clapisson's voice, manner and musical style, a piece entitled *L'Enterrement de Clapisson.* It began with a funeral march on the master's most banal theme: first the procession of mourners with the members of the Academy in solemn state at their head, then the funeral oration delivered by Ambroise Thomas, then the cheerful departure of the company, glad to have the tiresome ceremony over. The second part was called 'Apothéose'. Clapisson's soul, clad in full Academy robes with a sword at its side, finding itself alone, flies from the cemetery up to heaven. God, surrounded by the most celebrated composers, receives him with honour among the immortals (here the ceremony of admission to the Academy was parodied). Beethoven in his capacity of president greets him with the opening bars of his fifth Symphony, which Clapisson interrupts with a theme from *La Fanchonnette.* Beethoven, only momentarily disconcerted, resumes his Symphony (left hand), but Clapisson is not to be outdone and pours forth a stream of his choicest melody (right hand). So for some time the contrapuntal battle continues, till Beethoven as the wiser of the two gives in and *La Fanchonnette* is carried to a swelling apotheosis. This piece, which unfortunately has not survived, was in great demand at musical gatherings till Clapisson's death (1866), after which Bizet refused to play it. But he continued to amuse his friends with improvised fantasies on themes from Offenbach and Wagner and outrageous parodies of the Boieldieu school, adorned with every manner of embroidery and obsolete *fioriture*. He also set a newspaper to music, including the advertisements.

Early in 1862 Bizet was helping Gounod with the rehearsals and various instrumental arrangements of *La Reine de Saba*, which failed dismally at the Opéra at the end of February. In May he undertook a

[1] He also had a personal feud with Clapisson, who wrongly suspected him of playing a malicious practical joke and cut him in the street. Bizet drafted an indignant letter containing the sentence: 'Nothing could have prevented your seeing me this morning, unless perhaps it was the halo of glory encircling your brow.' See Curtiss, *Bizet and his World*, p. 66.

similar task for Reyer, whose *Érostrate*, together with Berlioz's *Béatrice et Bénédict*, was to inaugurate a new theatre at Baden in August. While Reyer finished his score at leisure in Baden, Bizet acted as his Paris agent, sending music to be copied, rehearsing and mollifying the singers, and performing other menial tasks. As a result he missed the *première* of *Béatrice et Bénédict*, which Reyer described to him in an interesting letter, but arrived in Baden a few days later. Here his fiery temper produced a spectacular explosion. Among the party from Paris were Gounod, the publisher Choudens and Émilien Pacini, joint-librettist of *Érostrate*, whom the others were in the habit of using as a butt to sharpen their wits. One day at dinner Pacini, perhaps under provocation, declared that *La Reine de Saba* had deserved its fate. The effect on Bizet was electric: he grew red in the face, waved his arms about, called the librettist every name under the sun and challenged him to a duel. Seconds were appointed before Gounod managed to intervene and point out that it was he, not Bizet, who had been insulted.

On the same visit Bizet is said to have set the cat among the pigeons by maintaining, in conversation with the critic Jouvin, that 'Wagner is Verdi with the addition of style'. In his Rome days he had thought little of Wagner. After reading two of his scores he wrote to his mother: '*There is absolutely nothing there.* They . . . are the work of a man who, lacking melodic inspiration and harmonic inventiveness, has created eccentricity; extraordinary that this innovator should have no originality, no personality. I like Verdi or Adam a hundred times more.' The Paris performances of *Tannhäuser* in 1861 may have converted Bizet, or he may have been pulling Jouvin's leg; but his habit of uttering outrageous and paradoxical opinions (and this statement would have been regarded as both in 1862), while no doubt it made his conversation stimulating, was not without its dangers. For the story and others to the same effect [1] soon got about, and they were used by the Paris critics as a stick with which to beat nearly all his work from *Les Pêcheurs de perles* to *Carmen*. In fact Jouvin gave the

[1] He was supposed to have challenged Scudo, the Wagnerophobe critic of the *Revue des Deux Mondes*, with the words 'You're an idiot—here is my card' at the Wagner concert of 25th January 1860—at which time he was still in Rome.

episode wide publicity immediately after the production of *Les Pêcheurs de perles*, adding that the captious remark ought to have scalded Bizet's tongue.

Another probable consequence of the visit to Baden has gone unrecognized. Reyer had promised to arrange with Bénazet,[1] the director of the Baden theatre, for the production of an opera by Bizet in 1863; in an unpublished letter [2] of 10th July 1863 (addressing Bizet as 'belliqueux jeune homme') he implies that Bénazet had agreed and asks what happened to the plan, which was entrusted to Choudens. For several reasons, too long to recount here,[3] it seems likely that Bizet composed this opera in the winter of 1862–3, and that it was the first, incompletely scored and only surviving version of *Ivan IV*.

Bizet's fourth and last *envoi* was a setting of a one-act *opéra-comique* by two of the leading purveyors (they usually hunted in couples), Jules Barbier and Michel Carré, entitled *La Guzla de l'Émir*. Bizet's original plan seems to have been a collaboration with Ludovic Halévy, whom he approached during his mother's last illness; twelve years were to pass before this came to fruition. Very little is known about *La Guzla de l'Émir*, which was probably composed early in 1862 and put into rehearsal at the Opéra-Comique a year later. This fact does not imply any success on Bizet's part or an enlightened attitude on that of the theatre. The Opéra-Comique received certain funds from the State on condition that it produced the one-act piece which the pensioners were obliged to submit. Only too often the production was long delayed [4] and confined to a single performance; often it was the only one of his works that the prize-winner saw on the stage. But Bizet's opera was never produced. The

[1] The first mention of Bénazet in Bizet's letters occurs as early as 22nd January 1859, when he spoke of returning from Rome via Baden and arranging 'a little matter of an *opéra de salon*'. There may be a link here with the mysterious *La Prêtresse*.

[2] The postscript records Reyer's first encounter with *Tristan und Isolde*. He read it at the piano and found it 'complètement fou. Je n'en retiendrai pas dix pages en dix ans'.

[3] See my study of *Ivan IV* in *Fanfare for Ernest Newman* (London, 1955) and p. 56 ff. below.

[4] For Bizet's own comment on the practice *see* Appendix E.

retiring Minister of Fine Arts, Count Walewski, had just given the Théâtre-Lyrique a subvention of 100,000 francs on condition that the management should produce every year a three-act opera by a young winner of the Prix de Rome. Bizet was the first to benefit under this scheme. The director of the theatre, Léon Carvalho,[1] was one of the few men of his position with a mind of his own. He had met Bizet soon after his return from Rome and been struck by his talents and his personal charm. He at once offered him the libretto of *Les Pêcheurs de perles*, by Carré and E. Cormon (pseudonym of Pierre Étienne Piestre). Bizet thereupon withdrew *La Guzla de l'Émir* from rehearsal at the Opéra-Comique and returned the libretto to its authors, an action that some writers have thought a fine example of artistic sincerity and others have damned as contemptible time-serving. The true explanation is simpler: one of the conditions attached to the subvention was that the composer should never have had a work staged, and the prior production of *La Guzla de l'Émir* would have invalidated *Les Pêcheurs de perles*. (*Le Docteur Miracle* did not count in this connection, either because it was an operetta or more probably because it was not given in a theatre with a State subsidy). The music of *La Guzla de l'Émir*[2] disappeared without trace. All we have is the opinion of the Academy judges, dated 4th October 1862. They picked out for special mention 'a prelude, serving the purpose of an overture, happy in form and very neatly scored' and 'a duet in which

[1] His real name was Carvaille (1825–97). He had begun as a singer of small parts, married a celebrated soprano and was director in turn of the Théâtre-Lyrique, Vaudeville (where he produced *L'Arlésienne*) and (after Bizet's death) the Opéra-Comique, where he was responsible for the revival of *Carmen*. He held the latter post for twenty-one years, broken by a spell in prison after the disastrous fire of 1887, which was adjudged to have been due to managerial carelessness. Saint-Saëns quotes some amusing instances of his passion for leaving his personal mark on every new production: during the rehearsals of *Le Timbre d'Argent* he wanted one day to introduce wild animals, the next to cut out all the music except ballet and choruses, and play the rest as straight drama. He revived *Così fan tutte* with a new libretto based on *Love's Labour's Lost*. His notorious extravagance brought most of his enterprises to financial ruin.

[2] The libretto was afterwards set by Dubois, whose version was produced in 1873.

is inserted an elegant serenade accompanied by a harp and a pretty design for flute' (possibly an earlier version of the duet in Act I of *Les Pêcheurs de perles*); and wound up as follows:

If this work still displays a little too much of the recondite and a certain tendency to sacrifice vocal interest to richness of accompaniment, we are happy again to recognize that loftiness of sentiment, vivacity of style and certainty of execution—in a word, those serious qualities of which M. Bizet had already given proof and which are today the assured guarantee of a brilliant future.

The qualification is significant: Bizet's reaction against the supremacy of the voice was already causing that uneasiness which was to culminate in the condemnation of his later operas as Wagnerian and anti-lyrical.

About this time Bizet made his début in the concert hall. His third *envoi* had been played at the Institut in November 1861, and the Scherzo was repeated (under Deloffre) at the Cercle de l'Union Artistique, an amateur club known as the Cercle des Mirlitons, during the following year. These had been private performances, but on 11th January 1863 Pasdeloup, who in his day played the part of a French Henry Wood and had just begun to include contemporary works within the classical programmes he was trying to popularize, introduced the Scherzo at one of his public concerts at the Cirque Napoléon. Most accounts agree that he was a very indifferent conductor. Saint-Saëns, who was present, says that Bizet's Scherzo was 'badly performed and badly listened to, falling upon general inattention and indifference'. According to Pigot it was received with hisses; and although the rest of the programme, which included Mozart's E flat Symphony and Beethoven's *Egmont* music, was eminently respectable, Pasdeloup was deluged with correspondence from angry subscribers threatening to withdraw their subscriptions. The few press notices scarcely bear out this account. The *Revue et Gazette Musicale* found the Scherzo charming; J. Lovy in *Le Ménestrel*, the organ of the music-publishing firm of Heugel, described it as 'a very pleasing piece, written with a certain verve but with something lacking in the peroration'. Both say it was applauded. On the following Sunday (the 18th) it was repeated under Bizet himself in a concert given by the Société Nationale des Beaux-Arts,[1] an institution (apparently short-lived) whose aim was to cater for young composers. Also included in the programme were parts of a Symphony by Saint-Saëns and Félicien David's symphonic ode *Le Désert.* This time *Le Ménestrel* in the person of Paul Bernard found the Scherzo prolix and lacking in melodic inspiration, but the *Revue et Gazette,* though critical of Bizet's conducting, praised the music for 'a wholly French clarity and grace' and contrasted it favourably with the distorted and far-fetched style of Saint-Saëns. Three weeks later (8th February) the Société Nationale des Beaux-Arts gave what appears to have been the only public performance of *Vasco de Gama,* again conducted by the composer. It had a thoroughly bad press. The *Revue et Gazette* damned it as a lamentable failure, congested in harmony and full of banal phrases and commonplace rhythms. 'Comparisons are useless when one is confronted with a work of such limited scope and, even worse, such imperfection. . . . Everything lacks breadth, colour and originality.' Scudo, discussing the season's music in the *Revue des deux Mondes* (15th June), called it a flagrant imitation of David's *Christophe Colomb.*

The contract for *Les Pêcheurs de perles* (originally entitled *Leïla*) was signed early in April 1863,[2] with the production fixed for mid September. This did not give Bizet much time; it is hardly surprising that he borrowed material from *Ivan IV.* The greater part of *La Guzla de l'Émir* probably went the same way. Gounod advised him to imitate the tortoise rather than the hare and not to drive himself too fast on the pretext that he must hurry. After urging him to be very much himself ('that is the way to be all alone today, but to have the world round you tomorrow') he continued in reply to some query of Bizet's:

> You regret that the laws do not permit the assassination of certain musicians? But they certainly do permit it, and the divine laws *order* it. Only

[1] To be distinguished from the more famous Société Nationale founded in 1871.

[2] The letter of 28th March 1863 from Berlioz to Marmontel, which Maurice Emmanuel (*Revue de Musicologie,* Nov. 1938, p. 140) relates to this opera, must—if it concerns Bizet at all, which is by no means certain—refer to *Ivan IV.*

you must agree over the means. We are all killing: the butchers kill meat; the lazy kill time or flies; journalists kill the dead; and good works kill bad ones. In twenty years from now Wagner, Berlioz, Schumann will reckon plenty of victims. Haven't we already seen some, and famous names at that, half slain by the last blows of Beethoven? There was a grand assassin! Try to be in the camp of the assassins; there is no middle way between that and the camp of the victims.

These were wise words well directed: Gounod's precept was better for Bizet than his example. The score was completed early in August, and Bizet promptly quarrelled with Choudens over its publication. His relations with publishers were subject to frequent storms and recriminations; on this occasion, after he had denied in print that Choudens had secured the rights, all was amicably settled. The first performance, fixed for 14th September, was postponed till the 30th owing to the indisposition of the Leila, Léontine de Maësen, who was still not quite fit on the first night. The part of Nadir was sung by Morini, Zurga by Ismaël and Nourabad by Guyot. The opera was moderately well received, though the audience seems to have been more surprised than pleased by the vividness of the scoring and the boldness of certain harmonic effects. Bizet was called on at the end and greeted with enthusiastic applause (there is no evidence whatever for Landormy's suggestion that the ovation was due to a careful dissemination of his friends in the audience). Louis Gallet, who was seeing Bizet for the first time, described him as

a little dazed; his head was lowered and revealed only a forest of thick curly fair hair above a round, still rather childish face, enlivened however by the quick bright eyes which took in the whole hall with glances at once delighted and confused.

According to another member of the audience, Pierre Berton, Bizet was already hailed by his contemporaries as the leader of the young French school: 'In the man himself there were such rare and charming qualities that one forgave the artist his disturbing superiority.' This may help to account for the tone of the press, which (with one notable exception) was frigid and patronizing. Bizet was taken severely to task for imitating Wagner, Félicien David and the 'violent effects' of the new Italian school (i.e. Verdi); he was accused of 'harmonic bizarreries born of a misdirected search for originality' and of the unspeakable sin of 'enthusiasm'; he was told that his talent approximated to that of Grisar, one of the most trivial of the *opéra-comique* composers, and should never attempt the pathetic. Jouvin in *Le Figaro* found the opera an orgy of noise and Gustave Bertrand in *Le Ménestrel* ended with a pompous rebuke to Bizet for appearing at the end: if he had to appear, he ought to have been dragged on—or at least have made a pretence of being dragged on. Johannès Weber in *Le Temps* indulged in the same type of captious irrelevance. The one exception—and he was an exception to almost everything in France at that time—was Berlioz, who devoted his last critical article in the *Journal des Débats* to *Les Pêcheurs de perles*. His appraisal was remarkably discriminating. He picked out for warm approval some of the most original items, such as the opening chorus and dance and the delightful chorus behind the scenes at the beginning of Act II, and greatly praised the subtlety and novelty of the scoring, while condemning the chorus 'Ah, chante, chante encore', 'whose rhythm is one of the things one doesn't dare write nowadays'. He observed with typical irony that Bizet had come back from Rome without having forgotten music, and summed up:

> The score of *Les Pêcheurs de perles* does M. Bizet the greatest honour, so that we shall be forced to accept him as a composer despite his rare talent as a sight-reader.

But Berlioz, as usual, was playing a lone game, and the opera, though it had a certain *succès d'estime* with artists,[1] was a failure with the paying public. For a time it was played alternately with *The Marriage of Figaro*, but after a total of eighteen performances (the last on 23rd November) it dropped out of the repertory till 1886, when Bizet was both dead and world famous. Carvalho's next production (4th November), the notorious emasculated version of *Les Troyens à*

[1] Ludovic Halévy, after hearing the opera three times and discerning 'the rarest virtues', wrote in his diary: 'There is in this first work an assurance, a calm, an easy powerful handling of the choruses and the orchestra which certainly announce a composer.' Paladilhe in a letter to his father described the opera as far superior to the work of the older generation of Auber and Thomas.

Carthage, which was all Berlioz ever heard of his masterpiece, again nearly involved Bizet in a duel. An obscure musician named Victor Chéri, conductor of the band at the Variétés Theatre, took offence at Bizet's public championship of *Les Troyens*, which he chose to consider a personal affront, and sent him a challenge.[1] Bizet dispatched his seconds to Chéri, who hastily withdrew.

[1] For his incoherent and perhaps inebriated letter, see Curtiss, p. 144. Bizet's praise of *Les Troyens* had provoked odious comparisons with a piece by Chéri called *Turlurette*.

CHAPTER IV

THE YEARS OF STRUGGLE (1863–9)

THE next few years were a period of constant and increasing frustration for Bizet, all the harder to bear for its promising start. Immediately after the production of *Les Pêcheurs de perles* Carvalho gave him a commission for *Ivan IV*. About the same time, on 3rd October 1863, Adolphe Bizet bought a small piece of land at Le Vésinet,[1] a few miles down the Seine from Paris. Here he built two small bungalows, known as Nos. 8 and 10 Route des Cultures, which served as summer residences for himself and his son (in the winter they continued to live in Paris where their address was now 32 Rue Fontaine-Saint-Georges). The bungalows were small and very simply furnished, and father and son did their own cooking, helped by an ample kitchen garden. Galabert describes the pleasure Bizet took in this place and in walking along the wooded banks of the Seine, accompanied by his great black-and-white watchdog Zurga, called after a character in *Les Pêcheurs de perles*. But this idyllic picture does not reveal the whole truth.

Although he had achieved something in having a three-act opera put on the stage, Bizet found himself at the age of twenty-five both financially and artistically insecure. Now that his Rome pension had run out he had to make a living, and this meant a great deal of uncongenial work. His pupils, who seem to have consisted largely of the talentless children of the upper classes who wished to acquire the social grace of playing a pretty piece on the piano, merely bored him. (Among his papers are several pages of notes for an elementary course of lectures.) He was employed by Perrin and Carvalho to play through the scores submitted to the Opéra and Théâtre-Lyrique. In April 1864 he had the more rewarding task of accompanying

[1] He paid 3,800 francs for an area of 4,697 square metres. Land was cheap in the district owing to the building of a railway, on which the purchasers were offered a free pass for three years.

rehearsals for *L'Enfance du Christ*, and a little earlier he and Saint-Saëns had supported (on piano and harmonium) a private performance of *Mireille* at Gounod's house. But his income was chiefly derived from hackwork for the publishers Heugel and Choudens. This consisted of piano transcriptions of all kinds, for two and four hands, vocal scores of operas, orchestrations of song hits of the day and even the composition of third-rate dance music. The transcriptions are models of their kind, far above the general level of the period, which they did much to raise; but Bizet had no illusions about the dance music. In a letter to Galabert (September 1866) he gives an amusing account of his scoring of a certain 'ignoble waltz':

> It is maddening to interrupt the work I love for two days in order to write cornet solos. One must live! I had my revenge. I have treated this orchestra more scurvily than nature intended. The cornet utters yells worthy of a low public house, the ophicleide and big drum pleasantly mark the first beat of the bar with bass trombone and cellos and basses, while the second and third beats are pounded out by the horns, violas, second violins, the two first trombones and the drum! Yes, the drum!

As late as 1869 Choudens asked him to compose a waltz on motives from the new ballet in *Faust*; he apologized to Galabert for perpetrating such filth on the back of one of his songs.

The list of works arranged by Bizet that poured from the presses during the sixties is astonishing: it includes *Le Pianiste Chanteur* (6 series; 150 pieces from all schools, for which Heugel paid him 2,100 francs), arrangements for piano solo or duet (or both) of *Faust*, *Hamlet*, *Don Giovanni*, *Mignon*, *Roméo et Juliette*, Nicolai's *Merry Wives of Windsor*, *L'Oca del Cairo* [1] and other operas, and a vast number of lesser pieces. It is perhaps arguable whether labours of this kind impaired his musical style and sense of artistic direction; there is no doubt whatever that they damaged his health. He speaks of working sixteen hours a day and even more, of periods of exhaustion and of frequent recurrences of his throat trouble; the effect of this on a constitution never robust is not difficult to estimate.

Nor was his creative career making progress. Conditions in the Paris theatres became less and less favourable to young composers.

[1] Victor Wilder's version of Mozart's unfinished opera, produced in 1867.

Late in 1863 a government edict ostensibly guaranteed them the freedom of the theatres. The management of the Opéra and the Opéra-Comique interpreted this as freedom to exclude them. Camille Doucet, Director-General of State Theatres, to whom Paladilhe appealed, declared that the minister had forbidden the Opéra-Comique to fulfil its traditional obligations: the freedom of the theatres meant the right of any individual to build a theatre and stage what he liked in it. There remained the Théâtre-Lyrique; and Carvalho certainly did his best. In 1864, instead of commissioning an opera, he offered a libretto, *La Fiancée d'Abydos*, for competition among Prix de Rome winners.[1] Bizet of course was disqualified by his selection the previous year; but the competition helped to seal the fate of *Ivan IV*. The winning opera, by Barthe, was staged late in 1865 and failed so badly that Carvalho's shaky financial position still further deteriorated. He put on *Don Giovanni* and *The Merry Wives of Windsor* as money-raisers, gave up commissioning new operas from winners of the Prix de Rome, and postponed *Ivan IV* so often that Bizet lost heart.

The libretto of this ill-fated work, by François Hippolyte Leroy and Henri Trianon, had been written for Gounod, who set it for the Opéra in 1855–8. The production was repeatedly put off and eventually abandoned, and Gounod borrowed from his music in *Faust* (Soldiers' Chorus), *La Reine de Saba* (march) and *Mireille* (air 'Le jour se lève').[2] On 10th March 1864 *Le Figaro* announced that

[1] Paladilhe's experience with Carvalho exactly anticipated that of Bizet with Perrin a few years later. Carvalho assured him that his entry would win the prize, and even if it did not it would be produced—but Samuel David's would not be produced even if he won. *See* below, p. 77. For years Paladilhe's career ran parallel with Bizet's: he wrote a symphony for Pasdeloup in the late sixties, and in 1872 his one-act opera *Le Passant* (with Galli-Marié) met the same rough treatment from de Leuven and the Opéra-Comique orchestra as *Djamileh* a month later.

[2] The autograph of Gounod's *Ivan*, running to 687 pages but with only a few numbers complete, was No. 31 in the Paris sale of his manuscripts on 27th November 1963. It was withdrawn and destroyed by his descendants when it was found in a list of works he did not wish preserved, apparently because he feared unauthorized arrangements after his death.

Bizet's opera—which it called *Ivan le Terrible*, a title incorrectly adopted in Pigot's and later biographies, including the first edition of this book—would follow *Mireille* (produced 19th March) at the Théâtre-Lyrique. During the next eighteen months the press continued to predict its imminent arrival. In the late autumn of 1865 Bizet told Galabert that the score was at the copyist's and the opera would come on in January or February 1866. Carvalho consulted Nestor Roqueplan, former director of the Opéra, about methods of paying for it, but without success. Bizet grew more and more impatient. '*Ivan* is still held up!' he wrote to Galabert in December. 'The Théâtre-Lyrique hasn't a penny, and I have to wait for the powers that be to gild the intelligent director a little.' And later in the same month: 'I have finished with the Lyrique. *Ivan* withdrawn. I am in negotiation with the Grand Opéra.' He sent the score to Perrin, director of the Opéra, accompanied by sour reflections on the lot of a composer.

Here again he was unlucky. A departmental memorandum from Doucet to the Minister of Fine Arts, dated 11th December, states that the Opéra is fully committed and Bizet would be better advised to stick to the Lyrique. 'By its very subject matter, this *Ivan IV* has more chance of success at the Théâtre-Lyrique than at the Opéra'; Doucet and Perrin are 'not at all disposed to compete with the Théâtre-Lyrique in a manner dangerous to the work and to its young composer'. Since the libretto had been written for the Opéra, and its subject and treatment are nothing if not Meyerbeerian, and since Doucet knew all about Carvalho's financial position, this must be put down as a shameless piece of bureaucratic hypocrisy. Three months later Perrin was forced to resign and *Ivan* disappears from the records, except for a couple of references in letters of February 1869. There was then some question of Bizet submitting the score to Pasdeloup, who had succeeded Carvalho at the Lyrique; but his short tenure (1868–70) was even more precarious than his predecessor's. The fact that Bizet never mentioned the opera in conversation with Galabert suggests that it was a sore subject. According to Pigot he burned the score, and this may be true. For the surviving autograph, containing passages used in *Les Pêcheurs de perles* and with the last act incomplete, is certainly not the version submitted to Carvalho and Perrin. Like Gounod's setting, the opera was used as a quarry for other works. For its subsequent fate *see* page 287.

This experience puzzled and embittered Bizet. In January 1866 he wrote to Choudens: 'More and more rebuffs and disappointments surround me, and I can't understand why.' A little later (31st March) we find the first signs of what later amounted almost to persecution mania. 'I am convinced from our conversation yesterday that somewhere around me there is hidden dung. I sense it, I feel it. It smells to high heaven.' There is no evidence that Bizet was the victim of any particular conspiracy, though the general corruption of the Second Empire lay heavily on ambitious young artists. But we can see how he felt himself cornered between impoverished directors on the one hand and prosperous publishers (who paid no royalties) on the other.

At the same period Gounod too became disillusioned with the theatre and declared [1] that the recently completed *Roméo et Juliette* would be his farewell to the stage (it was in fact his last operatic success). He introduced Bizet to the *salon* of Princess Mathilde, the daughter of Napoleon's brother Jerome, King of Westphalia. This enabled Bizet to shine as a pianist—on one occasion he played at an official reception at the Louvre—and may have encouraged him to compose for the instrument. In December 1865 Heugel paid him 600 francs for the six *Lieder sans Paroles* [*sic*] on poems by Méry entitled *Chants du Rhin*—though he tried to exclude the best of the set, *La Bohémienne*. Bizet sent a copy to Thomas, who expressed great enthusiasm for *Les Rêves*. Heugel also published *Chasse fantastique*, which reads like a transcription from an orchestral score and may be a rehash of the overture *La Chasse d'Ossian*. The three *Esquisses musicales* for harmonium (the piano version may not be by Bizet), hitherto attributed to 1866, had appeared as early as 1858. Galabert mentions an abortive opera of this period, called *Nicolas Flamel*, for which Bizet sketched a scene at the piano in the presence of himself and the librettist, Ernest Dubreuil. He dates this 'before he had begun *La Jolie Fille de Perth* . . . probably in May 1865.'

Edmond Galabert, who met Bizet early in that year and became his

[1] In a letter to Meilhac, 10th March 1866.

pupil in June, was a young musical amateur from Montauban. For several years Bizet gave him lessons by correspondence. Galabert, who later published a much-edited version [1] of the letters he received from Bizet, gives an illuminating account of his methods as a teacher. Before taking him on, Bizet examined him closely in literature as well as music, asking particularly what books he had read in French and foreign languages. When Galabert gave him a list, including Goethe and Schiller, Bizet replied: 'That settles it. People think you don't need any education to be a musician. They are wrong; you have to know a great deal.' [2] After lessons had been going on for a year Galabert broached the question of fees, on which nothing had been arranged. Bizet cut him short:

> Don't ever mention that again. I give lessons for money because they bore me. . . . With you, we are simply talking of things that interest us, things that we love. We are swimming in the same waters. I have been at it longer than you. I know the bad places, and I say to you only: Don't go there, it's dangerous.

In fact Galabert paid Bizet with gifts of wine from his father's vineyards at Montauban. All references to this were suppressed in the published correspondence.

Bizet was a conscientious and modest teacher. After giving Galabert the text of a Prix de Rome cantata to set, he called in Guiraud to hear it played, telling Galabert afterwards that he wanted a second opinion in case his teaching was on the wrong lines. He urged Galabert to study Mozart's and Weber's operas and to aim at emotional expressiveness, sacrificing the strict principles of harmony and counterpoint if necessary. 'Let yourself go, aim at the emotions, avoid dryness, don't turn up your nose at the sensuous, you austere philosopher. . . . Let us have fantasy, boldness, unexpectedness, enchantment—above all, tenderness, *morbidezza*!' He particularly emphasized the double profit, spiritual and technical, to be derived

[1] Or rather two versions, one in 1877 and another, somewhat fuller, in 1909. The full texts were recently recovered by Mina Curtiss.

[2] This alone should dispose of Landormy's preposterous charge, repeated by others, that Bizet had no cultural or outside interests and only financial ambitions.

from a study of Bach's preludes and fugues and remarked how modern some of them were in feeling, instancing the B flat minor from the first book. Orchestration in his opinion gained by not being too thick. When Galabert played something that had impressed him as effective, Bizet replied: 'No, that lacks air, and in the orchestra you must have air.' To another pupil he wrote: 'Let each part have around it sufficient room to move.' His somewhat cautious advice on the use of wind instruments has been held against him, with little reason; he preferred and recommended the old natural brass instruments, and sought (very successfully) to obtain new effects from original grouping rather than by extending the technical possibilities of each instrument.

In 1868 he gave Galabert the libretto of *La Coupe du Roi de Thulé*, which had been set for a competition by the Opéra and which he later tackled himself. His remarks on this subject are of great interest. He laid emphasis on the practical requirements of the theatre, such as giving the characters time to get on and off, and still more on the frame of mind in which a dramatic composer should work. He must get inside the skin of each character and interpret his or her feelings at each moment of the action; he should never set two stanzas in differing moods to the same music; and he can greatly heighten the dramatic tension by bringing back motives associated with a particular person or incident. Bizet at once seized on the character of Myrrha as the centre of the action—'this feline and terrible character . . . no heart, but a head and something else'. He upbraided Galabert for failing to make the most of her, and went on:

> She is an old-style courtesan, sensual as Sappho, ambitious as Aspasia; she is beautiful, quick-witted, alluring. . . . In her eyes must be that greenish look, the sure sign of sensuality and egoism pushed to the length of cruelty. . . . Yorick by himself is free; he sings his love with passion and frenzy; he tells it to the clouds and the stars. With Myrrha present he is extinguished. . . . She comes in (for the first time) slowly, dreamily, absent-mindedly; she turns her glance on all around her, and fixes it almost disdainfully on Yorick.

What is this but the Carmen-José situation, throwing its shadow years before the event? The still more interesting musical parallels are discussed in Chapter IX.

Céleste Mogador

Another new friend of 1865 may also supply a link with *Carmen.* In September an acre and a half of wooded land adjoining Bizet's cottage at Le Vésinet was bought by Mme la Comtesse de Moreton de Chabrillan, who made Bizet's acquaintance on the train while supervising the construction of her house. This was no common countess. Born in 1824, Céleste Vénard, the daughter of a loose mother and an unknown soldier, had fled from home in her teens to escape the attentions of her mother's lover, and in the course of a remarkable career had been by turns prostitute, actress (her stage name was Céleste Mogador), circus rider, novelist, dramatist and author of a volume of memoirs (though she had no idea of spelling and could hardly hold a pen). In 1854, after an assortment of dukes, musicians and authors, including Alfred de Musset, had reposed at her feet, she made a romantic and scandalous marriage with Comte Lionel de Moreton de Chabrillan, scion of an old aristocratic family. After his death in 1858 in Australia, where he was French consul at Melbourne, she returned to the stage in order to pay his debts, and in 1864 had enjoyed a triumph in a dramatization of one of her own novels by Alexandre Dumas *père.*

A second and recently discovered volume of memoirs, written in phonetic French, gives a portrait of Bizet from an unexpected angle. It is not certain, though probable enough, that the obvious explanation of their relationship is the correct one (in some respects the memoirs are more remarkable for what they omit than for what they include). She leaves the matter in doubt; but it is difficult to imagine any other link. She can hardly have helped him on the artistic plane; her cultural level seems to have been that of the drawing-room waltzes he had to score for publishers.[1] He did not get on with her friends, a Bohemian crew including a pianist who 'thumped like a beast', or with her mother, who hated both the piano and Bizet's habit of knocking on Céleste's window as he went home from the station at night (for which, on one occasion, she took a medieval revenge with a

[1] Among the songs she was then singing at cafés was Yradier's 'Ay Chiquita!' a copy of which remains in Bizet's music library (*see* Appendix G). It is a pathetic song of a girl dying for love, said to be based on an incident in the life of a cousin of Malibran.

well-aimed receptacle from an upper room). Yet he spent much time in her company, often working for hours on end in a room, complete with piano and music paper, which she put at his disposal. According to her account, she was the only woman he invited to the small musical gatherings in his bungalow, at one of which he played through the whole score of *La Jolie Fille de Perth*. Her picture of him does not suggest a contented man; though she calls him in a happy phrase 'the aristocratic savage', she also says 'I never saw him laugh freely' and more than once remarks that he 'was not very cheerful at this time'. She adds a delightful glimpse of Bizet senior, that *'saint homme'* uniquely careful of his son's independence and as reverent towards him 'as the Holy Virgin must have been towards her son conceived through the operation of the Holy Ghost'. This portrait of an unsmiling Bizet, taken when off his guard, is very revealing of the character behind the ironical mask which he presented even to his friends.

Equally striking, from a different angle, is Céleste's picture of herself:

> Moderation is no part of my nature. Joy, sorrow, affection, resentment, laziness, work—I have overdone them all. My life has been one long excess. . . . When I want something, I am willing to gamble ten or twenty years of my life to get it as quickly as possible. . . . Two defects in my character have protected me. I have always been capricious and proud. No one, among women whose tendency it is to say *yes*, derives more pleasure than I do from saying *no*. So the men to whom I have given the most are those who asked least of me.

The recurrence of such a character at the heart of Bizet's greatest music from *La Coupe du Roi de Thulé* to *Carmen* may not be due to coincidence.

The contract for the production of *La Jolie Fille de Perth* was signed with Carvalho in July 1866, and Bizet at once set about composing the music. The librettists were J. H. Vernoy de Saint-Georges, one of the most fashionable of Scribe's successors and as tiresome as he was incompetent, and Jules Adenis; the libretto was the worst Bizet was ever called upon to set. He had no illusions about this; he quoted some of the choicest verses to Galabert, remarking that he did not use the words for composing or he would never find a note (this may account for the bad prosody, a persistent but venial fault in all his operas). His method was to seize the general sense of each section and concentrate on the emotions rather than the utterances of the characters —a method that might have been fatal if applied to a work of art, such as Boito's libretti, but could hardly be said to constitute an injustice to Saint-Georges. He set himself deliberately to repair the faint characterization of the latter's creatures, and certain alterations in Act I (the suppression of a romance for Smith following the opening chorus and the substitution of Mab's *couplets*, one of the best numbers, for a duet between Mab and Smith) were probably due to his insistence. So, certainly, were many passages in Act III, of which the manuscript libretto survives, covered with his corrections and alterations. But it is unfair to condemn Bizet for not rejecting a libretto he despised; he was bound by contract with Carvalho, and the result of a young composer's rejection of a fashionable librettist's work (however inept) might have been no libretto at all.

The music of Act I was finished by September, Bizet declaring himself satisfied with it; he said, in mitigation of Saint-Georges's treatment of Scott, that the original was a detestable novel but an excellent book. His industry at this time was astonishing. The opera was not by any means the only work he had on hand. He was up to his neck in correcting proofs for publishers (which, he said, multiplied by spontaneous generation), scoring waltzes and composing songs.[1] The six songs published by Heugel under the title *Feuilles d'album* were composed this September; several others, including the admirable *Adieux de l'hôtesse arabe*, date from about the same period. In June he had resumed a project dear to his heart, the Italian symphony subsequently known as *Roma*; but though he told Galabert a month later that it was finished, this was by no means the end of its history. Two other works probably dating from the spring of 1866 are a two-part fugue, written for Galabert, which has disappeared, and a setting for male voices of Victor Hugo's 'Écoutez. Je suis Jean', written for a Belgian choral festival. By October Act II of *La Jolie*

[1] Apparently to commission: *see* the ninth letter to Galabert (July 1866).

Fille de Perth was ready, and the complete work was scored and dispatched to Carvalho on 29th December. No wonder Bizet complained of insufficient sleep.

But his worries over this opera were not at an end. For one reason or another its production was delayed for a full year, although Carvalho put on five new operas (including Gounod's *Roméo et Juliette*) during that period. Bizet, overworked, seething with impatience and quick-tempered at the best of times, was certainly unjust to Carvalho. His letters of the early part of the year, with their cries of 'rehearsal or the law-courts', are cantankerous in the extreme.[1] The Théâtre-Lyrique was in very low water, though the rumour (reported by Paladilhe) that its overdraft amounted to 1,600,000 francs in June 1866 may have been exaggerated. Some of the operas produced in 1867 were paid for by their composers—to the fury of Bizet, who rejoiced at their abject failure. *Roméo* on the other hand was an immense success, and this did not please him either since Carvalho naturally kept it running. Bizet, while arranging the vocal score, told Galabert that its authors had done everything possible to postpone and even compromise *La Jolie Fille de Perth.* To Choudens he complained that everyone was conspiring to destroy him: 'If I die of worry, discouragement, and also of hunger one of these fine days, it will occur to someone to do something about *La Jolie Fille* and *Ivan.*'

In January Carvalho had prevailed upon him to revise the contract, though Christine Nilsson, for whom the part of Catherine had been written, was re-engaged. In March Bizet went to Bordeaux to hear a new tenor, Massy, whom he engaged for the part of Smith. But

[1] To this period (March 1867) belongs his condemnation of Verdi's *Don Carlos*. 'It is *very bad.* You know I am eclectic; I adore *Traviata* and *Rigoletto. Don Carlos* is a kind of compromise. No melody, no expression; it aims at style, but it only aims. It made a disastrous impression. It was a complete and utter *flop.*' And in another letter: 'Verdi is no longer Italian; he wants to write Wagner. . . . It has neither head nor tail. He has discarded his faults, but his virtues have gone with them. He aims at style and achieves only pretentiousness.' He admitted that the attempt did credit to Verdi's integrity as an artist, and in later years he greatly admired *Aida*. 'You will find in it things that will astonish and delight you,' he wrote to Guiraud.

then Nilsson, preferring to create Ophelia in Ambroise Thomas's *Hamlet* at the Opéra, threw over her contract with the Théâtre-Lyrique and left two operas, including Bizet's, without a heroine. The next candidate, Jane Devriès,[1] who subsequently created the part, satisfied Bizet but not the rest of the syndicate, who wanted Mme Carvalho. Saint-Georges, whose vanity provoked a stream of ironical asides in Bizet's letters, and who according to Paladilhe could not distinguish between triple and common time, was particularly obstructive. But Bizet, though told he might lose 10,000 francs thereby, stuck to his guns; and rehearsals began in June with the first night planned for September. Two more postponements on account of Christine Nilsson's success in *Martha* were followed by a longer one at Bizet's own instigation. There was a Grand Exhibition in Paris that summer, and he preferred to wait until the cosmopolitan public, whom he suspected of following only the great names, had dispersed. After a very successful dress rehearsal on 10th September, which brought Bizet welcome publicity, including a caricature on the cover of the popular weekly *Diogène* and a puff from its editor (28th September), the opera was put away till December, with the result that more than one admirer of Bizet had to leave Paris without seeing it. However he had the satisfaction of selling the score to Choudens on excellent terms, which he said rivalled those given to Gounod. He was to receive 3,000 francs at the first performance, 1,500 at the thirtieth; if he had 120 performances within three years he would get 16,000 francs in all. It is doubtful if *La Jolie Fille de Perth* has yet reached 120 performances.

Meanwhile in the spring the organizers of the Exhibition had offered prizes for the best cantata and the best hymn, each composed on a given text: 10,000 francs for the hymn, 5,000 francs per performance of the cantata, plus a medal worth 1,000 francs for each winner. The distinguished jury included Berlioz, Verdi, Rossini (who failed to turn up), Auber, Thomas and Félicien David, as well as Carafa, Théophile Gautier and Saint-Georges. But the affair was typical of the Second Empire in that no one emerged with credit—

[1] She had just made a very successful début in *La Sonnambula* at the age of seventeen. Her dramatic intelligence was highly praised by Gustave Bertrand in *Le Ménestrel* of 16th June.

least of all Bizet, whose horror of humiliation led him to extreme lengths. He entered for both competitions, using Galabert's Montauban address and the pseudonymn Gaston de Betsi [*sic*] as well as the motto that was supposed to ensure anonymity. He gives an amusing account of what happened when he and Guiraud delivered their entries.

> The porter received us very unceremoniously. 'Oh! So everyone is a musician! Good Lord, it's time that was stopped!' I replied drily: 'I am no more a musician than you are, I would have you know; but a poor fellow whom I'm looking after entrusted me with this parcel, and I ask you to deliver it faithfully.' All the staff then bowed on learning that we were not musicians. What a coward I am!

According to Galabert Bizet and Guiraud took the cantata seriously but tried to be as vulgar as possible in the hymn. For this there were 823 entries, including two (one under his father's name) by Paladilhe, who remarked that the prize would probably go to one of the jury. The latter, however, declared themselves swamped by numbers and annulled the contest. The cantata competition (the piece was called *Les Noces de Prométhée*) was won by Saint-Saëns. There were 103 entries, of whom Bizet was among the first fifteen. While the jury were deliberating he had written to its secretary Ernest L'Épine, an old friend, drawing attention to his own and Guiraud's entries and identifying them by their mottos. Afterwards he was furious that his handwriting had been recognized and his participation known. His letter of congratulation to Saint-Saëns included the words: 'I regret not having competed. I should then have had the honour of being beaten by you.' Bizet and Paladilhe both said that Saint-Saëns had submitted his entry on foreign paper (though they disagreed about the nationality) and were convinced that this had influenced the result. But it availed the victor little in the long run: he was never paid, since the authorities omitted to perform his cantata, substituting one by Rossini, the absent juryman.

Soon after this Bizet arranged the vocal score of Saint-Saëns's opera *Le Timbre d'Argent*, which he greatly admired, describing it to Guiraud as 'true *opéra-comique*, slightly tinged with Verdi'. He was on excellent terms with its composer, with whom he used to discuss his difficulties. Saint-Saëns once suggested that as they were not welcomed in the theatre they should go back to the concert hall. 'That's all very well for you,' replied Bizet. 'I am not made for the symphony; I need the theatre, I can do nothing without it.' This was not always his opinion; he was apt to change his mind on such matters, and when taxed with inconsistency would reply: 'Yes, but since then I've been thinking.' Saint-Saëns well expressed the difference between his approach to music and Bizet's: 'We pursued a different ideal, he seeking passion and life above all things, I running after the chimera of purity of style and perfection of form.' On one occasion Bizet was working in his study at Le Vésinet when he heard a tenor voice declaiming the romance from *Les Pêcheurs de perles* in the street. It was Saint-Saëns, who, not knowing the number of Bizet's house, chose this method of attracting attention. Bizet liked Massenet, admiring in particular his oratorio *Marie-Magdeleine*, and wrote of him: 'We must pay attention to this little chap, he's going to leave us standing.' He respected Thomas, but could not abide Auber. Once when both composers had had an opera produced within a short interval Auber met him in the street and said, in the tone of one repeating a banal formula: 'I've heard your work. It's very good.' Bizet replied: 'I accept your praise, but I do not reciprocate it.' Then, as Auber made a face, he added quickly: 'A private soldier may receive the praises of a marshal of France; he does not return them.'

Early in 1867 he acquired another correspondence pupil. This was a young composer named Paul Lacombe, who lived at Carcassonne and wrote to Bizet without introduction. He was much more of a musician than Galabert and a man of wide culture, an author in prose and verse and a collector of pictures. Bizet introduced him to Paris musical life, and he became a close friend of Massenet, Chabrier, d'Indy and Duparc. Bizet's letters to him, if they tell less of his personal life, are of greater musical interest. In the first letter,[1] writing to a man he has never seen, he makes an engagingly frank statement of his position.

I am 28 years of age. My musical baggage is pretty slender. An opera

[1] Dated 1866 by Imbert, but almost certainly belonging to the early months of 1867.

very much discussed, attacked and defended—in fact a failure, honourable, brilliant if you allow me the expression, but none the less a failure. Some songs—seven or eight piano pieces—some symphonic fragments performed in Paris—and that's all. In some months' time a big work, but that is to count my chickens—don't let's speak of it.

The final sentences give a picture of the man and his preoccupations:

As for terms. I don't know what answer to give. I don't like dealing with that side. If I had money of my own, I would be happy to give you some of my leisure. I should think myself amply paid by the progress I should be helping you to make. Unhappily I have no leisure. Lessons, vast quantities of work for several publishers, extensive correspondence—all that swallows up my life. I am thus forced to accept, not the price of my advice, but the price of the time I spend on you. I charge 20 francs for my lessons. On an average, my time is worth 15 francs an hour to me. Will you base our arrangement on this consideration? We shall be able to work out a general average on the amount of work you send me. . . . The important thing is that we should talk no more about it, for these details are particularly disagreeable to me.

In the summer he found a more public opportunity of stating his views of music. The editor of *La Revue Nationale et Étrangère*, recently converted from a monthly to a weekly in order that more space could be devoted to current affairs, asked him to take the vacant post of music critic. He agreed, and his first article appeared on 3rd August under the pseudonym Gaston de Betzi (this time with a *z*), an anagram of his name. This witty and sensible piece of criticism [1] contains much that is still apposite. It also shows that Bizet had a real literary gift, a fact confirmed by the publication of his letters. It is a forcible plea for honesty and impartiality in musical criticism. 'I shall tell the truth, nothing but the truth, and as far as possible the whole truth.' He protests against the increasing tendency to judge music according as it conforms or fails to conform to a preordained system, whether national, philosophical, political or purely musical. 'For me

[1] Printed as Appendix E, p. 283. Frédéric Robert reproduced it for the first time in French as a prologue to his *Georges Bizet* (1965). Bizet had used the pseudonym as a private joke as early as 1865.

there are only two kinds of music—the good and the bad.'[1] Two further sins, as green as ever today, receive no less trenchant treatment: the habit of praising one composer only by damning several others, and the fashionable admiration of good taste at the expense of genius.

Let us be unaffected [*naïfs*] and genuine, not demanding from a great artist the qualities he lacks but learning to appreciate those he possesses. When a passionate, violent, even brutal personality like Verdi endows our art with a work that is vigorously alive and compounded of gold, mud, blood and gall, don't let us go up to him and say coldly: 'But my dear sir, this lacks taste, it is not gentlemanly [*distingué*].' Gentlemanly! Are Michelangelo, Homer, Dante, Shakespeare, Beethoven, Cervantes and Rabelais *gentlemanly*?

This is a truth that needs to be uttered from time to time in the history of art. We do not know how Bizet's article was received; but it was his last as well as his first venture into journalism. Immediately after it appeared the editor of the paper retired, and his successor endeavoured to censor Bizet's second contribution. He took exception to some criticism of Azevedo, Rossini's biographer, and asked him to cut out a passage about Saint-Saëns. Bizet, true to his principles, refused and resigned his post; this may have cost him some sacrifice, for it was particularly well paid. Whether he would have made a good composer-critic like Berlioz is doubtful; but he was aware of the dangers. 'Once and for all', he wrote to Choudens in 1866, 'never attach too much importance to the judgment of musicians, even the best. They identify themselves with the work; they see it from a special point of view. They are prejudiced without knowing it, and it blinds them.'

In October 1867 he wrote a jubilant letter to Galabert:

I am completely happy! Never did an opera have a better start! The dress rehearsal produced a great effect! The piece is really very interesting; the interpretation is most excellent! The costumes are rich! The settings are new! The director is delighted! The orchestra and singers are full of keenness! And what matters more than all that, dear friend, the score of the *Jolie Fille* is a GOOD PIECE OF WORK! I mention it to you *because*

[1] Chabrier, who had much in common with Bizet, later in a similar context added a third kind—the music of Ambroise Thomas.

you know me! The orchestra gives it all a colour, a relief, that I admit I didn't dare hope for! I am sticking to my path. Now, forward! I must climb, climb, always climb. No more evening parties! No more fits and starts! No more mistresses! All that is finished! Absolutely finished! I am talking seriously. I have met an adorable girl whom I love! In two years she will be my wife! From now on nothing but work and reading; thinking is life! I am talking seriously; I am convinced! I am sure of myself! The good has killed the evil! The victory is won!

The girl was Geneviève Halévy, second daughter ot Bizet's old teacher, and within two years she was indeed his wife; but no sooner was the engagement made than the Halévy family broke it off, plunging Bizet once more into despair. 'The hopes I had formed have been broken. The *family* has resumed its rights! I am very unhappy' (October). 'I am still very much depressed. The blow I have received takes away all the hopes that were dear to me' (November). We can only guess at the cause, which may have been personal or financial. Bizet said later that the Halévys regarded him as 'a Bohemian and an outsider', an odd objection from a family bristling with artists and eccentrics. It is possible that some breath of scandal about Céleste Mogador had reached their ears: in a letter of December Bizet refers to 'the disasters of Le Vésinet'.[1] Nor do we know when they eventually agreed to the marriage; probably not till shortly before it took place, in June 1869.

It was in this gloomy mood that Bizet wrote an act for an anonymous joint operetta called *Malbrough s'en va-t-en guerre* (words by Siraudin and Busnach). He described the circumstances in a letter to Lacombe:

I sent the Athénée packing. But they came weeping to me, and I polished them off the first act. Legouix is charged with the second, Jonas with the third and Delibes with the fourth. The secret was well enough guarded; but a woman has just revealed it, all is lost. I shall disown it shamelessly.

---

[1] In 1872 he had to reassure his mother-in-law that he would never allow women of the theatre to cross his threshold, and proclaimed his agreement with Dumas *fils* that unfaithfulness is as deplorable in a husband as in a wife. He also wrote to Dumas congratulating him on his treatment of moral issues and on preaching a single standard for both sexes.

I have a mind to hiss the first act—apart from the fact that the public will do it quite well without me! I have been totally dished and done for. I was reproached with not keeping my word, they set up a wail, and I *gave* them my first act. It won't bring me in a brass farthing. I certainly don't make much progress in business matters.

Delibes in a letter to Mme Trélat, who seems to have been the woman involved, gives a rather different account: Busnach (a cousin of Bizet's future mother-in-law) offered the libretto first to Delibes, and when he hesitated to Bizet, who accepted on condition that his authorship remained unknown. Carvalho heard of this and pointed out that his name was bound to come out and would not help *La Jolie Fille de Perth*. As a result Bizet withdrew, handing over the first act unscored and praising the piece so exorbitantly to Mme Trélat that she wrote Delibes a letter of congratulation. It was produced at the Athénée on 13th December with considerable success; at least two reviewers mentioned Bizet's name, and the *Revue et Gazette Musicale* particularly admired his contribution.

Pigot says that at some period during the next two years Bizet wrote music for another piece of the same kind, with the illuminating title of *Sol-si-ré-pif-pan*, which was produced, also anonymously, at the Menus Plaisirs. The only discoverable work with this title, a so-called 'bouffonnerie musicale' in one act by William Busnach, was produced at the Château d'Eau on 16th November 1872 with music by one H. Vincent. There was a contemporary Viennese composer called H. J. Vincent who did write operettas (and devised a new system explaining the principles of harmony by reference to geometry), but it is not impossible that the name was a pseudonym of Bizet's. The music of both operettas has disappeared [1]—a matter for little regret.

Deloffre conducted the first performance of *La Jolie Fille de Perth* on 26th December 1867. It seems to have been well performed and well received—though the duet for Smith and Catherine in Act IV was interrupted by an outbreak of fisticuffs in the gallery. Lutz as Ralph and Massy as Smith were excellent; Devriès (Catherine) began

[1] According to Pigot an attempt was made to reconstruct *Sol-si-ré-pif-pan* from the orchestral parts after Bizet's death.

nervously, but was at her best from the middle of Act III; the Gypsy Dance was encored. Bizet wrote cheerfully to Galabert:

> My work obtained a genuine and serious success! I was not hoping for a reception so enthusiastic and at the same time so severe. . . . I have been taken seriously, and had the great joy of moving and gripping an audience that was not predisposed in my favour. . . . The press is excellent! Now, are we going to make money?

This was the one opera of Bizet's that was reasonably well received by the press. H. Moreno's enthusiastic notice in *Le Ménestrel* called the second act 'a masterpiece from beginning to end'. Eugène Tarbé in *Le Figaro* praised the orchestration and the dramatic perspective, but found the work, judged by the highest standards—and he maintained that Bizet deserved to be so judged—lacking in originality. Reyer in *Le Journal des Débats* considered the style eclectic, but excused the concessions to public taste and to the whims of the prima donna on the ground of Bizet's youth and unestablished position. He gave high praise to the Gypsy Dance and Ralph's song in Act II. Gautier in *Le Moniteur Universel* acclaimed Bizet for following the dramatic action instead of cutting the music into catchy snippets for applause. 'Richard Wagner must be his favourite master, and we congratulate him on it.' Gautier looked forward to the promised production of *Lohengrin*, for which Paris had to wait another twenty years. The severest critic was Johannès Weber in *Le Temps*, who pointed out that, so far from the charge of Wagnerism being justified, Bizet was in danger of lapsing too far the other way; and he instanced Catherine's Act I polonaise and the entry of Catherine and Glover in Act III with its *ensemble* in quadrille rhythm [1] in the style of Auber accompanied by copious *roucoulades* from the soprano. Bizet, who was never afraid of criticism provided it was fair, at once wrote to Weber, whom he did not then know:

> No, sir, no more than you do I believe in false gods, and I will prove it to you. This time, I admit, I have made some concessions [2] which I regret.

---

[1] This is to be found only in the 1868 vocal score: *see* p. 289.

[2] He told Galabert that they had been forced upon him.

I should have plenty of things to say in my defence—you can guess them. The school of *flonflons*, trills and falsehoods is dead—dead as mutton! Let us bury them without tears, without regrets, without emotion and—forward![1] Needless to say, sir, this letter is not an advance which would be as unworthy of my character as I am convinced it would be of yours, but I repeat, your criticism pleased me, and I felt the need to tell you so sincerely.

But a good press did not save *La Jolie Fille de Perth*. It had eighteen performances, the same number as *Les Pêcheurs de perles*, and then disappeared from the Paris stage till 1890. There were several reasons for this: the remoteness of the theatre in the Place du Châtelet to which Carvalho had recently transferred his enterprise, a series of indispositions in the cast, and the imminent collapse of the Théâtre-Lyrique (Carvalho's bankruptcy was announced on 6th May 1868). *La Jolie Fille* gave way to *La Fanchonnette*; Clapisson had his posthumous revenge. According to Berton, Bizet at this time lost his pristine high spirits and assumed an air of anxiety that he never lost. He spent the early weeks of the year making three reductions of Thomas's *Hamlet*; he groaned under the labour, which brought him 900 francs from Heugel, but admired the opera.[2] He failed to persuade Litolff, through Choudens, to conduct excerpts from *La Jolie Fille* at a concert. But the *salon* of Mme Trélat, a trained singer who patronized many young musicians as well as the leading executants of the day, gave him some recreation. The St Valentine chorus soon became popular there. On 14th April *La Jolie Fille de Perth* was produced at Brussels. It was a success with the public and press, but Bizet, after attending the dress rehearsal, was so disgusted with the conducting (he praised the orchestra and singers) that he preferred to spend his time in the art galleries of Brussels and Antwerp. He told a Belgian critic that most of the music was distorted beyond recognition.

[1] It is typical of Vuillermoz's treatment of facts that he should sneer at Bizet for saying this 'just at the time that he was writing without remorse' the passages Weber had complained of. He had written them over a year before, and was now abjuring them!

[2] There is a palpable echo in *L'Arlésienne* of a theme in Thomas's play scene.

Bizet's musical activities during the next three years are bewildering. He began or projected at least eight operas; the only one he finished he kept so dark that the facts were not revealed for ninety years. In August 1867, in connection with the Exhibition, the three opera-houses each announced a competition. The Théâtre-Lyrique invited a work on any libretto the composer chose; the Opéra-Comique put forward a libretto by Saint-Georges, *Le Florentin*; while the Opéra began with a preliminary libretto competition. Bizet's first reaction was typical: 'If I compete, no one except you [Galabert] and Guiraud will know of it, and *my copying will not be recognized*.' In April 1868 the Opéra announced that its winning libretto (out of 168 submitted) was *La Coupe du Roi de Thulé* by two young authors, Louis Gallet and Édouard Blau. Bizet advised both Galabert and Lacombe to set the piece as an exercise, adding (June): 'It is more and more probable that I shall not compete.' The reason for this was that Perrin, the director of the Opéra, was pressing him to set a piece, still in scenario, by Arthur Leroy and Sauvage. Its title is not known. At the same time he refused a request from Bagier of the Théâtre-Italien to write an opera in the old Italian style by asking the exorbitant fee of 6,000 francs. He spent the summer in a state of vacillation.

> I am very much embarrassed at the moment; I don't know what to do. If I compete without getting the prize, I'm afraid the good opinions that are held of me may be modified to my disadvantage. If I win the prize, that will put off my big affair for two years, perhaps. If I do not compete and my big affair miscarries I shall find myself between two stools!

The big affair was presumably the Leroy and Sauvage opera, over which he was at first very enthusiastic. While waiting for the libretto he concentrated on other compositions. During the summer he at last finished *Roma*, completely rewriting the first movement, which had been a set of variations, and finding that the second theme of the finale fitted 'marvellously' in the middle of the andante. The first movement 'bears no resemblance to any known first movement. It is new, and I count on a good effect'. He considered, however, that the finale was not up to the standard of the rest, and later upbraided Guiraud for not telling him how bad it was. He also composed some songs,[1] which did not greatly please him, and some piano music, which did. This (inspired, according to Galabert, by his hearing Delaborde play on one of Erard's pianos) comprised the *Variations chromatiques*, based on a theme sketched the previous winter, the *Nocturne* in D major and probably *Marine*.

In July, and again in August, he had very severe attacks of quinsy ('forty tiny abscesses in the gullet, etc., etc.'), accompanied by some kind of spiritual crisis.

An extraordinary change is taking place in me. I am changing my skin, as artist and as man; I am purifying myself, I am becoming better: I feel it! Come, I shall find something in myself if I look hard enough. . . . A change so radical from the musical point of view is taking place in me that I cannot risk my new manner without preparing myself several months in advance. I am making use of September and October for this trial.

He was making 'a summary study of the history of philosophy from Thales of Miletus to the present day'. This was not his first attempt to chart his philosophical position. In 1866, disgusted by the battle of Sadowa and the aggressions of Bismarck ('aided by cholera, his worthy colleague in mincemeat'), he had tried to formulate his views on progress, political, religious and artistic. He saw no hope in nationalism—he was convinced that 'notre belle Frrrrance' would soon be soiling her hands in the fray—and organized religion, though it had served a purpose, seemed to him outmoded and misused.

Religion is for the strong a means of exploitation against the weak; religion is the cloak of ambition, injustice and vice. This progress of which you speak moves slowly but surely; it destroys little by little all superstitions. Truth breaks free, science is popularized, and religion totters; soon it will fall, in the course of centuries—that is, tomorrow. That will be all right, but don't let us forget that this religion, with which you can dispense—you and I and some others—has been the admirable

---

[1] These were the six originally published by Hartmann in 1868: *Pastorale*, *Rêve de la bien-aimée*, *Ma vie a son secret*, *Berceuse*, *La Chanson du fou* and *La Coccinelle*. *Berceuse* was written for Mme Trélat, who chose the poem.

instrument of progress; it is religion, and above all the Catholic religion, that has taught us the precepts which enable us to dispense with it today. . . . The Jews had to have altars, Sinais with Bengal fire, etc. One had to speak to their eyes; later it was enough to speak to their imagination. In good time we shall only have to deal with reason.

But this prospect had its drawbacks too.

I believe that the whole future belongs to the perfecting of our social system (with which politics are always so confoundedly mixed up). Society once perfected, no more injustice, and so no more malcontents, hence no more assaults on the social system, no more priests, no more policemen, no more crime, no more adultery, no more prostitution, no more inflamed emotions, no more passions—but wait! no more music, no more poetry, no more legion of honour, no more press (bravo for that!), above all no more theatre, no more error, and so no more art! . . . The societies most deeply tainted with superstition have been the greatest promoters of art. . . . Art decays in proportion as reason advances. . . . The imagination lives on chimeras, on visions. You suppress the chimeras, and goodbye imagination!

Faced with this dilemma, or with the greater implied dilemma that lay beneath, Bizet for a time took refuge in something approaching sheer pessimism ('Don't count on anything! The longer I live, the more I mistrust our poor human kind'). His survey of 1868, superficial as he admitted it was, brought him a conclusion of sorts. He found

talent, genius, outstanding personalities . . . but not a philosophical system that stands up to examination. With morality it is different. Socrates (that is to say, Plato), Montaigne (excellent, because he has no system)—but spiritualism, idealism, eclecticism, materialism, scepticism, all are downright useless. Stoicism, despite its errors, did make men. In fact, the true philosophy is: examine known facts, extend scientific knowledge and ignore *absolutely* everything that is not proved up to the hilt! That positivism is the only rational philosophy, and it is grotesque that the human spirit should have taken nearly three thousand years to discover it!

However inadequate an answer this may seem on the part of Bizet the man (and it is hard to think he really believed it), it is possible that it was a help to Bizet the artist. Gounod, faced with a more acute conflict between the fleshly and the spiritual, developed something like religious mania, with disastrous effects on his music.[1] Bizet remained critical, detached, half idealist, half sceptic; and in the remaining years of his life he wrote music that showed a remarkable power to enter into and interpret, as it were from within and without at once, the emotional and psychological states of all manner of persons, from an Arabian slave-girl to Parisian children at play, from young men turned into criminals by a passion stronger than themselves to a couple of old peasants meeting at last to declare the love they have concealed for fifty years.

The results of what he described as this changing of his skin appear in *La Coupe du Roi de Thulé*. The Leroy-Sauvage libretto still hanging fire, Perrin prevailed upon Bizet 'with the *compelling authority* which a director of the Opéra exercises over a composer whom he holds between finger and thumb' to enter for his competition. Two acts were written by October, and Bizet was at first greatly pleased, considering them far superior to anything he had done before.[2] Yet though Perrin assured him that whatever the jury decided he would see that he got the prize, Bizet was still suspicious.[3] He thought that Perrin's object was to make sure of getting a tolerable score, but that if he received one better he would be quite pleased to drop Bizet's; and he found himself up against the old problem: 'Not to get the prize would be annoying and a black mark as far as the Opéra is

[1] The few references to Gounod in Bizet's letters of this period are sharply critical, though he still found his early operas 'full of verdure and sap'. In October he lamented that Gounod's election to the Institut was 'leading him astray'. In December 1868 he wrote to Lacombe: 'Gounod is leaving for Rome to take orders. He is absolutely mad! His last compositions are dreadful. To hell with Catholic music!'

[2] Though as usual he soon wavered. 'I have reviewed my first act of *La Coupe* on two different occasions,' he wrote to Guiraud. 'The first time I found it altogether admirable; the second time it seemed to me nauseating!'

[3] He may have been justified. Perrin—who was to pronounce a fulsome eulogy at the inauguration of Bizet's monument in 1876—was described by Sardou in a letter to du Locle as 'the most volatile, the most capricious, the most changeable of men'.

concerned. To let it be carried off by a gentleman who would do less well than I would be galling. What am I to do?' In December he told Lacombe he was thoroughly sick of the subject. Nevertheless he finished his score, probably early in 1869, and sent it in (the closing date was 1st September). Late in the summer something happened to revive his suspicions, for he wrote a disgusted letter to Guiraud telling him to go to Perrin and pretend that he (Bizet) had not entered. 'For two sous, if I were not afraid of losing, I should withdraw my effort. It's all settled in advance, you can be sure. They will choose the one that offers the biggest chance of failure.' Although he could not withdraw his entry, he contrived to recover the sealed envelope containing his name and address and to substitute another with his new address (he had since married) and this statement: 'In the event of my score, even though it be judged the best in the competition, not being considered worthy to be staged at the Opéra, I wish to remain anonymous and to give up the prize of 3,000 francs.'

On this occasion all Bizet's suspicions were abundantly justified. The conduct of the jury was scandalous. It consisted of Perrin and seven composers, all nonentities except Saint-Saëns; only three of them had had an act performed at the Opéra, and each had failed. There were forty-two competitors, including Massenet, Guiraud and Paladilhe (who found the subject 'horribly difficult and not very musical'), besides Bizet. On 21st November the result was announced: the winner was an amateur, Eugène Émile Diaz de la Peña,[1] followed (in order of merit) by Massenet, Guiraud, Barthe and the Prince de Polignac. Bizet was one of the next two. Adolphe Jullien heard a member of the jury telling a colleague, a month before the judgment, that Diaz would win. According to Paladilhe, it was common knowledge that most of his score was the work of Victor Massé, his

[1] A pleasant story is told of his getting into difficulties with the scoring of his opera. He went to Bizet and Guiraud and said: 'Shall I have the flute accompanying here, or the horn?' Bizet suggested the horn, Guiraud the flute. Diaz, perplexed, went to his father, an elderly and distinguished painter, who pondered hard and replied: 'Don't run any risks, my boy. Have them both.' Diaz had already experienced a disastrous failure at the Théâtre-Lyrique with an opera called *Le Roi Candaule*.

teacher and one of the jury. Massenet [1] and Guiraud were so disgusted that they refused to allow the minister to publish their names. Massé told Massenet that his score contained such an abuse of Wagnerian formulae that it engendered nothing but weariness and fatigue, and it is possible that the same charge was brought against Bizet's, which makes a more elaborate use of *Leitmotive* than any of his other operas. When Diaz's opera was produced at the Opéra on 10th January 1873, after being touched up during rehearsal by Massé, the singer J. B. Faure and others, it failed abjectly,[2] as it deserved: its dreary insipidity would be difficult to parallel even in the annals of mid-nineteenth-century France. Bizet's, so far as can be judged from the surviving fragments, would have ranked among his operas second only to *Carmen*.

Two more abortive operas of this period merit a brief mention. In September 1868 Bizet was in negotiation with Léon Halévy, brother of the composer and father of Ludovic, over a five-act piece called *Les Templiers*. He spent a week on Halévy's scenario, which he found 'superb', and declared himself ready to undertake it. 'How happy I should be if you would be willing in collaboration with M. de Saint-Georges to write this magnificent opera-poem for me.' He may have been swayed by a desire to stand well with the Halévy family; but although he went to see Perrin about the opera, nothing came of it. The subject seems as unsuited to his gifts as that of *Vercingétorix*, which he considered late in 1869. He told the librettist, Émile Délérot, that he had long been in love with the idea, 'but the insurmountable obstacle is Caesar! These wretched emperors are generally not too musical!' Bizet's muse certainly was not equipped to deal with emperors. There is also an undated letter expressing 'infatuation' with

[1] The events of this year put a strain on Bizet's friendship for Massenet, whom he described as 'atrocement intrigant'. A year later he wrote him a most enthusiastic letter about his *Cahier bleu*, praised his *Suite d'orchestre* and *Poème du souvenir*, and thanked him for the gift of the overture to *Die Meistersinger*.

[2] So did the winning entries in the Opéra-Comique and Théâtre-Lyrique competitions. The latter was won by another nonentity after the jury had reached stalemate over two much better operas, one of them Lalo's *Fiesque*.

what he calls a modern subject in costume, set in the Caucasus in 1840, containing 'battles (offstage), love, jealousy, treason, fanaticism' but requiring only moderate scenic resources and the personnel of the Opéra-Comique. The statement [1] that Bizet sent in a setting of *Le Florentin* for the Opéra-Comique competition seems to be untrue; it is not mentioned in his letters.

In February 1869 Bizet told Mme Trélat he had suffered a misfortune that struck him to the roots of his pride as an artist, but his own interest demanded a prudence foreign to his character. This probably refers to the abandonment of the Leroy-Sauvage libretto with which he had hoped to conquer the Opéra. It did not fulfil the hopes of its scenario, and was apparently rejected by Perrin. Bizet fell into a state of profound depression and was unable to compose. He poured out his woes in a long letter to an unidentified woman:

> I spend my nights wondering whether life is not a cruel joke, if intelligence and sensitivity are not malformations of the moral system, burdens we must bear. I have never felt as disgusted as this. What is the point of going on with such an existence? I would like to fly the country, escape from my kind, from this hateful world to which I am riveted. This so-called artistic *milieu* is no better than the gutter. I see no one in it I can like or even respect.

Nevertheless this was the moment when, unperceived, the tide began to turn. Camille du Locle, a man of progressive ideas but no great musical understanding, had just joined de Leuven in the management of the Opéra-Comique. He at once wrote to Bizet about a possible work in three or four acts. Bizet was eager to co-operate: 'I shall be delighted to drop the competition and try to change the *genre* of *opéra-comique*. Down with *La Dame blanche*!' Much time was spent in finding a libretto; Sardou and du Locle were busy with one piece, probably *Grisélidis*, while Bizet was keener on another. It was some time before he was sure he had found the right path.

On 28th February 1869 Pasdeloup—who had expressed an interest in *Ivan IV*, but Bizet was too discouraged to play it to him—performed three movements of the Italian symphony under the title *Fantaisie symphonique, Souvenirs de Rome.* This title, as well as those of the individual

[1] Soubies and Malherbe, *Histoire de l'Opéra-Comique*, vol. ii, p. 202.

movements, was concocted at the last minute, possibly by Pasdeloup, who omitted the scherzo, apparently because of its dubious reception six years earlier. This was against Bizet's wish, but Pasdeloup said that as soon as the work obtained the success it deserved he would 'slip in the scherzo like a letter into the letter-box'. The performance went quite well. Bizet reported the public reaction concisely: 'First movement: a round of applause, some hisses, second round, a whistle, third round. Andante: a round of applause. Finale: great effect, applause three times repeated, hisses, three or four whistles. In fact a success.' This was a modest ration of hisses for a new work at this date; in the same year the overture to *Die Meistersinger* was twice nearly howled down by Pasdeloup's audience.[1] But despite the fair reception the Symphony was ignored by the press,[2] apart from the *Revue et Gazette Musicale*, which applauded its technical skill, 'above all a lively feeling for orchestration', but found the ideas and the style derivative. Bizet tried to persuade Pasdeloup to revive it in the winter of 1872; but it was not heard again till 1880, five years after Bizet's death, when the scherzo was restored. The publication of the score, prepared in 1869, was also delayed till 1880, when the work appeared under the title *Roma*.

[1] The first Paris performance of *Rienzi*, at the Théâtre-Lyrique in April 1869, also baffled the public. Bizet gave Galabert an amusing description of the dress rehearsal; he described the opera, not inaptly, as 'a noise of which nothing can give you an idea', but 'on the whole an astonishing work, prodigiously alive. . . . Genius without proportion, without order, but genius!'

[2] Perhaps because it coincided with the death of Berlioz and the first performance of *Faust* at the Opéra. *Le Ménestrel* (28th February) announced it as *Souvenir de Rome* (in the singular).

CHAPTER V

MARRIAGE AND WAR (1869–71)

ON 3rd June 1869 Bizet married Geneviève Halévy. Until the recent discovery of their private papers this was regarded as a union of unadulterated happiness,[1] a conclusion deliberately fostered by the suppression of facts and the destruction of documents. It is true that the early months were happy, and that both parties were deeply in love. But temperamental factors made friction almost inevitable. Geneviève had a heritage of nervous instability from both parents, especially her mother, who belonged to a family of rich Jewish bankers in Bordeaux and was twenty-one years younger than her husband. Léonie Halévy had conspicuous social and artistic gifts (she was an amateur sculptor), but suffered from periodic attacks of insanity which required her confinement.[2] Her extravagant tastes created chronic domestic upheavals, and her relatives were more than once compelled to sell part of her property to pay her debts.

Geneviève's childhood was darkened by tragedy. Her father died after a long illness when she was thirteen. Two years later her gifted sister Esther, who was engaged to her cousin Ludovic, died suddenly at the age of twenty. Léonie in a fit of mental derangement accused Geneviève of being responsible for Esther's death, and the child was never afterwards able to live with her mother. For the next few years, covering the period of her brief engagement to Bizet in 1867, she stayed with different relations. It is scarcely surprising that her early diaries reveal a character haunted by fear. In 1864, after attending Esther's funeral, Paladilhe wrote to his father: 'The mother has been mad for several months, and Bébé [Geneviève's pet name], who is

[1] In later years Geneviève invented fantasies about it, including the statement that Bizet had asked her father for her hand, a chronological impossibility.

[2] Geneviève's aunt Mélanie lived permanently in a sanatorium for the same reason.

now a woman, is more and more unbalanced.' Her diary entries in the early months of 1868, after the breaking of the engagement, are marked by a desolate loneliness verging at times on total despair.

Geneviève's explicit dread of the future developed into a constant demand for support and reassurance from all around her, most of all of course from her husband, whose ambition and consciousness of his own powers were themselves undermined by sensations of insecurity and persecution. Well might Paladilhe senior write to his son on hearing of the renewed engagement (22nd May 1869):

> Like you I am glad it is Bizet, not you, who is marrying Mlle Halévy, although she is the daughter of your master. Even when I knew her as a child, it was not difficult to recognize the seeds of a mental instability that did not bode well for the future.

Bizet indeed shouldered a heavy burden. In the next few years both Geneviève and her mother made endless demands on his time and sympathy; from the summer of 1870 his letters show a persistent concern for Geneviève's health, mental rather than physical. The experience matured him: the many interesting letters to his mother-in-law and other Halévy relations published by Mina Curtiss reveal a character balanced and sympathetic and utterly different from the raw youth of the Rome correspondence. But it must also have impaired his resistance to his own illness and disappointment. In discussing his death Mrs Curtiss observes perceptively:

> He lacked the instinct for self-preservation. . . . An artist has only two alternatives: either he cultivates his sense of self-protection to a degree that may well make him seem a monster of selfishness to non-creative human beings; or, if he is incapable of the ruthlessness necessary to protect the integrity of his inner core from the onslaughts of daily existence, he compensates for this lack by finding the right person to protect him.

Wagner and Verdi did both; Bizet, so far from doing either, saddled himself with 'a mother and daughter incapable of conducting their own lives, unaware of or indifferent to the burden they imposed on others'.

The marriage was a civil ceremony; neither party was a religious believer. Four months later Bizet described Geneviève to Galabert as 'an adorable creature whose intelligence is open to all kinds of progress and reform, who believes neither in the God of the Jews nor in the God of the Christians, but in honour, duty, in a word morality'. As Mrs Curtiss points out, this is rather a reflection of his own character than an accurate appraisal of his wife's. Bizet's father attended the ceremony, but not Geneviève's mother, who was once more prostrated in a sanatorium. Bizet told Galabert that the dowry would be between 150,000 and 200,000 francs, with 500,000 to come later; by the terms of the contract Geneviève was to enjoy all her father's royalties. The honeymoon was spent near Enghien in the house of Mme Halévy's brother Hippolyte Rodrigues (1812–98), who seems to have been largely responsible for gaining the family's consent to the marriage. A stockbroker, religious scholar, author and amateur composer (of an opera, *David Rizzio*, among other works), Rodrigues was a loyal friend to Bizet for the rest of his life.

This summer, and the following, Bizet was a member of the jury chosen to award the Prix de Rome; with him were the ancient Auber and a number of nonentities. In the autumn he settled down at 22 Rue de Douai, sharing the house with some of his wife's relations, including her cousin Ludovic Halévy, already known for his collaboration with Henri Meilhac in libretti for Offenbach. His first major task after marriage was the completion of his father-in-law's biblical opera *Noé* (libretto by Saint-Georges). The dying composer had wanted Gevaert to finish it, but Bizet was approached through Ambroise Thomas as early as December 1862. He did nothing then, and a first attempt in 1868, probably a placatory offering to the family, was equally fruitless. In October 1869 he was furnishing his flat by day and working on *Noé* at night. He had a contract with the Théâtre-Lyrique (now under Pasdeloup), binding him to complete it by the end of November, but a clause allowed him to postpone the production until he was satisfied with the cast. He at once availed himself of this; the Théâtre-Lyrique went bankrupt; the Franco-Prussian War broke out; and *Noé* was not produced till Mottl staged it at Karlsruhe in 1885.[1] It has never been played in France.

The fruit of his deliberations with the Opéra-Comique was not

[1] In the summer of 1871 Bizet had hopes of a performance at the Opéra (*Musical Quarterly*, July 1950, p. 406).

one projected opera, but three; and again, though all seem to have been begun, not one was finished. During the winter he was much taken with *Calendal*,[1] a libretto by Paul Ferrier based on an epic poem by the Provençal Frédéri Mistral. The attraction of the Provençal subject is noteworthy, especially as Bizet had been considering it for some time. He wrote more than once that *Calendal* had been '*commissioned* by the director of one of our important lyric theatres', and contradicted a rumour in a gossip column that Gounod held the rights in the libretto. The other two pieces were *Grisélidis* by Sardou and *Clarissa Harlowe* by Philippe Gille, based on Richardson. Nor was this all. Further projects mentioned in his letters are a grand opera *Rama*, with libretto by Eugène Crépet from the Indian epic *Ramayana*, and a set of 'musical interpretations' based on Eugène Manuel's volume of poems *Pages intimes*.

All these plans were still-born. Apart from *Noé*, the only work Bizet is known to have completed between *La Coupe du Roi de Thulé* and *Djamileh*, a period of nearly three years, is the unpublished and unperformed *cantique La Mort s'avance*, a choral curiosity based on two Chopin studies. But the reasons were as much public as personal. In June 1870 he went to Barbizon for the summer, taking all three *opéra-comique* libretti and concentrating on *Grisélidis* as the most urgent. He was soon overwhelmed by events that menaced the very existence of France.

On 19th July 1870 Napoleon III, provoked by Bismarck, declared war on Prussia and began the disastrous campaign that terminated his own dynasty and lost Alsace and Lorraine. Within a few weeks the Second Empire had fallen, the emperor himself was a prisoner, and Paris was besieged. Bizet's reaction to these events was not that of most Frenchmen; the jingoism of his Rome days had given way to a broad detachment that does him credit. Eschewing the cheerful bellicosity of his countrymen, he wrote sadly to Galabert:

> And our poor philosophy, our dreams of universal peace, world fraternity and human fellowship! Instead of all that we have tears, blood, piles of

---

[1] So much so that he copied out the libretto in different-coloured inks, one for each part. It was this copy that he sent back to Ferrier, who gave it to his widow after his death. The libretto was set later by Henri Maréchal.

corpses, crimes without number or end! I can't tell you, my dear friend, in what sadness I am plunged by all these horrors. I remember that I am a Frenchman, but I cannot altogether forget that I am a man. This war will cost humanity five hundred thousand lives. As for France, she will lose all!

Still more revealing of his unhappiness and unsatisfied longings is a dream he recounted to Guiraud:

I dreamed last night that we were all at Naples, installed in a charming villa; we were living under a purely artistic government. The Senate consisted of Beethoven, Michelangelo, Shakespeare, Giorgione and people like that. The National Guard was replaced by an immense orchestra under the command of Litolff. The suffrage was withheld from idiots, spongers, intriguers and ignoramuses. I need not tell you it was thus the most limited suffrage imaginable. Geneviève was a little too friendly with Goethe, but despite this inconvenience waking up was a cruelly bitter business.

As a Prix de Rome winner Bizet was exempt from military service. But a few days after the outbreak he went to Paris and enlisted in the sixth battalion of the National Guard, complaining loudly of Napoleon's failure to rouse and arm the nation ('the *uncle* at least knew where to find the enemy'). As a precaution he ordered two casks of red wine from Galabert ('not good enough to be expensive or cheap enough to be undrinkable') and prepared to live economically in the knowledge that neither his operas nor Halévy's could be performed. The proclamation of the Republic on 4th September delighted him, and he took his military duties seriously despite the suspicion that his rifle would inconvenience himself more than the enemy. He remained in Paris with his wife throughout the four months of siege; he refused to leave on the ground that it was more dangerous to be a coward than to do one's duty. Work did not come easily. He shrank from writing a popular song on the Marseillaise pattern, but considered setting Victor Hugo's 'Ceux qui pieusement sont morts pour la patrie' under the title *Morts pour la France!* Choudens, whose efforts to preserve a satisfactorily escapist frame of mind are amusingly described in a letter to Guiraud, dissuaded him from this, but demanded songs about spring, love and roses. Not surprisingly Bizet could not oblige. By December he was living on horse, and Geneviève dreamed every night of chickens and lobsters (as for Choudens, he had given up eating and was growing fat). Nevertheless he could still applaud the fall of the Empire and the removal of 'the thick coat of shame and ordure' with which it had bespattered the country.

After the armistice of 26th January 1871 Mme Halévy, who was in Bordeaux, asked Bizet to bring Geneviève down for a visit. Bizet hesitated—the only meeting of mother and daughter since the marriage, in the asylum at Ivry, had been far from propitious—but a week later he yielded to the persuasion of Rodrigues. The result was disastrous. Two days in her mother's company reduced Geneviève to such a state of nervous prostration that she begged Bizet to take her away at once or she would die in the same way as Esther. Back in Paris Bizet described the circumstances in a long and moving letter to Ludovic Halévy.[1] Mme Halévy thought that Geneviève was indulging in childish histrionics and that Bizet was much too gentle with her. Bizet, convinced that 'it is her life or Geneviève's', recognized that both women were ill and not to be blamed. He feared his motives would be misunderstood by the family, and sure enough some who had reproached him with trying to keep mother and daughter apart now accused him of taking Geneviève to Bordeaux and risking her health to protect himself from criticism. In a letter to Rodrigues he expressed bitter regrets 'for having, out of human respect, taken a chance in which the stakes were Geneviève's life. I knew by intuition and from all the doctors I consulted that it was essential for Geneviève never to see her mother again. . . . Her terror went beyond any bounds we could have imagined. She was perpetually haunted by incessant dreams that were all the more harmful because she did not dare tell me about them.' He could not leave her alone for an instant. 'The external manifestations of her nervous shock are frightening. I can't give you any idea of the extent of the nervous tics.' Geneviève retained a facial tic till the end of her life. Bizet said nothing of this to his friends, though he told Galabert that the closing of the theatres had temporarily ruined him, and asked him and Lacombe about the chances of renting a house in the south for the summer.

[1] 24th February 1871 (Curtiss, pp. 273–4).

Instead of a holiday he was to undergo further harrowing experiences. The Prussians entered Paris on 1st March and withdrew to the outskirts on the 3rd, leaving the field open to revolution. Bizet was an eye-witness of the events leading to the proclamation of the Commune at the end of the month and, as a member of the National Guard, a participant in some of them. His letters on the subject are of considerable interest. At first he was appalled by the sheer inefficiency, stupidity and cowardice on both sides. All discipline had collapsed; Bizet was among those who put their services at the disposal of the Government, but after being in position for eighteen hours during which they neither saw a superior officer nor received an order, they were advised to go home. He found the citizens out on holiday, cigar in mouth. The position, he said, would have made him burst with laughing were it not the sure sign of the death of a society. He was no reactionary; he admitted that the Communards were better disciplined than the garrison, and confessed that his greatest fear was a Catholic monarchy. At first he declared that Paris had fallen too low for bloodshed ('We no longer have revolutions, merely parodies of revolutions!'), but he was soon proved wrong. On the outbreak of fighting at the barricades, looting and political murder, he took Geneviève to Compiègne and then to Le Vésinet, where for weeks they listened to the cannonade of the guns of Paris, which was loud enough to keep them awake at night. At Le Vésinet they were safe, thanks to the German garrison, a circumstance on which Bizet commented bitterly. He was disgusted by the excesses of the Commune ('it is assassination and incendiarism raised to the level of a political system'), though still afraid of the reaction: he lost his temper with a man at Versailles who spoke of the return of the emperor. He began to feel that there was no future for the arts in France.

> Between the fury of the whites and the reds there will be no place for honest men. There is no future for music here. We must go abroad. Shall I go to Italy, England, America? . . . Germany, the country of music, is impossible for anyone who bears a French name and heart. It's all very sad. Life had begun so well for us!

This was on 19th April; a month later he was taking a more philosophical attitude and noting the great powers of recovery that France always displayed on the morrow of disaster. On 24th May MacMahon's army entered Paris, and within four days the civil war was over, though not before the Communards had shot their hostages, including some of Bizet's friends and the Archbishop of Paris.

These events had caused Bizet much heart-searching, and not only in regard to his material future. In April, responding to Mme Halévy's expressed interest in his career, he reviewed progress.

> To tell the truth, I have never been spoiled. That is doubtless due to the lack of flexibility in my character. I have little affection for what is known as the world, and even less esteem. So-called *honours*, *dignities* (in the plural), *titles*, etc., would profoundly disgust me if I were not indifferent to them. Of all my comrades I am one of the two or three who have obtained good artistic results, slender enough in truth, but seriously and honourably acquired.

He has seen colleagues obtain lucrative appointments by backstairs methods which he would disdain to use; he is prepared to face a future that holds out no prospect of official encouragement. He goes on to criticize, with ample reason, the administration of the state theatres and the Conservatoire. 'Saint-Saëns, Guiraud, Massenet, myself and some others could rejuvenate this school, which Monsieur Auber has turned into a house I shall not qualify honourably because it is not honourable.' A few weeks later he heard of Auber's death and recognized it as the end of a period: 'The poor man could not survive the destruction of all that life meant to him.' In his place the Commune appointed Salvador Daniel, the music critic of a radical paper, who was shot by Government troops ten days later. His successor, as Bizet had hoped, was Ambroise Thomas, whose *Hamlet* he regarded as 'a great work that conceals all the little musical weaknesses of this kind and honourable man'.[1] Of Gounod, who had fled to London in 1870 and written to the Crown Prince of Prussia craving protection (in vain) for his property at Saint-Cloud, Bizet remarked in the same letter that his private life was not sufficiently pure for him to be trusted with a school for young girls.

[1] Bizet's letter of congratulation to Thomas is printed by Marc Pincherle, *Musiciens peints par eux-mêmes* (1939).

Bizet looked forward to his future career with a certain sober confidence.

The doors are opened to me, and opened by me. But as for begging something from whosoever it may be, that I shall never be able to do at any price. Ten years ago I believed in the world, consorted with it and, I confess, was amused by it. Today I am not misanthropic, I am indifferent: I do not hate, I despise. . . . The road I have taken is long, but I know where it is leading me.

And a little later he reviewed the old question of success, immediate and ultimate. 'The beautiful, that is to say the union of idea and form, is always beautiful,' but few contemporaries can assess it.

What makes success is *talent*, not *ideas*. The public (and I speak of intelligent people, the rest don't count: that's democracy for me)—the public only *later* understands the *ideas*. To reach this *later*, it is necessary for the artist's talent, by means of an attractive form, to make the road easy for him and avert an immediate repulse. Thus Auber, who had any amount of talent but few ideas, was nearly always understood, while Berlioz, who had genius without any talent, was scarcely ever understood. . . . The artist does not find his true level till *a hundred years* after his death. Is it sad? No. Merely stupid.

It is significant of his detachment from prejudice, whether musical or national, that he should be able at this time to give a balanced opinion of Wagner. He had for some time admired the musician but been repelled by the man. In 1868 he had been furious with Wagner ('this cardboard republican', who was equally ready to accept money from the King of Saxony one year and take a shot at him from the barricades the next) for calling Gounod's *Faust* 'musique de cocottes'. 'Genius certainly, but what a poseur! what a bore! what a blackguard [*goujat*]!' In 1871 he bade his mother-in-law set aside Wagner's political writings, particularly *Eine Kapitulation*, the typical and revolting piece of tactlessness he had just perpetrated on the fall of Paris.

It is the fate of great geniuses to be misunderstood by their contemporaries. Wagner is no friend of mine, and I hold him in indifferent esteem; but I cannot forget the immense pleasure I owe to his innovating genius. The charm of his music is unutterable, inexpressible. It is voluptuousness, tenderness, love! If I played it to you for a week you would be infatuated! Besides, the Germans, who alas! are quite our equals musically, have understood that Wagner is one of their strongest mainstays. The German nineteenth-century spirit is made incarnate in that man. You personally know well enough what cruelty disdain brings to a great artist. Happily for Wagner, he is endowed with a temper so insolent that criticism cannot touch his heart—even admitting that he has a heart, which I doubt.

He dismisses the claim that Wagner's work is the music of the future, a meaningless term: it is 'the music of all time, because it is admirable'. And in a postscript he answers one of the favourite charges of his critics.

Of course if I thought I was imitating Wagner, despite my admiration, I would not write another note in my life. *Imitation* is a fool's job. It is much better to write bad music of one's own than other people's. And besides, the finer the model, the more ridiculous the imitation.

Meanwhile, uncertain of the future of the theatres, but seeking distraction, he resumed work on *Grisélidis* and *Clarissa Harlowe.* The former had been well advanced by February, though Sardou wanted to change the last act; *Clarissa Harlowe* was then hardly begun. His plan was to complete both by the autumn, and he tackled them conjointly throughout May and June. *Calendal* had apparently been scrapped because du Locle took a dislike to the subject. Of *Clarissa Harlowe* at least one act was composed, for Bizet wrote to Guiraud:

My wife says it is good; as for me, I know nothing about it whatever. I await your opinion before having one of my own. I am always the same! Yesterday my act seemed to me bad, this morning mediocre, and just now excellent. I am dropping it and remaining under this last impression, which a new examination will clearly modify.

Although Bizet's flat in Paris, to which he paid a short visit early in June, was fortunately intact, he was assailed by domestic anxieties throughout the summer. Geneviève's physical health improved, but the prospect of her mother's leaving Bordeaux for Versailles brought on a relapse of her nervous breakdown; she developed a 'strange terror' of her husband, perhaps because he tried to remain on good terms with both parties.[1] He was now required to co-operate with a lawyer (whose competence he doubted) over Mme Halévy's business affairs, and in particular to arrange for the transport to Bordeaux of the furniture from her house at Bas-Prunay, which had been damaged during the war. He spent endless time and trouble over this (a voluminous correspondence survives) and offered to modify his marriage settlement to her advantage when she feared she would be left in straitened circumstances. Although she had constantly pressed gifts on him, most of which (except Halévy's old piano) he refused, she repaid his generosity by accusing him of carelessness over the furniture and of withholding or losing some of her property. He was deeply wounded, but replied with pages of facts and figures and a final paragraph of great dignity, ending: 'Let us hope that this letter is the last I shall write to you about your household goods. We will discuss art, a subject which is perhaps less alien to me.' It is no surprise to hear that in this month (September) he was threatened with what he called his eleventh attack of quinsy.

Mme Halévy had also been intervening in his affairs. Vauthrot, the old chorus-master at the Opéra, had died in April, and Bizet decided to apply for the post, which he expected to bring in five or six thousand francs a year. Mme Halévy urged him to set about lobbying in the Second Empire manner, not only for this position, but for one at the Conservatoire. She sent him a letter singing his praises to be forwarded to Thomas and a special gift for the Prime Minister, Thiers. Bizet, to whom such procedure was repulsive, refused to touch either: 'For many reasons I need absolute moral independence.' Nevertheless she went ahead on her own account and approached Mme Perrin, the wife of the retiring director of the Opéra. Bizet was very angry and wrote her a stern letter of rebuke. 'Everyone in the know in this affair will think I am playing a part I would never be willing to accept. I have a horror of being defended, supported,

[1] Mrs Curtiss's conclusion (p. 298) that his affection for Mme Halévy 'seems to have been quite as real and strong as his love for his wife' appears to me to go beyond the evidence. He certainly liked his mother-in-law and enjoyed arguing with her about music; but Geneviève's jealousy, if it existed, was a product of her illness.

recommended. . . . I would rather renounce any position than not achieve it *by myself* and completely on my own.'

In the event his appointment was confirmed by Perrin and his successor, Halanzier, early in July, but kept secret until the necessary funds could be voted. Bizet expected to take up his duties at the beginning of October and rejoiced at the prospect of a steady and adequately paid position. Yet there is no mention of the appointment in the official records, and someone else was given the job from 1st November. Mrs Curtiss's conjecture that Bizet resigned because of the scandalous treatment of Reyer's *Érostrate*, which was chosen to open the season on 16th October but taken off without warning after two performances,[1] is probably correct. A letter reproduced in Vuillermoz's biography proves that he was actively engaged in the rehearsals of this opera.

The many family letters of this period published by Mrs Curtiss in her biography and in the *Musical Quarterly* (July 1950) are the most important evidence we have of Bizet's character in later life. They show a persistent effort to establish his moral integrity, a task as formidable as it was advisable for a man who had struggled through the corruption of the Second Empire, and a degree of self-knowledge that can be linked with his growing artistic maturity. The suspicion that his standards may have slipped once or twice seems to have strengthened his resolution to stand on his own feet. In refusing to lobby politicians he wrote to Mme Halévy:

> You regard people in general as kindly, good, generous, sincere and human. I regard them as almost universally malicious, wicked, greedy, false and cruel. You have faith in people, I am suspicious of them. . . . I am on the defensive physically and morally, always. I have every reason for this, and it is to my advantage to take precautions.

This is the tone not of a misanthrope or a neurotic but of a man who has digested some harsh lessons. When his mother-in-law protested at his refusal to accept all her gifts, his reply showed just how much he had learned about his own nature.

> I am in no way reluctant to admit the great flaw in my character! I am,

[1] For the full story, which involves the prima donna's bizarre confusion between Aphrodite and hermaphrodite, see Curtiss, pp. 315 ff.

I know, exaggeratedly sensitive; I readily believe myself the object of suspicion; I am often conscious of being the victim of persecution which probably exists only in my own mind. It is really a sickness, and I can only ask those who love me not to expose a very painful nerve which some trifling thing too easily sets in vibration.

Grisélidis was abandoned during the summer because the Opéra-Comique refused to mount it on grounds of expense. This theatre was now under the joint direction of two men of very different temperament. The one, Adolphe de Leuven, had been the librettist of certain operas by Adam, which he accordingly regarded as the most up-to-date works in the repertory; he was a true-blue conservative with a fanatic horror of innovation.[1] Camille du Locle, on the other hand, Perrin's nephew, wished to break with the Auber-Scribe tradition and create a form in which exoticism, poetry and the symphonic element had a large part; unfortunately, although he wrote libretti for Reyer and was part-author of Verdi's *Don Carlos*, he does not appear to have had great musical perception or much understanding of the drama. He was at heart a sceptic and a dilettante who desired the credit for introducing novelties without the bother of believing in them. Needless to say the collaboration was not happy. After a flop at the Opéra-Comique du Locle would be seen grinning and whispering to his friends 'That's one of Leuven's!' After the next flop de Leuven would return the compliment.

Du Locle had acquired rights in several of Gounod's operas from the Théâtre-Lyrique, and since the failure of that concern he was trying to attract the young composers who had begun to make their name there. He now hit upon Bizet as his chosen instrument, and on the withdrawal of *Grisélidis* offered him in compensation a piece by Louis Gallet (originally in two acts, later reduced to one) based on Alfred de Musset's *Namouna*. This, like *Grisélidis*, had been in the hands of one Jules Duprato, who had expressed himself charmed but

[1] His real name was Count Adolph von Ribbing. He had been writing for the theatre since 1825, often in collaboration with Saint-Georges: his stage works number over a hundred and fifty, and occupy seven pages of the British Library catalogue. His father had been one of the conspirators against Gustavus III of Sweden and is familiar to operatic audiences as Samuel in Verdi's *Un ballo in maschera*.

omitted to set it to music. Du Locle recalled the libretto and shortly afterwards induced Gallet to change the title to *Djamileh*,[1] a name he had met on one of his periodical visits to Cairo. Bizet was told to get busy at once—he spoke to Galabert of pistols pointed at his head—but at first he had doubts about the subject, which he found 'charming but horribly difficult', and asked for time to make up his mind. On 22nd July, however, he described it to Mme Halévy as 'very distinguished, very noble, artistically very significant; it will enable me to be not entirely forgotten by the public and will at the same time, I hope, be *good business*'. He composed the score in a few weeks, drawing on *La Coupe du Roi de Thulé*, while struggling with inventories of his mother-in-law's furniture.

As an instrument for changing the *genre* of *opéra-comique* and delivering Bizet's counterblast to *La Dame blanche*, an opera in his opinion fit only for sappers, nursemaids and porters, *Djamileh* was not a fortunate choice. Gallet, though a cultivated man and a great improvement on Saint-Georges, was more fitted to supply du Locle's requirements than Bizet's. In his preface to the libretto of *Thaïs*, where he abandoned strict metre, he wrote: 'A lyrical poem is a work in verse that is handed over to a musician to convert into prose.' He thought more of poetry and atmosphere than of the stage. He left a delightful picture of Bizet at Le Vésinet during the composition of *Djamileh*:

> He walked about in a straw hat and loose jacket with the easy assurance of a country gentleman, smoking his pipe, chatting happily with his friends, receiving them at table, with a conviviality that always had a touch of banter in it, between his charming young wife and his father, who was his host and spent all day gardening as a change from the fatigue of giving lessons.

It was Bizet's habit always to converse or talk business on the move, either in the open air or walking about the room; it was a bad sign if anyone found him sitting down. A cigar-smoker in early years, towards the end of his life he was seldom seen without a pipe in his mouth.

Djamileh was not his only care this year. He was still working at

[1] Du Locle, according to Pigot, inspired the whole thing, subject, words and music: both are dedicated to him.

Clarissa Harlowe, and *Roma* seems to have undergone further touching up. A small but important new venture was the set of twelve pieces for piano duet entitled *Jeux d'enfants*. This was sold to the publisher Durand for 600 francs on 28th September 1871; the date 1872 usually assigned to the composition is due to a mistake of Imbert's in dating the eighteenth letter to Lacombe. The assumption that the *Petite Suite d'orchestre*, Bizet's orchestral version of five of the pieces, was later than the duet version is unproven. Certainly the orchestral suite was finished by September, when the duet pieces numbered only ten, as specified in the contract with Durand. *Les Bulles de savon* and *Les Quatre Coins* were written later; *La Toupie* was originally *La Toupie d'Allemagne*, and *Trompette et tambour* appears (if indeed it is the same piece) as *Les Soldats de plomb*. Bizet names *Les Chevaux de bois* as one of the pieces already scored, though it was subsequently replaced by *Trompette et tambour*, taken from a march in *Ivan IV*. He also scored and expanded *Les Quatre Coins*, intending to use it as the finale of the suite. One if not two of these pieces thus await rediscovery in their orchestral form.

CHAPTER VI

MATURITY (1872–5)

THE production of *Djamileh* was delayed, partly by a dearth of suitable singers and partly by Offenbach's *Fantasio*, which Bizet resented because he suspected Sardou of having been more assiduous over its libretto than over *Grisélidis*. He spent a harassed winter struggling with lessons and rehearsals and, as he put it, strengthening himself against the little emotional upsets of life. At last on 22nd May 1872 the opera was produced. It was not a success. Du Locle had taken immense trouble with the settings and costumes, going to the length of pedantry in his effort to achieve an authentic background. He even installed a special multicoloured lamp for the sunset. He was much less successful with the singers. Bizet had wanted Priola or Galli-Marié to play Djamileh, but the choice lighted on one Aline Prelly, pseudonym of the Baroness de Presles, whose physical potentialities were overwhelming, and indeed notorious, but seem to have been her only qualification to appear on the stage of the Opéra-Comique. This voiceless Venus, as Vuillermoz aptly terms her, was splendid at her first entrance, when she does not have to sing; but she jumped thirty-two bars in the Ghazel, and the orchestra, under Deloffre, had a desperate race to catch her up. The tenor Duchesne (Haroun), an inexperienced singer at the outset of his career (Bizet had wanted Lhérie), was also weak, and Potel (Splendiano), though a good artist, had little voice. Bizet watched in the prompt box and said to Gallet at the end: 'There, a complete flop!' The scene in front of the curtain is amusingly described by Adolphe Jullien:

> It's infamous! cried one. It's odious! cried another. It's very funny! said a third, more philosophically. What cacophony! What audacity! He's making fun of us all! That's where the Wagner cult leads to—to madness. Neither tonality nor shape nor rhythm! It's no longer music—it's macaroni. What! Is it Italian music then? Not a bit, I mean it has neither beginning nor end.

Djamileh struggled on for eleven performances (not four or ten, as sometimes stated) and then disappeared from the French stage till Bizet's centenary in 1938.

This was a tragic fate for a charming work, full of music as original as it is delightful; but though much may be set down to the inadequacy of the singers, there was an artistic weakness as well. De Leuven in his own way had put his finger on it when he suggested that the action might be gingered up if one of the characters suddenly dropped a plate. Bizet himself wrote a month later that the poem was anti-theatrical. Du Locle and Gallet in their love for atmosphere had forgotten that the stage also requires action. The press was not slow to point out this and other supposed deficiencies. Bizet, surprisingly, expressed satisfaction with his press notices; perhaps he did not read many: for the majority were overwhelmingly antagonistic. All but three or four renewed the charge of Wagnerism at full blast; even Reyer detected a whiff of *Die Meistersinger*. Moreno in *Le Ménestrel*, generally favourable to Bizet, complained of 'the absence of tonality'. Others condemned the opera as pretentious, monotonous and incomprehensible. Albert Wolff in *L'Avenir National* expressed the majority opinion when he wrote that it breathed 'an odour of boredom that only the composer's friends can resist. . . . From first to last *Djamileh* is a succession of laments. . . . The composer seems to have but one aim, to render his art incomprehensible.' Frédérick in *Paris-Journal* found no trace of an original idea in this 'laborious' score, but 'an aspect dim, vague, confused, without relief, contour or colour'. F. de Lagenevais in the *Revue des deux Mondes* considered it a disappointment after *La Jolie Fille de Perth*: 'It is not even one act, it is an *entr'acte*.'

Certain numbers came in for particular attention. The slaves' march that opens the overture, declared Jouvin in *Le Figaro*,

> lacks character, melody and rhythm. The tonality in an affected manner eludes the comprehension of the ear that would grasp it. To make this clear by a bodily parallel, imagine the listener walking on a mass of superimposed dissonances and losing his balance in following the musician as he steps off into air.

Perhaps no more could be expected from a writer who described the chorus of Haroun's friends as 'fugué'. The critic of *Le Soir*, after accusing Bizet of 'the pitiless and deliberate suppression of every sign of rhythm and tonality', pounced on Djamileh's lament. He analysed the bold progression at the beginning ('one of those audacities of which M. Wagner would be jealous'), apologizing for the technicalities, and added: 'This is so horrible, so savage in its effect, that I could not resist pointing it out for the edification of persons possessed of sufficient musical instruction to understand me.' But the height of absurdity was touched by Félix Clément in his imposing *Dictionnaire des Opéras*. To him the music was

> so extraordinary, so bizarre—in a word, so disagreeable that one might suppose it the result of a wager. Wandering in the tracks of M. Richard Wagner, he has exceeded his model in bizarrerie and strangeness. That melody is absent goes without saying. . . . But that the successions of sounds and chords, the processes of harmony and accompaniment, belong for the most part to no known or classified system of composition is an error of judgment very regrettable in a composer so skilful as M. Georges Bizet.

As for the overture, the music of the age of Rameses and Sesostris could not have appeared more extraordinary to modern ears, and the whole opera was 'packed with dissonance and harmonic cacophony in comparison with which the audacities of Berlioz were mere child's play'.

This was not the whole story, but it is curious to find the most favourable critics concerned about the extent to which Bizet had removed the centre of interest from the voice to the orchestra. Joncières (*La Liberté*), in an appreciative notice in which he applauded Bizet for turning his back on conventional *opéra-comique*, remarked that even the common herd, lost in the new lands to which Bizet was leading them, seemed not unmoved by the subtle atmosphere they encountered there. The most discerning criticism came from Guillemot in *Le Journal de Paris*; he picked out the two great qualities of *Djamileh*, the charm and freshness of the oriental colouring with its novel harmonic and orchestral effects, and the presentation of the heroine herself. Jullien too was favourable, finding fault only with the final duet. Whereas the others detected traces of Wagner, he complained (with more justification) of the preponderance of Gounod. He found the opening of the overture 'extremely original and picturesque', praised the scoring and the dramatic aptness of the music, and summed up the work as showing 'a curious spirit, in search of novelty but afraid of the banal. He is still searching; one day maybe he will find.' But perhaps it was Reyer who gave Bizet most pleasure. He noted traces of Wagner, Schumann and Gounod in the music, but defended Bizet on the sensible ground that 'the composer who stumbles in taking a step forward is worth more attention than the composer who shows us how easily he can step backwards'. He praised the treatment of the exotic element, which never transgressed the boundary separating art from realism, and acclaimed him as the leader of the young French school.

There is in this work more than the manifestation of a talent, there is the expression of a will. And I think that if M. Bizet knows that his work has been appreciated by a small number of musicians judging without prejudice, he will be more proud of that than of a popular success.

One of this small number was Massenet, who wrote Bizet a letter full of enthusiasm. Another, Saint-Saëns, paid his tribute in the unexpected form of a sonnet, in which 'Le bourgeois ruminant dans sa stalle serrée' opens one glassy eye, eats a sweet and goes to sleep again, bored by this 'perle aux porceaux jetée'.

Bizet felt that *Djamileh* despite its failure was a great advance, and he was right. 'What gives me more satisfaction than the opinion of all these gentry,' he wrote to Galabert on 17th June,

is the absolute certainty of having found my path. I know what I am doing. I have just been ordered to compose three acts for the Opéra-Comique. Meilhac and Halévy are doing my piece. It will be *gay*, but with a gaiety that permits style.

This was the genesis of *Carmen*, though the subject was not yet chosen; de Leuven produced three scenarios, one of them entitled *L'Oiseau bleu*. It was Bizet himself who suggested Mérimée's novel to his new collaborators. There were other projects too. 'It seems decided that I shall be asked for something for the Opéra. The doors are open; it has taken ten years to get there. I have ideas for oratorios, symphonies, etc.' In July he was nominated to the jury of a fugue competition and wrote to Marmontel: 'A wrong answer is in my opinion only a very slight fault, especially if the mistake makes the answer more *musical*, more *genuine*. Long live Bach! If Saint-Saëns is on the jury, he will probably think as I do, but the others!' And as if to multiply his high spirits and hopes, on 10th July Geneviève Bizet gave birth to a son, Jacques,[1] who instantly became a vocal force to be reckoned with in the household.

The next commission was not long in arriving. After his failure at the Théâtre-Lyrique Carvalho had migrated to the Vaudeville, a theatre where straight plays were the staple diet. He decided to revive the almost extinct form of *mélodrame*, that is, a play with incidental music. Although Gounod had written music to Legouvé's *Les Deux Reines* in 1866, the form had fallen into the hands of mediocrities whose stock device, according to one writer, was to accompany every mention of the Virgin Mary with a banal tune on violins, two clarinets and three cornets in unison over a tremolo on one cello and one double bass. Carvalho invited Bizet to write music for Alphonse Daudet's play *L'Arlésienne*. For reasons of economy he was allowed an orchestra of only twenty-six players, though he was given latitude in his choice of instruments. This restriction seems to have stimulated rather than hindered him: he produced a masterpiece of dramatic insight and orchestral balance and wrote the whole score in a matter of weeks, despite interruptions from his wife's quarrelsome family. Mme Halévy, prevented from seeing Geneviève, took to waylaying her infant grandson in the Parc Monceau and trying to force barley-sugar on him; the nurse and the park keeper had to be mobilized in his defence.

Bizet's collaboration with Daudet was singularly happy and

[1] He was the only child of Bizet's marriage and bore a striking likeness to his father. He inherited the instability as well as the charm of his mother's family and embarked on several careers: medical student, journalist, author of light dramatic pieces, secretary of a commission appointed by the Minister of Fine Arts in connection with the Paris Exhibition of 1900, founder of the first garage in France to let cars for hire. He died by his own hand on 3rd November 1922. Shortly before this, after showing Henry Malherbe round the house at Bougival where Bizet died, he had entered a gypsy caravan to have his fortune told. In 1908 he asked Romain Rolland to write his father's life.

intimate. Not only was Daudet a gifted artist and a passionate lover of music; he had much in common with Bizet. Théodore de Banville's description of him as 'a young savage who will become a *dandy*' might have been applied to the composer.[1] The imagination of both was haunted by the central situation of *L'Arlésienne*, which was based on a real event, the frustrated love and suicide of a young relative of the Provençal poet Mistral. Daudet took the words in which the hero Frédéri describes his love for the heartless girl from Arles from an autobiographical novel written a year earlier. For the offstage chorus at the end of Act I he used a song by Mistral; the speech in which the jealous and possessive Mitifio proclaims his rights in the girl seems to have been contributed by Bizet.[2] Six charming letters from Daudet to Bizet survive, and each presented the other with an affectionately inscribed copy of his printed work.

Once more Bizet was unlucky on the night. Carvalho intended to open his season with a play called *Madame Frainex* by Robert Halt, and the advance press notices dealt with this. On 21st September it was suddenly banned, and *L'Arlésienne* was put forward at the last minute. The first performance took place on 1st October before a bored and unappreciative audience. The overture and *entr'actes* were drowned by perpetual chatter, people coming and going, doors opening and shutting, and chairs being pushed back; a group of literary folk demanded loudly why this confounded Wagnerian Bizet had to interfere with his orchestral cacophony. 'They're not even listening,' Bizet whispered to Daudet in great agitation. Only the Intermezzo (the Minuet of the first Suite) made a hit. At the entry of Mère Renaud, to Bizet's exquisite C minor *mélodrame*, the editor of the *Figaro* slammed the door of his box and exclaimed: 'What a bore all these old women are!' Daudet told Bellaigue that as the evening advanced he and Bizet had the sensation of drowning with a collar of stones hung about their necks. He left the theatre 'discouraged, disheartened, with the inane laughter that punctuated the tragic scenes still ringing in my ears, and . . . resolved to write no more theatre pieces'. A little later he informed Bizet that he was 258 years

[1] In one of his first letters from Rome Bizet had described himself as the dandy of the Academy. *See also* p. 62.

[2] Curtiss, p. 336.

old, but offered to discuss an idea for an *opéra-comique* he had found in an English novel.

The production was not at fault; the acting seems to have been good and the scenery admirable. The orchestra, according to Reyer, played with rare perfection and irreproachable *ensemble*, like a handful of virtuosos—which indeed they must have been to realize the delicacy and subtlety of the score. The chorus was not thought good enough to be seen on the stage (the only number in which it should so appear, 'Le flutet se marie' in the last act, was cut), but it seems to have given satisfaction in the wings, where it was accompanied on the harmonium by Bizet or Guiraud or occasionally Antony Choudens, the publisher's son. The conductor was Constantin, of the Athénée theatre. The *mélodrame* form had such a low reputation that with two exceptions the music critics of the daily press did not attend (Reyer put in a special request to his dramatic colleague Jules Janin), and Bizet's work, which ran for twenty-one performances to empty houses, passed almost unnoticed. Reyer, however, acclaimed it as a masterpiece, and both he and Johannès Weber noted the skill with which rare artistry was subordinated to the psychological demands of the drama. Gustave Bertrand too wrote a discriminating notice in *Le Ménestrel*. Reyer ended by sounding a challenge:

Go and hear *L'Arlésienne*, you young musicians who as yet hold out no hopes to your professors, and perhaps you will be encouraged and more assiduous in your studies when you see the degree of talent reached by one who, only a few years ago, was sitting like you on the school benches.

It is interesting to observe that Francisque Sarcey, the leading dramatic critic of the day, in a long article devoted to demolishing Daudet's claims as a dramatist, dismissed the music as 'in no respect integral with the work; it is an addition applied afterwards' (the ineffable Clément made the same charge). In criticizing the 1885 revival at the Odéon Sarcey attributed the great success wholly to the music. Bizet was a frequent sufferer from this time-serving kind of criticism; the grotesque contortions performed by Arthur Pougin with regard to the libretto and score of *Carmen* make fascinating if disillusioning reading.

Four extracts from *L'Arlésienne*, forming the familiar first Suite, were rapidly rescored by Bizet for full orchestra and performed by

Pasdeloup on 10th November. This time the success was immediate, the Minuet being encored. The Suite was repeated by Colonne at the Châtelet on 9th November 1873, at two different concerts on 18th January 1874 and at the Concerts du Conservatoire on 21st February 1875. There were now more openings than at the outset of Bizet's career. The war of 1870 had been followed by a national revival in the arts: operetta and *salon* virtuosity, symbols of the giddy Empire, were replaced by more substantial forms. The great date in this movement was 25th February 1871, when Saint-Saëns and a professor of singing named Bussine founded the Société Nationale de Musique, which (under the slogan 'Ars Gallica') had as its object the encouragement of young French musicians and the performance of their works. The original committee included Franck, Guiraud, Fauré and Lalo, and one of the earliest members was Bizet. The society prospered from the first, for it was rooted in fertile soil. Soon it was giving an average of nine or ten concerts a year, devoted entirely to contemporary French music (in 1886 Saint-Saëns and Bussine resigned in protest against a proposal to let in the classics); the earlier concerts were confined to chamber music,[1] but orchestral works quickly followed. Nor was the society's influence confined to direct encouragement. Before the new demand the old institutions began slowly to open their doors (all except the Opéra, whose doors had rusted into a solid barrier). Pasdeloup was soon playing a French work at every concert; du Locle at the Opéra-Comique put on pieces by Saint-Saëns, Massenet and Paladilhe as well as Bizet (he proved to be too far in advance of his public, the most notoriously backward in Paris, which took acute exception to all of them); and early in 1873 a new society, the Concert National, began to function at the Odéon under the conductor Édouard Colonne. It was at the first of Colonne's concerts, on 2nd March 1873, that the *Petite Suite d'orchestre* from *Jeux d'enfants* was first played in public.[2] Bizet derived great

[1] For one of them Bizet arranged the finale of *Roma* for two pianos, eight hands, and played it with Guiraud, Saint-Saëns and Fissot.

[2] Bizet had previously offered it to Pasdeloup but withdrawn it after three rehearsals. He described Pasdeloup in 1869 as 'a sorry musician'.

benefit from these new outlets; unfortunately he had little time in which to enjoy them. Had he lived a few years longer he would doubtless have made further attempts to realize those symphonic projects which he never ceased to cherish; he might even have left posterity in debt to that unexplored talent for chamber music that lurks in the pages of *Jeux d'enfants* and *L'Arlésienne*.[1]

Immediately after the production of *L'Arlésienne* Gounod, who had returned to London, asked Bizet to take charge of the negotiations for the revival of *Roméo et Juliette* at the Opéra-Comique. In a long reply full of erasures Bizet tried to chart their relationship, perhaps with the idea of finally breaking the spell.

> The ties that bind us are of the kind that neither absence nor silence can relax. You were the beginning of my life as an artist. I spring from you. You are the cause and I am the consequence. I can tell you now that I was afraid of being absorbed, and you must have noticed the results of this uneasiness. Today I believe I am more master of my craft, and I feel only the benefit of your salutary and decisive influence.

Gounod professed himself much astonished. Bizet went on to declare that

> the moment has come to organize grand choral concerts in Paris. You alone have the necessary authority to bring this job to a good conclusion. How many years before one of us feels strong enough to introduce our Parisians to the overwhelming beauties of Bach and Handel?

Roméo was given on 20th January 1873, and Bizet received a charming letter of thanks from the composer.[2]

It seems to have been about this time that he began work on *Carmen*. He had spoken in September of rehearsals being planned for October 1873, adding: 'I feel that the hour for production has come, and I do not want to lose a day.' The first act (and probably a good deal more) was finished before the summer, but some hitch with the Opéra-Comique intervened, and he turned elsewhere. His collaboration

[1] A letter of September 1872 confirms that he had this intention. His only known chamber work is a little duet for bassoon and cello dating from 1874.

[2] Later in the year he performed the same service for Gounod's incidental music to Barbier's *Jeanne d'Arc*, produced at the Gaîté Theatre in November.

with Gallet over *Djamileh* had borne fruit in an unexpected quarter. Jean Baptiste Faure, principal baritone at the Opéra, had proposed that Gallet and Édouard Blau should write a libretto for Bizet to compose and himself to sing in. The first suggestion was Musset's *Lorenzaccio*, but Faure did not like the moral character of the hero (on hearing this, Bizet said 'He wants everything. Not only must he be great, handsome, generous and strong, but the other characters must be praising him when he's not on the stage'). The next idea came from Bizet. He found a translation of Guilhem da Castro's *La Jeunesse du Cid* and told Gallet:

> That's what I want to do. It's not Corneille's *Cid*, it's the original Cid with real Spanish colouring. There is one scene, that with the beggar, which is marvellous. Have a look at it. Faure, I'm sure, will be satisfied. The Cid amorous, filial, Christian, heroic, triumphant—what more could he want?

Bizet insisted that there should be no quotations or echoes of Corneille and that the piece should have a new title. It was accordingly named *Don Rodrigue*. He composed the whole five acts during the summer and autumn, which he spent at 17 Rue de Paris, Port-Marly. His correspondence with Gallet during this period throws light on his methods. He took immense pains over details and was always asking for minor alterations in the libretto, emphasizing (as he had done to Galabert years before) the vital importance of dramatic timing. On one occasion he asked pardon for rewriting the verse, excusing himself on the ground that the music sometimes came 'with an authority that I would call inspiration if the word were not ridiculously pretentious'. The scene in which Rodrigue, at the lowest ebb of his fortunes, protects a beggar and is rewarded by a vision in which Lazarus foretells the turn of the tide, he regarded as the climax of the opera; Massenet, when he came to set a revised version of the libretto, omitted it altogether. Towards the end of October Bizet invited Faure, Guiraud and the librettists to hear him run through the work at the piano. He played from a score containing only the vocal parts, supplying the accompaniment from memory. Gallet speaks of the vivid expression he infused into every part, though his voice was a poor reedy tenor, and says that he played all five acts at a sitting with scarcely a pause. The listeners were much impressed by the passion and colour of the music, as more than one of them left on record, and the outlook for the future seemed bright. On the following day Bizet wrote Gallet an anxious note: 'What is your impression of yesterday's session? What did you say when you went home? What are your hopes and fears?' Another note reports the cordial attitude of Faure, whose influence it was hoped would thaw the frozen portals of the Opéra. But it was left to a stronger agency to achieve this: on 28th October the Opéra was burned down. The company migrated to the Salle Ventadour and began to play for safety; after a period of suspense the management announced that the reputation of neither Bizet nor his librettists was sufficiently established, and in place of *Don Rodrigue* put on *L'Esclave*, a work of profound obscurity by one Membrée, whose immediate failure drove them farther than ever behind the entrenchments of tradition.

Don Rodrigue was probably not such a loss as Guiraud and others imagined. Only the vocal parts and a few half-legible indications of the scoring survive in the autograph—presumably the one from which Bizet played to his friends—and these fragments, so far as it is fair to judge them, show less character than might be expected from a work on a Spanish subject written at the same time as *Carmen*. But Bizet was thoroughly discouraged, swore he would have nothing more to do with the stage (*Carmen* was still held up), and asked Gallet to prepare him the text of an oratorio to be entitled *Geneviève de Paris*. The immense success of Massenet's *Marie-Magdeleine*, first performed on Good Friday 1873 and acclaimed as a second *Enfance du Christ*, probably influenced him here. Bizet had congratulated Massenet, addressing him (not inaptly) as 'you brazen musician!' He was aware of the sycophantic strain in Massenet and on one occasion lost his temper with him in public for flattering Guiraud with fulsome praise of his ballet *Gretna Green*, which everyone agreed was a failure. Bizet's anti-theatrical mood may not have lasted long; at some point he said to Guiraud: 'Your place is at the Opéra; I'm afraid of making a poor showing there, of not having the necessary fullness. I shall shine at the Opéra-Comique; I shall enlarge and transform the *genre*.'

Meanwhile Pasdeloup, true to the spirit of the time, had commissioned three symphonic overtures, from Massenet, Guiraud and

Bizet. The results of this were *Phèdre*, *Artewelde* and *Patrie*. Bizet composed the last during the winter of 1873–4, taking its main theme from a march in Act V of *Don Rodrigue*. There is some mystery about the title. It has nothing to do with Sardou's play *Patrie*, then being converted into an opera by Paladilhe. Pigot says that this rumour was put about by malignant persons who wished to suggest that Bizet wanted to set Sardou's work, but had been rejected in favour of Paladilhe. It may be so; but Pigot goes on to say that Bizet, though he had the war of 1870 in mind, did not wish to reopen a sore subject in an age of appeasement, and so by a poetic fiction substituted for France 'the mighty shade of Poland in her death agony, always conquered but always resurgent, whose ineffaceable memory and sacred name live for ever in the hearts of her scattered children'. But did Bizet bring Poland into it? There is no such hint in the score, which is merely entitled *Patrie!* [*sic*] Possibly a note was inserted in the programme at the first performance. At any rate, the real inspiration was the war of 1870. *Patrie* was first played under Pasdeloup on 15th February 1874, and met with immediate favour. It was repeated more than once in the same year, and so this most dramatic composer enjoyed his only unqualified success with two concert works for orchestra—one a suite torn from its context, the other the feeblest and most uncharacteristic progeny of his later years.

Some time during the winter things began to move at the Opéra-Comique. Even during the composition of *Don Rodrigue* Bizet had continued to work at *Carmen*, and there was talk of rehearsals beginning in December. They were put forward to August 1874, and Bizet, after a renewed and very acute attack of quinsy, accompanied by the usual abscesses, left for the country to finish the score. This year he found a new summer residence at Bougival (1 Rue de Mesmes [1]), a quiet spot on the Seine. Here *Carmen* was finished, and the 1,200 pages of full score were orchestrated in two months. He was pleased with the result. He said to a friend:

They make out that I am obscure, complicated, tedious, more fettered

[1] Now 5 Rue Ivan Tourgueneff. The house carries a commemorative plaque.

by technical skill than lit by inspiration. Well, this time I have written a work that is all clarity and vivacity, full of colour and melody. It will be amusing. Come along; I think you will like it.

He told Lacombe that for three or four years he had been dreaming of a piano concerto, but could not bring himself to write piano and symphonic music at the same time. During the winter, thinking perhaps of his oratorio, he attended César Franck's organ class at the Conservatoire, where his silent attentiveness made an impression on the young d'Indy. Till the eve of the production of *Carmen* none of the pupils knew the identity of the stranger in their midst. It is interesting to speculate on what fruit Franck's teaching might have borne had Bizet lived longer.

We catch a vivid picture of Bizet at the time of *Carmen* through the eyes of a twelve-year-old American girl to whom he gave piano lessons during the last two years of his life.[1] As a teacher he was exacting and sparing of compliments; he made no secret of his dislike of the whole business, in particular his embarrassment at being paid, and naturally the pupil was terrified of him. She described him as always on the move during lessons, 'uneasy as a lion in a cage', impatient, excitable, fastidious to a fault in his dress but invariably unpunctual. Though absent-minded in practical matters—he would go off without his hat or coat or the twenty francs he had just been paid—he pounced on any slip in her performance and could detect the slightest error in fingering while apparently studying a picture on the wall. A more human trait was his passion for cakes and sweets. Later, when he was too busy to go out, she visited his flat and found a different personality. Instead of hurrying through the lesson he would spend half the afternoon over it; he seemed delighted to entertain, and would show off his pictures and Jacques and play the piano, which he never did in a pupil's house. She heard much of *Carmen* before she had any idea what it was.

Another child visitor was Jacques Émile Blanche, the future painter, who was impressed by Bizet's 'enormous head, a Diocletian

[1] Stuart Henry, *Paris Days and Evenings* (London, 1896), quoted by Curtiss, pp. 345–7.

with glasses'. Wearing Turkish slippers and a red scarf he played *Patrie* on the piano and moved the boy to tears. He was not usually alarming to children, and often had his own in the room while he worked. Neither their games nor the voice of the family parrot nor the sound of other music disturbed his concentration. Jean Reiter recalled, sixty-five years later, his kindness when Jacques's toy balloon hit a candle in his study and burst.

Meanwhile *Carmen* was again postponed till the spring, perhaps because of difficulties anticipated in rehearsal. An earlier stumbling-block had been de Leuven's implacable hostility to the libretto. When Halévy first tackled him he flew into a panic at the mention of the subject: 'We have five or six boxes let every night for marriage interviews! Impossible!' Halévy pointed out that the story would be sweetened by the introduction of Micaela, and the final murder softened by ballet [1] and spectacle; but de Leuven could not reconcile himself to the murder and cut the Gordian knot by resigning early in 1874. There was also the problem of finding a leading lady. Zulma Bouffar, who had sprung to fame in Offenbach, seems to have been the librettists' first choice; she is unlikely to have pleased Bizet and was rejected by du Locle. A tentative approach was made to Marie Roze, whose refusal (in a letter to Bizet of 7th September 1873) sufficiently indicates her unsuitability. She had supposed that 'the very scabrous side of the character would be modified'; when she heard that Mérimée's conception was to be respected she prudently withdrew. It is clear that the former impression had been conveyed by Meilhac and Halévy, the latter by Bizet. The statement of Sutherland Edwards [2] that Bizet wrote the part for Marie Roze, who was only prevented from singing it by engagements in England, is not true.

Du Locle now approached Galli-Marié. Although she had never

[1] There was no ballet in *Carmen* as first produced; probably this was one of the many points at which Bizet resisted the sweetening process. The ballet in Act IV with music from *La Jolie Fille de Perth* and *L'Arlésienne*, which appears in the Choudens full score, was inserted by Guiraud for the Vienna production of October 1875. It is an unpardonable solecism.

[2] *The Prima Donna* (London, 1888).

heard of Mérimée's *Carmen*,[1] she admired Bizet's music; she told him she knew his last two operas 'almost entirely by heart, both voice and accompaniment'. Very soon she was as struck by the part as he was by her suitability for it; his chief anxiety was that she might refuse for financial reasons. However on 18th December 1873 she accepted: she was to create Carmen in October 1874 at a fee of 2,500 francs a month for four months, twelve performances a month. If her engagement was prolonged through the success of the piece she demanded a minimum of 300 francs per performance. On 2nd January she asked Bizet, through du Locle, to use the *tessitura* of Marguerite in *Faust* rather than that of Mignon, her most famous role.

According to Henry Malherbe, who drew his information from backstage gossip at the Opéra-Comique, Bizet had a love affair with Galli-Marié, punctuated by frequent quarrels. Her letters to him (including five in the summer of 1874 and one in May 1875) give no hint of such intimacy; she had for some years been living with Paladilhe. There are, however, indications that Bizet's marriage was increasingly unhappy. Early in 1874 husband and wife lived apart for a time, Bizet remaining in Paris while Geneviève stayed with her cousin Ludovic at Saint-Germain. Mme Halévy again tried to interfere with Jacques; she wanted to have the child constantly with her or not see him at all. Bizet decided on the latter, and wrote to Geneviève that the subject was beginning to besmirch him singularly.

There are several witnesses to his settled melancholy at this period; Henri Maréchal said he 'often sensed tears in his voice, but an immediate effort at self-control quickly suppressed them'. Malherbe thought that one cause was the assiduity with which the pianist Élie Delaborde, a neighbour at Bougival who shared Bizet's passion for swimming, made advances to Geneviève, who was said to be in love with him. According to Mrs Curtiss, Bizet welcomed this because it relieved him of the burden of her perpetual need for attention. There is no conclusive evidence for any of these conjectures. What is quite certain is that there was a deliberate attempt by the Halévy family and

[1] Her name nevertheless had already been linked with it. By a strange coincidence there is extant a letter from Victor Massé to Sardou projecting an opera on *Carmen* with Galli-Marié in the title-part. It is dated 11th August 1864.

others, including Galabert, to suppress the facts. Nearly all the family letters covering the last three years of Bizet's life were destroyed, as were many long entries in Ludovic Halévy's diary, including most of those covering the rehearsals of *Carmen*. It is impossible to say now whether the intention was to protect Bizet or Geneviève or Halévy. The readiness with which Bizet's family, heirs and publishers permitted biographers to repeat false information over many decades, to which Chantavoine drew attention,[1] was undoubtedly part of the same smoke-screen.

Rehearsals began at the beginning of October and, after two short gaps, continued almost daily from 12th November until (and even after) the dress rehearsal on 1st March. This was a trying period for Bizet. He met with hostility inside the theatre: d'Indy, who often attended, says that 'everyone from the director to the concierge turned his back on Bizet'—till the opera showed signs of success. The orchestra, accustomed to the routine scoring of the Auber-Adam school, resented the greater elaboration and difficulty of Bizet's music, even finding some passages unplayable, and Deloffre, the veteran conductor, though a conscientious musician, had little authority. It was the same with the chorus, who after two months' work declared their music in the cigarette girls' and quarrel scenes impossible to sing, especially as they had to act instead of following their usual practice of standing in a line with their eyes on the conductor. Early in February Bizet asked for six additional sopranos and four contraltos in Act I and offered to rehearse them himself (he was already accompanying many of the rehearsals and arranging the vocal score). Du Locle replied on the 13th that the request was not very reasonable and would condemn them to at least a week's delay, but offered with a bad grace to consult Halévy. Bizet's insistence won the day.

To understand the unhelpful attitude of the librettists we must remember that for them *Carmen* was a sideshow. Between late September and early December 1874 they had four other works staged in Paris and could seldom find time to attend rehearsals of the opera; as Halévy wrote shortly before the first night, 'the thing had

[1] 'Les Inédits de Bizet ou La Culte des Maîtres en France', in *La Vie Musicale*, Dec. 1951/Jan. 1952.

little importance for Meilhac and me'. Meilhac, who was responsible for the prose dialogue, especially the comic passages, and the design of the plot, was not interested in music. Both, as popular dramatists, had their eyes fixed firmly on the box office. Apprehensive of the outraged moral sense of the public, they prevailed on the singers to tone down their parts; they stopped Escamillo (at his first entrance) patting the cheeks of a couple of the gypsy girls in the chorus and tried to put some restraint on Galli-Marié. In this policy they were acting directly contrary to Bizet's wishes; the latter resisted every attempt to soften down word and gesture. He refused to change the end of the Flower Song or shorten the duet in Act II (which was thought too 'naturalistic') and break it up into sections for applause. In Act I he wished the chorus to enter by ones and twos instead of in a dense mass, but du Locle protested that this was against tradition.

Du Locle's attitude is puzzling. He seems to have liked Bizet personally, and he mounted the opera with great care, but he was unhappy about the libretto and he loathed the music. He kept repeating in his 'sour and derisive voice' (Saint-Saëns's phrase) that it was Cochin-China music, no one could understand it. Saint-Saëns accused him of deliberately sabotaging *Carmen*'s chances in order to leave the field clear for his favourites, Verdi and Gounod. This is probably unfair, but he certainly did not put his weight behind the work. When a minister applied for a box on the first night he invited him to the dress rehearsal, saying that the piece was so improper that before taking a box for his family he ought to see if it was suitable. The *première* happened to coincide with a ministerial crisis, the re-establishment of diplomatic relations between France and Spain after the Carlist Wars (the new Spanish ambassador was to call on President MacMahon that afternoon) and the celebration of the centenary of the American War of Independence. Du Locle shrank from inviting to *Carmen* any of the eminent public figures concerned. One reason for his behaviour (which unsettled the whole company) was no doubt the financial position of the Opéra-Comique. Early in March 1876 he was compelled to surrender the management, leaving a deficit of 100,000 francs, and perhaps he was already beginning to count up the results of the fiasco which he was convinced *Carmen* would be.

It has recently been suggested that Bizet, succumbing to the various pressures, made numerous cuts and other alterations in the score against his better judgment. There is no evidence whatever to support this. On the contrary, the accounts of many witnesses agree upon his adamantine resistance to any such compromise. It is true that many changes were made during rehearsals; but they can all be justified on artistic grounds.[1] Moreover, since Bizet was supported by his principal singers, especially Galli-Marié and Lhérie (José), who threatened to resign their parts rather than accept any censorship of this kind, there is even less need to impugn his artistic conscience by the gratuitous assumption that he bowed to dictation.

On 15th January 1875 Bizet sold the score of *Carmen* to Choudens for 25,000 francs; foreign royalties were to be divided equally between the two librettists, the composer and the publisher. On 3rd March the first performance took place at the Opéra-Comique. That same morning Bizet's appointment as chevalier of the Legion of Honour was announced in the *Journal Officiel*,[2] and the omen seemed favourable, although some wit put it about that the authorities made haste to decorate him in the morning as they would never dare to do so in the evening, owing to the scandalous nature of the new work. By now most of those taking part had been won round to enthusiasm, and the last rehearsals had been excellent. Ludovic Halévy in his diary records the initial mystification of those behind the scenes (including himself) at the novelty of the music and their subsequent confidence of its success. Perhaps it was too much to hope that the most notoriously conservative audience in Paris would reach the latter state of mind without passing through the former. At any rate the reception was disappointing—not openly hostile as has sometimes been stated, but frigid, shocked and uncomprehending. Halévy described it in a hurried letter to a friend the following day:

> Act I well received. Galli-Marié's first song applauded, also the duet for Micaela and José. End of the act good—applause, recalls. A lot of people

---

[1] *See* Chapter XI, p. 215 ff., and Appendix F, pp. 294–5.

[2] When Bizet heard of the coming award he wrote a graceful letter to Mme Carvalho, attributing the honour to her husband: 'It is to HIM that I owe it. I am not *forgetting* it and I shall NEVER FORGET IT.'

on the stage after this act. Bizet surrounded and congratulated. The second act less fortunate. The opening very brilliant [the *entr'acte* was encored]. Great effect from the Toreador's entry, followed by coldness. From that point on, as Bizet deviated more and more from the traditional form of *opéra-comique*, the public was surprised, discountenanced, perplexed. Fewer people round Bizet between the acts. Congratulations less sincere, embarrassed, constrained. The coldness more marked in the third act. The only thing applauded was Micaela's air, of old classical cut. Still fewer people on the stage. And after the fourth act, which was glacial from first to last, no one at all except three or four faithful and sincere friends of Bizet's. They all had reassuring phrases on their lips but sadness in their eyes. *Carmen* had failed.

The audience contained a number of composers, of whom Massenet and Saint-Saëns (but not Gounod or Thomas) sent Bizet letters of congratulation, and many fashionable followers of Meilhac, Halévy and Offenbach. The thirteen-year-old Jacques Émile Blanche, who sat in Gounod's box, left two accounts of the evening, including a devastating glimpse of the master's attitude to his favourite pupil. After overwhelming Bizet with embraces and admiration in the second interval, he ostentatiously applauded Micaela's Act III air and then leaned back with the remark: 'That melody is mine! Georges has robbed me; take the Spanish airs and mine out of the score, and there remains nothing to Bizet's credit but the sauce that masks the fish.' Blanche described this as his 'first lesson in duplicity'.[1]

The performance seems to have been fair, though the chorus, especially the women, were inclined to sing out of tune and put little conviction into their acting. Bouhy (Escamillo) and Mlle Chapuy (Micaela)—afterwards the wife of a general who became Minister for War—were good, and Galli-Marié excellent. Lhérie (José) was a poor actor and erratic in pitch. The orchestra was no more than moderate. There were the usual mishaps. Once when Galli-Marié was singing *pianissimo* the big-drum player, miscounting his bars, stupefied the house by coming in with two loud bangs. Some of the ladies of the chorus, accustomed to the unhurried entries and exits of

[1] Gounod's last communication with Bizet was an irritable note dated 5th May 1875 about a dispute with Choudens, whose part he suspected Bizet of taking (Curtiss, pp. 412–13).

La Dame blanche and obliged to dance and fight and even to smoke on the stage, were taken ill as a result. D'Indy, who with Camille Benoît was the lucky winner of a free ticket that Bizet had offered to Franck's organ class, went to congratulate the composer in one of the intervals. According to his account, which does not quite square with Halévy's, they found him and his friend the publisher Hartmann walking up and down on the pavement outside the stage door. Both seemed dejected. Bizet thanked them for their congratulations, adding: 'I sense defeat. I foresee a definite and hopeless flop. This time I am really sunk.' Benjamin Godard too found him in despair. When someone else mentioned his success he replied: 'Success! Don't you see that all these bourgeois have not understood a wretched word of the work I have written for them?' On catching sight of the critic Victor Wilder he broke through a circle of friends and begged him to say what he really thought of *Carmen*, as he was not the kind of man who had to be told that everything he did was admirable. After the performance he took refuge in du Locle's office, where some of his friends tried to comfort him, and he was one of the last to leave the theatre. Of what followed two flatly contradictory accounts have been given. According to Pigot, who had it from Guiraud soon after the event, Bizet took Guiraud's arm and wandered about Paris for half the night pouring out the bitterness of his soul. Halévy, on the other hand, thirty years later and when he was an old man of over seventy, stated that Bizet went quietly home with himself and Meilhac. Pigot's account is the more probable. Halévy, who was living with Bizet at the time, may have been thinking of another occasion, perhaps the dress rehearsal (his account is inaccurate in several other respects). For reasons that can only be guessed, he seems to have been at pains to minimize the depressing effect that the reception of *Carmen* had on Bizet; the evidence of others who knew him well—Guiraud, Gallet, Maréchal, Berton and Geneviève Bizet—points all the other way.[1]

The first press reviews of a work that has since been accepted as a masterpiece are always interesting; those of *Carmen* throw a light half lurid, half humorous, on French musical criticism in 1875. It would

[1] Galabert agrees with Halévy; but he was not present, and he seems to have had little contact with Bizet after 1872.

hardly be too much to say that both libretto and music caused something approaching pandemonium in the press. The general opinion was that Mérimée's novel was far too obscene to be staged, the characters were, in Arthur Pougin's words,[1] 'of an antipathetic nature and devoid of interest', and Galli-Marié over-emphasized the seamy side of her part to such an extent that 'it would be difficult to go much farther without provoking the intervention of the police' (François Oswald in *Le Gaulois*). The actress's gestures, wrote Léon Escudier in *L'Art Musical*, 'are a very incarnation of vice, and there is something licentious even in the tones of her voice'. Or, as succinctly put by Noël and Stoullig in their *Annales du Théâtre et de la Musique*: 'Quelle vérité, mais quel scandale!'

This in a sense is a tribute to the actress, but the critics found more scandal than truth in the music. The more conservative trumpeted about Wagnerism, the decrepitude of melody, the surrender of the voice before the confused and clamorous roar of the orchestra.

[1] Pougin is quoted rather than others whose vocabulary was even stronger, because in 1903 he published in *Le Ménestrel* an article (since much quoted) entitled 'La Légende de la chute de Carmen et la mort de Bizet', in which he posed as a great admirer of the libretto ('a masterpiece'), supported statements of Galli-Marié's (*a*) that Bizet was much less severely handled than the librettists, (*b*) that the success of *Carmen* was assured before Bizet's death, and concluded: 'It is absolutely untrue to say that the public understood nothing of the music and felt only indifference or disdain towards it.' The article is a complete distortion of the facts, apparently inspired by a guilty conscience. The second of Galli-Marié's statements was explicitly denied by Bizet's widow; the first is disproved by reference to the printed word. Pougin wrote two reviews of *Carmen* in 1875; in the first (7th March) he described Bizet as 'one of the most ferociously intransigent of our young Wagnerian school', but gave the music considerable praise; in the second (11th March) he was a good deal cooler. In 1878 he contributed the article on Bizet to Fétis's *Biographie universelle*. Having now, it appears, seen the writing on the wall, he became patronizing and contemptuous. Bizet is held up as 'the most deadly enemy of *opéra-comique*', and rebuked for having shown antipathy to 'the genius of one of its most glorious representatives in the past—Boieldieu'. The 1903 article completed the volte-face. In 1878 Pougin made the extraordinary assertion that the critics welcomed *Carmen* with the greatest pleasure.

It seems astonishing that *Carmen* of all operas should, even in a society notoriously hostile to new ideas, have been condemned for lack of melody, but that was the opinion of more than half the Paris press. Oswald remarked that the tunes were given to the orchestra, the accompaniments to the voice, and contrasted Bizet's erudite melody with the natural flow of Auber, Adam, Hérold and Boieldieu. Baudouin in *La République Française* spoke of 'complete absence of light—music dwelling from start to finish in a limbo of greyness'. Henry de Lapommeraye in *La France* found José's air behind the scenes (Act II) 'indecisive in shape and pretentious in harmony', though this is the one item in the score that is sung unaccompanied (it is possible however that the critic heard one of the later performances when d'Indy supported Lhérie with a harmonium in order to keep him in tune). Another charge, nearly as surprising, was that the music was not dramatic. A typical summing-up is that of Oscar Comettant, in *Le Siècle*, who thought that only Rossini could have done justice to so sensual a libretto.

> Certainly no one will accuse M. Bizet of melodic prodigality. . . . It is impossible to give musical expression to Carmen's erotic fury by ingenious orchestration; melody is the only thing that can realize MM. Meilhac and Halévy's brutally realistic characters. I do not mean to say that there are not what are called themes in M. Bizet's music. Unfortunately, as a rule, they are anything but original and they lack distinction. . . . There is no unity of style in *Carmen*, but its greatest fault is that it is not dramatic. . . . M. Bizet has learnt everything that can be taught, but unhappily he has much still to learn of what no one can teach him. He thinks too much and does not feel enough, and his inspirations, even when most happy, lack sincerity and truth, two qualities that are worth all the erudition in the world.

To the supporters of the Auber school everything that savoured of erudition was suspicious, and Bizet's scoring fell under this ban. Escudier, who could stomach neither scoring nor harmony, ranked *Carmen* below Bizet's first two operas.

> In *Carmen* the composer has made up his mind to show us how learned he is, with the result that he is often dull and obscure. He makes a point of never finishing his phrases till the ear grows weary of waiting for the cadence that never comes.

Chevojon

PORTRAIT OF BIZET BY GIACOMOTTI, 1860

BIZET AGED ABOUT TWENTY-FIVE

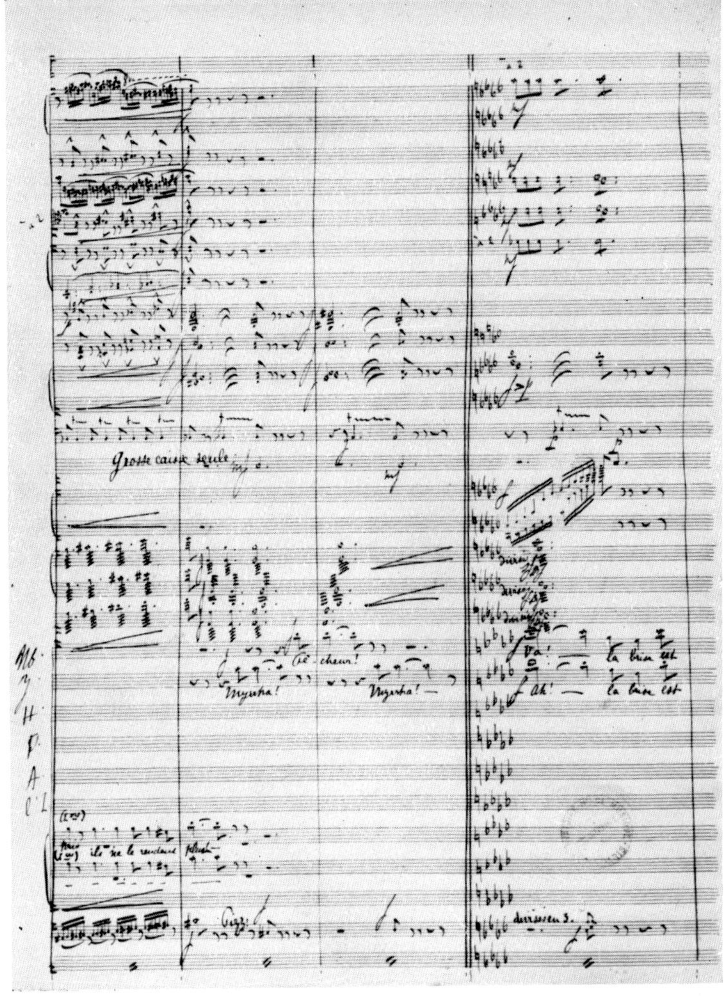

PAGE FROM THE AUTOGRAPH OF 'LA COUPE DU ROI DE THULÉ'
(ACT I, FINALE)

Musée du Louvre

PORTRAIT OF GENEVIÈVE BIZET BY
ÉLIE DELAUNAY, 1876

Carjat

GEORGES BIZET, AGED THIRTY-SIX (1875)

Cher ami

Que dites-vous donc lorsque
vous avez vu Rome et Naples?...
quel pays!
Vive en Italie même
sans musique, quel rêve!
Gounod va partir pour
Rome, afin d'entrer dans les
ordres!....
il est absolument fou!...
Ses dernières compositions sont
navrantes!
au diable la musique
catholique!
Pasdeloup va jouer ma
symphonie - du moins, il l'a dit

FIRST PAGE OF A LETTER FROM BIZET TO LACOMBE (DEC. 1868)

POSTER FOR THE 1875 PRODUCTION OF 'CARMEN'

L'amour est un rebelle
Et nul ne peut l'apprivoiser.
C'est en vain qu'on l'appelle
S'il lui convient de refuser

8 vers pareils aux quatre premiers. Le second, 4me, 6me, 8me, 10me et 12me vers commençant par un voyelle!!!

L'amour est enfant de Bohême...
Il ne connut jamais de loi.
Si tu ne m'aimes pas je t'aime!..
Si tu m'aimes... tant pis pour toi!..

L'oiseau que tu croyais surprendre
Battit de l'aile et s'envola.
L'amour est loin — tu peux l'attendre.
Tu ne l'attends plus — il est là.
Tout autour de toi, vite, vite
Il vient — il s'en va — puis revient
Tu crois le tenir — il t'évite —
Tu crois l'éviter — il te tient!

L'amour est enfant de Bohême
Il ne connut jamais de loi.
Si tu ne m'aimes pas, je t'aime!
Si tu m'aimes.. tant pis pour toi!

BIZET'S ORIGINAL DRAFT OF THE WORDS OF CARMEN'S HABANERA, WITH INSTRUCTIONS TO HALÉVY AND HALÉVY'S SUGGESTED VERSES

Most of these gentry allowed him a certain talent and occasional glimpses of inspiration, and nearly all had a kind word for Micaela; to Comettant she was 'the only decent and sympathetic character in the midst of this inferno of ridiculous and uninteresting corruption'. Many of them showed a remarkable ignorance of the history of music and the most elementary details of craftsmanship. It would be otiose to multiply quotations, except that an historian must take note of the climate in which an artist worked, and the voice of criticism is a potent element in this.[1] Pierre Berton thought that part of the press was bribed, and said he could name the most notoriously venal of the critics. Certainly some explanation is required of the simultaneous appearance in several papers, on the *morning* of the first performance, of short notices announcing that the Opéra-Comique could no longer be the theatre of marriage interviews and family parties owing to the impropriety of the new opera. Was this du Locle reinsuring against a possible scandal?

Carmen was not condemned in these terms by the whole Paris press. There was a section from which sounder judgment could be expected. Joncières in *La Liberté* praised most of the music, especially the card scene and the final duet, though he wanted more rage *à la* Verdi at the end. The subtlest appreciation came from the poet Théodore de Banville in *Le National*, who alone showed some grasp of Bizet's aims and achievements in *Carmen*: 'M. Bizet has sought to show (in place of the puppets of *opéra-comique*) real men and real women, with the orchestra, turned creator and poet, interpreting for us their agonies, jealousies and mad impulses.' He had special praise for the castanet dance and the 'irresistible and purely musical delight' of the moment when the retreat is sounded against it. Reyer in *Le Journal des Débats* wrote a rather dull article, less enthusiastic than his criticisms of Bizet's earlier work,[2] but ended with the much-quoted

[1] Bizet in a letter to Saint-Saëns complained particularly of the 'insults' of Comettant and Achille de Lauzières of *La Patrie*, who was a marquis and a failed composer. Both these scurrilous reviews are quoted at length by Mina Curtiss, pp. 399–404.

[2] He was never a great enthusiast for *Carmen*. In 1883 he found 'not a high enough affirmation of the doctrines the young composer professed'. In other words it was insufficiently Wagnerian.

sentence: '*Carmen* is not dead, and at the Opéra-Comique we have seen plenty of others come back to life after such an experience.' Weber in *Le Temps* was both cautious and captious. He thought the cigarette girls' chorus mediocre and the final duet too long, and came a bad tumble over the opening chorus of Act IV, which he damned as a mere quadrille despite the fact that it is in 3–4 time throughout. When the vocal score was published a week later he ate many of his words; Reyer also, and even Jouvin, took the opportunity of modifying their original coolness. Jouvin tried to keep an open mind while approaching *Carmen* in the gingerly manner a modern critic might adopt towards a new excursion by the *avant-garde*. He reached the startling conclusion that although parts of the score might not stand up to the theatre they would find a public in the *salons*.

There remains Jullien, who in *Le Français* uttered a piece of invective that left the efforts of the Comettant-Escudier school in the shade. He considered the work 'a vulgar *opéra-comique* with a dash of the pathetic and a final murder that is almost inexplicable' (his reason for this epithet is that Carmen had done nothing wrong, and if José was seduced by her it was his own fault!). Meilhac and Halévy had travestied Mérimée, and Bizet's music was always contemptible where he was in contact with the former, sometimes interesting when he was dealing with Mérimée. The quintet was banal, Act III 'bad almost from beginning to end'. In particular Jullien renewed the old charge about concessions.

> The composer has naïvely imagined that it would be enough for him to attenuate his preferences, repudiate his juvenile audacities, timid and modest as they were, rally openly to the traditional *opéra-comique genre*, whose sacred forms he had believed he could stretch or modify according to the exigences of his libretti—in fact to write plenty of lively *couplets* and easily memorized refrains, in order to win those precious praises that most of the critics obstinately refused to bestow on him. . . . This *opéra-comique* is nothing but a long string of compromises, in the poem as much as in the music.

Bizet, in fact, knew what he ought to do, but for discreditable reasons refused to do it. The flaws in Jullien's bombinations are obvious enough. It was a literal case of prejudice: Jullien, a passionate Wagnerian, had decided beforehand in which direction French music should go, and if Bizet tried to lead it elsewhere he was guilty of a sin not only against France and music, but against his own nature. Jullien was the first of many French writers to approach Bizet in this state of mind. There was, indeed, a certain duality in Bizet's nature, though it was not the pull of genius versus self-interest that Jullien maintained. And *Carmen* in 1875 did fall between two stools, though not the two so unctuously placed on either side by Jullien. Most of the critics expected a sort of apotheosis of Auber (or even Offenbach, for Meilhac and Halévy were known primarily as Offenbach's librettists) and, not finding it, damned the result as Wagnerian; while Jullien and his followers, desiring the exact opposite, waxed indignant when they saw a revitalized *opéra-comique*. There is no need to look farther than this to account for *Carmen*'s failure in 1875. As with *Pelléas et Mélisande* twenty-seven years later, neither the conservatives nor the radicals were satisfied, because neither party had envisaged the possibility of Bizet creating something equally remote from both of them.

And *Carmen* really was a failure in 1875, though attempts have been made to maintain the opposite. It is true that it had forty-five performances during the year (more than any other work at the Opéra-Comique), together with three more early in 1876. But it was nearly taken off owing to poor support after four or five nights, and there seems little doubt that, though its admirers increased, two things only kept it running: the attractive rumour that it was very shocking and Bizet's sudden death on the night of the thirty-third performance. It had at best a brief *succès de scandale*—an impression confirmed by the subsequent refusal to revive it till 1883, though its success at Vienna in October 1875 had led to a world-wide reputation. Towards the end of the run, too, the management was giving away tickets wholesale. The effect on the man in the street is illustrated by an experience of Charles Malherbe, later librarian of the Opéra. He was present on the second night, in a half-empty theatre; a gentleman entered and sat down by him, watched the first act with an expression of growing stupefaction on his face and beat a precipitate retreat (banging the door) when Galli-Marié broke a plate for her dance in Act II. Halévy tells a pleasant story of the ancient librettist Dupin, whose first work had been staged in 1808. He found *Carmen* a criminal breach of the Scribe tradition, for which he soundly rated his friends

Meilhac and Halévy, and declared that it would not be played twenty times. Yet he lived to see the three-hundredth performance in the ninety-sixth year of his age. Tchaikovsky on the other hand prophesied that within ten years it would be the most popular opera in the world.

Servières quotes figures for the receipts, which show that though *Carmen* did not empty the theatre, it seldom if ever filled it.[1] At no time did the takings equal those of the 1883 revival; they averaged about half and were sometimes down to a fifth. For a period the Opéra-Comique presented the strange spectacle of half-empty performances of *Carmen* alternating with seven packed houses for the Verdi Requiem, conducted by the composer. On the day of the second performance Bizet appeared at Franck's class and asked for a volunteer to attend regularly and play the harmonium to support José's song behind the scenes in Act II. When the request was received with amusement, Bizet explained that Lhérie was incapable of sustaining the pitch: 'He begins in G and finishes in E major—unless it should be E minor, or even (horrors!) E flat minor'. D'Indy undertook the task with enthusiasm and fulfilled it to the last. 'I saw the house gradually empty. I was present at the last performance in February 1876.'

According to Vuillermoz, quoting the *Figaro* of 10th March 1875, du Locle immediately after the first night commissioned another *opéra-comique* from the same three collaborators. Servières says that du Locle mentioned this at Bizet's funeral, as reported in the *Figaro* of 6th June. These references are wrong; but the story did appear in *L'Univers illustré* of 20th March (quoted by Malherbe, *Carmen*, p. 106). Whether it was true is however by no means certain.

Late in March Bizet had a severe attack of quinsy. Normally in these circumstances he would stay a few days in bed, and no one was worried. But this time his recovery was slow and incomplete, and was accompanied by extreme depression. Two or three weeks after *Carmen* Henri Maréchal, a young winner of the Prix de Rome who used to dine with him every week, found him so upset that he dared not mention the subject. Suddenly Bizet burst out: 'Ah! I've had

[1] There were eleven performances in March 1875, fourteen in April, seven in May, three in June (two others were cancelled), and thirteen between November and February 1876.

enough of writing music to surprise three or four comrades who then go and scoff behind my back!' He complained to the critic Weber about the perpetual outcry of Wagnerism. To Gallet 'he seemed to fall into profound melancholy, which showed itself in words that escaped his lips as if in his own despite', though on the surface he was his usual ironical self, 'speaking of everything in that same bantering tone which disguised so well from people who did not know him his sensitiveness and kindness of heart'. Berton described him as ultra-sensitive and impressionable, and all the more at the mercy of his emotions from his attempts to conceal them. He found him 'torn between the raging desire to curse his judges and his terror of believing them. Finally he shrugged his shoulders in a gesture of profound weariness and said "Perhaps they are right".' (Lhérie also spoke of finding him hesitant and dispirited, but this may have been during the rehearsals; he told Gelma that Bizet never returned to the theatre after the first night of *Carmen.*) Gallet added that even when in good health he harboured the idea of some grim catastrophe, and Perrin confirmed that he was haunted by the fear of early death.

One evening about this time he had some friends in and was running through *Carmen* with a young singer whose voice and musical aptitude had charmed him. Towards the end he suddenly interrupted and asked her to sing some Schumann. He listened in a corner with his head in his hands, greatly moved, till she finished something from *Manfred.*[1] Then he exclaimed: 'What a masterpiece, but what despair! It's enough to make you long for death [*C'est à vous donner la nostalgie de la mort*].' He went to the piano and played Schumann's funeral march (presumably the slow movement of the Quintet), followed by Chopin's—which not many days later played him to the grave.

Early in May Bizet met Comettant in the lobby of the Conservatoire and lost his temper with him over his review of *Carmen.* Saint-Georges, called in to arbitrate (surely an ironical choice), wrote Bizet a clumsy and obscure letter containing the suggestion that he ought

[1] According to another account she sang *Ich grolle nicht* and *Aus der Heimat* (presumably *In der Fremde*).

to apologize for his 'mistake in supposing that [Comettant's] article had the same malicious imputation as that of M. de Lauzières'. Bizet received this less than a week before his death and had little time to act on it. It is hard to believe in Comettant's good faith or the disingenuous protestations in his review of the *Carmen* revival of April 1883. In October of that year he executed a complete about-turn, saluting Galli-Marié as the personification of Mérimée's Carmen and Bizet as the liberator of the Opéra-Comique from bourgeois prudery.

When, about the beginning of May, the time came for going into the country, Bizet was still convalescent, and his wife tried to persuade him to wait till his recovery was complete. 'No, no,' he cried, 'let's go; I want to go at once; this Paris air is poisoning me.' He soon had another attack, accompanied by suffocation, an abscess in the ear and increasing rheumatism, which caused him to fall when getting out of bed; he could not rise unaided. An undated note to Guiraud tells its own tale: 'Colossal quinsy. Don't come on Sunday. Imagine a double pedal A flat–E flat going through your head from the left ear to the right. I'm quite done in. I shall write to you.' He recovered sufficiently to see Lamoureux about *Geneviève de Paris*; Gallet had read the poem to Lamoureux, who expressed lively interest. Bizet proposed to write the music in the first three months of the summer.

The libretto survives, with a few preliminary annotations in Bizet's hand. It is a frigid conventional piece that seems quite antipathetic to his genius. There are three characters, Geneviève, Bishop Germain of Auxerre and the Spirit of Evil, who appears under four disguises, and four scenes: (I) Geneviève as a child receives the Bishop's blessing; (II) she resists carnal temptation and, reassured by unseen voices, consoles fugitives fleeing from the approach of Attila; (III) she defies a storm conjured up by Satan (Bizet wanted to alter this) and with supernatural aid leads a flotilla of food ships into the besieged city of Paris; (IV) the Spirit of Evil stirs up the population against Geneviève, who prepares for martyrdom but is saved by the approach of the Bishop and Roman forces under Aetius. The finale was to be a *Te Deum*, accompanied by bells and organ. Bizet named the latter instrument in the margin, with the words 'Te Deum'; it looks as if he meant to use his Rome setting. Not a note of the music was written, and it is difficult to agree with Tiersot that French music here lost one of its supreme masterpieces.

Late in May Gallet visited Bizet for the last time; it was the only occasion on which he remembered him conversing seated. Guiraud called on the evening before his departure for Bougival and in response to Bizet's invitation sat down at the piano to play passages from *Piccolino*, the opera he was then composing. Bizet stopped him; in a shrill and shaky voice that horrified Guiraud he said he could hear nothing with his left ear, and came round to the other side. They discussed Guiraud's music and other things, till at midnight the visitor rose to go. At the bottom of the staircase he remembered something he had promised to discuss, and for twenty minutes they chatted, Guiraud at the bottom, Bizet at the top in his dressing-gown, with a candle in his hand. That was the last Guiraud saw of his friend.

There is some slight doubt about the chronology of Bizet's last days. Eugène Gelma, a professor of psychiatry at Strasbourg, wrote two articles [1] on his illness and death, largely based on the testimony of Jean Reiter, whom he knew well. Galabert's account [2] was derived from conversation with Guiraud. Mrs Curtiss says that Bizet and his household left for Bougival on 28th May; Galabert gives the date as the 31st, Gelma in both articles as Thursday the 27th. The last seems the most likely. The first day passed well; husband and wife went for an enjoyable walk along the Seine with Delaborde, and later Bizet was rash enough to bathe in the river for longer than was prudent.[3] On the 30th he suffered a violent and incapacitating attack

[1] 'Quelques souvenirs sur Georges Bizet' in *L'Alsace Française* (10th Dec. 1938) and 'La Mort du Musicien Georges Bizet' in *Cahiers de Psychiatrie* (Strasbourg, 1948).

[2] 'La Maladie et la mort de Bizet' in *Le Passant* (Feb. 1888).

[3] This detail came from Daniel Halévy, who presumably had it from his father Ludovic. Ever since his Rome days Bizet had a passion for swimming. He gave lessons to Jean Reiter and frequently swam in the Seine with Lhérie when the tenor came to Bougival to study the part of José during the summer of 1874. He had a shower-bath fitted up behind curtains in his study.

of rheumatism, accompanied by high fever, great pain and depression. After a partial recovery this was followed on the night of 1st June by a severe heart attack. A doctor was hastily summoned from Rueil and returned on the morning of the 2nd, when he declared that the crisis was over and there was no further danger; only calm and rest were needed. He seems to have attributed the symptoms largely to imagination, for he said there was no point in disturbing him in the event of another crisis. During the day Bizet was still restless with a high fever, but seemed better when his two sons visited him in the evening. Later he had a second heart attack of equal severity. Delaborde and the doctor were sent for, but took their time in arriving. While waiting for them Bizet spoke anxiously to Marie Reiter about his father and then lost consciousness. When the doctor arrived he was dead.

According to the death certificate he died at 2 a.m. on the morning of 3rd June,[1] the sixth anniversary of his marriage. An hour or two earlier the curtain at the Opéra-Comique had fallen on the thirty-third performance of *Carmen*. When playing the scene in Act III in which Carmen reads her death in the cards—'moi d'abord, ensuite lui, pour tous les deux la mort!'—Galli-Marié had been overcome with foreboding and fainted on leaving the stage. She managed to continue, but burst into tears at the end and refused to be comforted.[2] Du Locle, suspecting some personal crisis, was more amused than upset—till a few hours later he received Halévy's telegram. By an odd chance the same day saw signal honours paid to two of Bizet's pet aversions, a gala performance of *La Dame blanche* for Boieldieu's centenary at Rouen and the inauguration of a monument to Auber at Caen; and in the evening *La Dame blanche* was substituted for *Carmen* at the Opéra-Comique because Galli-Marié was too ill or too upset to appear.

The exact cause of death has never been determined. During the

[1] Jean Reiter and Gelma thought he died before midnight; Ludovic Halévy, who spent the night in the house, put the time at 3 a.m. He at once took Geneviève to his own house at Saint-Germain, and telegraphed the news to Rodrigues, Guiraud and du Locle in the morning.

[2] This telepathic experience is vouched for by Reyer and Guiraud.

last illness there was talk of an open abscess of the throat;[1] but neither this nor the quinsy seems likely to have proved fatal. Gelma was probably right in suggesting a cardiac complication of articular rheumatism, aggravated by a chill. Bizet may always have had a defective heart. He complained of palpitations in Rome and could never climb the five flights of stairs to Guiraud's Paris flat without pausing for breath. It is of course fanciful to attribute his death to the bad reception of *Carmen*—just as it is fanciful to suppose that Keats was killed by reviewers—but worry and disappointment after the prolonged strain of the rehearsals may well have sapped his resistance to an ailment which he had been able to throw off when in better health. Modern research has proved that psychology is more intimately concerned with physical illness than was once supposed, and even in the eighties one doctor[2] suggested that 'physical and moral depression brought on by the failure of *Carmen*' may have been the last straw. Unfortunately Gelma's discussion of this point is valueless. He preferred to ignore many independent witnesses and trust the word of Jean Reiter, Robert Dreyfus, Louis Ganderax and Daniel Halévy that Bizet in his last days was not in any way unhappy or depressed. But all except Ganderax were children at the time, and the last three at least, intimate members of the Halévy circle, had something to conceal of which Gelma knew nothing—the breakdown of Bizet's marriage. Gelma also assumed, without evidence, that Bizet in the last week of his life was hard at work on *Geneviève de Paris* and asked how this resumption of creative activity could be reconciled with depression—a considerable *non sequitur*.

The funeral took place on 5th June at the church of La Trinité in Montmartre. Four thousand people attended. The musical arrangements were in the hands of Pasdeloup, who had hurried back from Caen, where he was conducting a regional festival, and got together the programme in a few hours. It was remarkable for loyalty rather than taste. The organist Bazille played fantasies on themes from *Les Pêcheurs de perles* and *Carmen*; Pasdeloup's orchestra contributed the

[1] Antony Choudens's misinterpretation of this when he saw the body seems to have been responsible for the rumours that Bizet committed suicide.

[2] G. Lefèbvre, quoted by Pigot.

Patrie overture and the Adagietto and second half of the Prelude from *L'Arlésienne* (besides Chopin's funeral march); the vocal numbers consisted of the now notorious *Agnus Dei* and a *Pie Jesu* arranged by Guiraud from the duet in Act I of *Les Pêcheurs de perles*. The pall-bearers were Gounod, Ambroise Thomas, Camille Doucet (President of the Société des Auteurs Dramatiques) and Camille du Locle; behind them came Bizet's old father,[1] leaning on Ludovic Halévy's arm, and a distinguished company that included Alexandre Dumas *fils*, Léon Halévy, Massenet, Guiraud and Paladilhe. Among the wreaths was one from the young competitors for the Prix de Rome, who could not attend because their examination was in progress.

At the interment in the cemetery of Père Lachaise speeches were made by Jules Barbier, du Locle and Gounod, who after quoting a statement of Geneviève Bizet's that there was not an hour or a minute of her married life that she would not gladly have again,[2] broke down and was unable to continue. The special performance of *Carmen* that night was, according to all accounts, almost unbearably moving; and the press which had so damned the opera three months before for a whole week proclaimed its composer a master. A year later, on 10th June 1876, a monument of red Jura stone was unveiled at Père Lachaise; it was designed by Charles Garnier, with a bust by Paul Dubois after the well-known Carjat photograph.[3] A replica of the bust, which is described as an excellent likeness, was set up in the foyer of the Opéra-Comique, but perished in the fire of 1887. Among the eighty-three subscribers were many names famous in the theatrical and musical world, and the proceedings were graced by eulogistic

[1] He lived till 19th December 1886. In that year (8th October) Geneviève Bizet married Émile Straus, a well-known advocate. The Strauses became intimate friends of Marcel Proust. Proust's portrait of the Duchesse de Guermantes is said to have been modelled on Madame Straus, who died on 22nd December 1926 at the age of seventy-seven, four years after Proust and her son Jacques, and more than half a century after her first husband.

[2] This was probably camouflage. Geneviève was in bed at Saint-Germain, too ill to attend the funeral, and is unlikely to have seen Gounod. For his draft speech *see* Curtiss, p. 423.

[3] Dubois (1829–1905), a fellow pensioner of Bizet at Rome, was rewarded with the autograph score of *Djamileh*

speeches from Barbier and Perrin. The city of Paris named a street in the district of Passy after Bizet.

A few words may be added on the posthumous history of *Carmen*. The day before his death Bizet signed a contract for its production at Vienna. This took place on 23rd October in a version for which Guiraud had replaced the spoken dialogue by recitatives.[1] It is from this Vienna production, highly praised by Brahms and Wagner among others,[2] that the popularity of *Carmen* dates. It had fair success at Brussels in February 1876; in 1878 it triumphed in St Petersburg, London, Dublin and New York. In London it narrowly missed performance by two companies simultaneously. (The impresario Mapleson gives an amusing account of its first performance here—by an Italian company. The tenor returned the part of José, saying that he would do anything to oblige, but could not think of undertaking a role in which he had no romance and no love duet except with the *seconda donna*. The Escamillo and the Micaela declared that their parts must have been intended for one of the chorus. For the methods, worthy of a company promoter, by which Mapleson ensured the success of the opera with the public, see *The Mapleson Memoirs*.)

For the next few years *Carmen* continued to sweep Europe and America, often with Galli-Marié in her original part (at Genoa in 1881 she was wounded in the cheek by the knife of an over-realistic José); but Paris, though it heard many of Bizet's works in the concert-hall,[3]

[1] Not all of them were used, however, the director (Jauner) preferring a mixture of spoken dialogue and recitative. Guiraud's version or Jauner's compound seem to have been the only ones used outside France till about 1928, when various German theatres began to restore the spoken dialogue. For later practice *see* p. 220. A letter of 7th July 1875 from Massenet to Paul Lacombe suggests that Bizet himself intended to compose recitatives for 'Belgium and Germany' (*La Revue Musicale*, Aug./Sep. 1937).

[2] Tchaikovsky saw one of the last Paris performances, early in 1876, but he had already received the vocal score from his pupil Vladimir Shilovsky, who was an enthusiastic spectator on the first night. For his interesting reactions to the opera, see his *Life and Letters* by Modeste Tchaikovsky, translated by Rosa Newmarch.

[3] On 12th December 1880 Colonne gave the first performance of the *Marche funèbre* from *La Coupe du Roi de Thulé*, which the critics found worthy but rather crude. The neglect of this fine work is surprising.

steadfastly refused to revive *Carmen*. The first attempt, by Ludovic Halévy in 1876, met with a firm refusal from Carvalho, du Locle's successor. In 1878 Carvalho drew the line at Galli-Marié, preferring a 'calmer' interpreter. In 1882 a lively campaign on behalf of *Carmen* developed in the Paris press, led by Maurice Lefèvre in *Le Clairon*, who called personally on the director and the librettists. He found all three hostile. Carvalho objected to the representation of a brothel on the stage of the Opéra-Comique, and Meilhac and Halévy expressed horror at the idea of engaging Galli-Marié, whom they blamed for the original failure. 'Mme Galli-Marié may have played Mérimée's Carmen, she did not play ours!' (It does not seem to have occurred to them to consider whether she played Bizet's.) The singer herself approached Geneviève Bizet and Carvalho independently. She too found the librettists cool, and on 6th June 1882 she wrote an eloquent letter to Geneviève begging her to use her influence on behalf of the opera and offering to discuss and modify her interpretation. It is clear that Halévy, who now had higher ambitions than that of theatre librettist, was afraid that his reputation might suffer.

All this pressure led to a disastrous compromise. Carvalho's revival on 21st April 1883 was reluctant, half-hearted and under-rehearsed. He seems to have been terrified of his public, for he watered down the production in a manner to make Bizet turn in his grave. The title-part was entrusted to Adèle Isaac, a light *coloratura* soprano pungently described as an elephant who had swallowed a nightingale; she could not sing the notes, and she acted in a style of demure respectability. Lillas Pastia's tavern-cum-brothel emerged as a glorified Corner House café, with sixty to a hundred guests and at least twenty dancers. The fight with knives became a token duel, and the music was prettified and dragged. No trouble was taken with the dramatic side, for Carvalho was sure it would be a failure. He must have had the shock of his life. The public flocked to see it, and the critics—many of them survivors from 1875—raised an uproar, not this time against the opera, but against the director who had dared to travesty one of the masterpieces of the French stage.

Various explanations have been given for this odd behaviour by a man who had always supported Bizet: that he was unwilling to revive a work associated with his predecessor, that there was no part for his wife, that he wanted to set his stamp on the production by being different, that the Opéra-Comique received 20 per cent of its takings from bridal couples, who used it as a rendezvous with their families—and how could a decent man take his betrothed to see the illicit amours of Carmen? Whatever is the truth, Carvalho was quick to see his mistake. On 27th October of the same year he brought back Galli-Marié in a rejuvenated production, and since that time *Carmen*'s success has been as assured in France as it was already elsewhere.

CHAPTER VII

ORCHESTRAL MUSIC

AT THE head of Bizet's output stands a work which, for sheer precocity of genius, rivals the juvenilia of Mozart and Mendelssohn. The Symphony in C major, begun on 29th October 1855 and finished by the end of the following month, has had a curious history. For nearly eighty years the autograph lay unknown to the world. Geneviève Bizet gave it, with several others (including *La Jolie Fille de Perth*), to Reynaldo Hahn, a close friend and member of her *salon*, who found it of no interest.[1] In 1933 he deposited it at the Paris Conservatoire, and in August of that year Chantavoine described it in the first of his articles in *Le Ménestrel*.[2] Soon afterwards D. C. Parker, author of the first English life of Bizet, brought it to the attention of Weingartner. Since its first performance under that conductor, at Basle on 26th February 1935, it has made up in popularity for its long years of neglect. Tardy performances of unknown works by eminent composers often bring a sense of anticlimax; Schumann's violin Concerto is an example. Bizet's Symphony made all the greater impression since there was no evidence that at the age of barely seventeen he either had produced, or was capable of producing, music of such quality. Vuillermoz, for whom any stick was good enough to beat Bizet with, had maintained without challenge that the last thing that could be claimed for him was precocity. The discovery therefore helped to correct a wrong perspective.

The Symphony is in the classical four-movement form and is

[1] This need not surprise us. Hahn's superficial view of Bizet is brutally exposed in three articles written for the centenary in 1938 and republished in *Thèmes variés* (1946). He thought Carmen should be played as a frivolous flirt, and could not understand how serious musicians could rank Bizet above Thomas, Gounod or Saint-Saëns.

[2] *See* Appendix F, p. 288.

scored for an orchestra of moderate size, without trombones or harp. Any seventeen-year-old composer is bound to lean on his models, and Bizet's are clear at once. The simple construction of the opening theme on a rising arpeggio of the tonic chord tells of a grounding in the Haydn-Beethoven tradition. The *crescendo* in the bridge-passage with its *tremolo* strings and repeated rhythm on the trumpets is a memory of Rossini (there are others later). Touches here and there recall the Mozart whom Bizet loved so much, and the deftness of the scoring perhaps owes something to Mendelssohn. But the principal model was Gounod's first Symphony in D major, performed earlier the same year, which Bizet had just been arranging for piano duet. The parallels, in all the movements except the scherzo, are sufficiently prominent to account for the suppression of Bizet's work. Many of the procedures—fanfares, rushing string figures (especially at the approach to cadences), sequential development, even the fugato in the slow movement—are common to both symphonies, and there are thematic echoes too. This is not the Gounod of *Faust*, still less of the church music, but a younger composer revelling in the tradition of Haydn and Mozart, a charming orchestrator and a spontaneous melodist. He was a much better model for Bizet than the later Gounod; even so his pupil already surpasses him in vitality and concentration.

The modern listener to Bizet's Symphony is more likely to be struck by the resemblance to Schubert. This must be wholly fortuitous (Schubert's instrumental works were not then known in Paris, and Bizet, though he later acquired some of Schubert's music,[1] never mentions him in his letters). It is an affinity of genius, not shared by Gounod's Symphony. The second subject of the first movement has two characteristics that at once recall Schubert: the momentary glance at the relative minor and the unexpected extension of the melody (this also appears in the main theme of the slow movement). The corresponding theme in the finale, after a similar glance at the relative minor, proceeds to modulate with an absence of clamour thoroughly Schubertian into the remote key of B flat major and back again. More pervasive, though less tangible, is a general similarity of temper

[1] *See* Appendix G, p. 296.

—the flow of singing melody, the gay impulsiveness of rhythm, the tendency in the development section to repeat the material in contrasted keys instead of treating it organically (a habit shared by Schumann). On the other hand the long-windedness that might have been expected in a youthful work on this scale (compare Schubert's early symphonies) is absent; there are already signs of a terse epigrammatic quality, typically French, that was to come to full flowering in *Jeux d'enfants* and *L'Arlésienne*.

Of Bizet's four movements, the *Adagio* is the most prophetic and the scherzo the most perfect. The former opens with a brief introduction, built on a figure:

which, besides raising a nice sense of expectation, is used with considerable subtlety later in the movement. The main theme, played by the oboe over pizzicato violas:

marks the first appearance of a type of melody that runs all through Bizet's work. In *Les Pêcheurs de perles* and perhaps *L'Arlésienne* it might be taken to have an exotic significance, and it may be influenced by current French experiments with oriental colouring, such as

David's *Le Désert*; but it is clear from its appearance here that it represented something in Bizet's musical make-up and was not simply turned out when he was confronted with a demand for local colour. It is one of many signs that Bizet's preoccupation with themes remote from the Parisian scene was not an exterior thing, a searching for novelty in the Meyerbeerian sense, but corresponded to a need in his own nature. The tune is admirably treated and extended, and is followed by a soaring string melody that recalls Gounod at his most attractive and looks forward to such things as the flower song in *Carmen*. The fugal central section has been condemned as academic, and it hardly fits the context. But the fault lies not in the fugue itself, which is academic only in the sense that it is extremely skilful, but rather in the fact that the young composer, having hit on the happy idea of developing his subject from the introductory figure, could not resist the temptation to drag it in regardless of the unity of the movement. Even so he disarms criticism by the neatness of his return, the oboe melody being at once combined with the opening, thus tying it not only to the introduction but to the fugue as well. Towards the end there occurs another prophetic passage, a slow descending chromatic scale over a tonic pedal, which adds a wonderful touch of colour:

This device was to become very characteristic of the mature Bizet; like the 'exotic' oboe melody it formed a part of his musical personality from the earliest years.

The scherzo (it is marked only *allegro vivace*), apart from typifying the exuberance that Bizet brought into French music, has unusual technical features. The first theme with its gay rhythm that breaks refreshingly away from the four-bar and eight-bar phrase, not only supplies a counterpoint to the delightful tune for strings in octaves that follows, but forms the chief material for the trio as well. This is no barren ingenuity; the music sounds entirely spontaneous. The use of the device at all is hard to parallel at this date (though Schumann in his D minor Symphony had built the trio of his scherzo on a theme from the slow movement); for a boy of seventeen to bring it off triumphantly—however well it reflects on his teachers at the Conservatoire—betokens a native talent of no common order. The whole movement, especially the trio with its drone-bass, is admirably finished.

The opening subject of the finale:

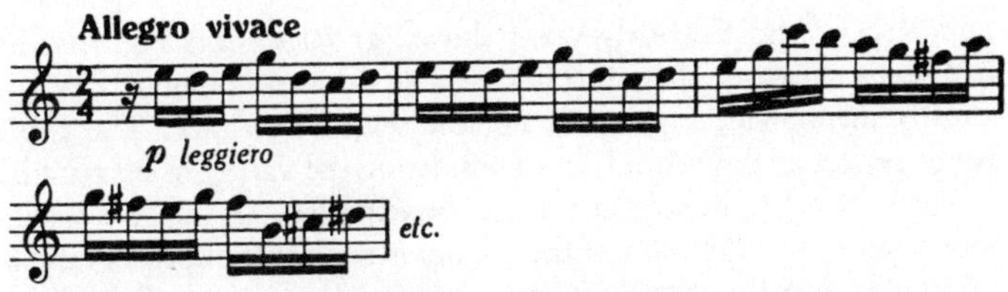

looks forward to the bull-fighting music in *Carmen* as surely as the march-like bridge theme does to the chorus of street urchins in the same opera:

In some ways, indeed, the whole Symphony seems closer in spirit to *Carmen* than to many of the works that intervene. The lilting second subject leads by a brilliant extension to a cadence that, for all its derivation from a similar feature in Gounod's Symphony, carries Bizet's personal stamp:

The weakness of the movement is the development, which belies its name, the themes, especially the second subject, being merely repeated in a variety of keys.

However, the surprising thing is not that the work has too little of the genuine symphonic quality, but that it has so much. In later years Bizet told Saint-Saëns that he could do nothing without the theatre; he was not made for the symphony. Yet his early letters are full of symphonic as well as operatic projects. He began and abandoned at least two symphonies in Rome, apart from the scherzo that grew into *Roma*. And this early work shows, as *Roma* does not, that he had some talent in that direction. Apart from its obvious failings, already mentioned, it shows a notable sense of balance. The *adagio* is not perfect in this respect, but considering the variety of its material it keeps its figure better than might be expected. In the two sonata movements the exposition of the themes is neither cramped nor overweighted, and the recapitulations are shortened just sufficiently to give conciseness to the summing-up of the argument. Bizet makes no innovations in the symphonic form, but he manages it easily and pours into it a wealth of music that varies in originality but never degenerates into padding or bad taste. Also, it is clothed in an orchestral dress that matches it for lucidity and charm. Bizet was a born orchestrator: like Mendelssohn, he seemed to have an instinctive grasp of the potentialities of each instrument. There is no superfluous doubling, no smudging of the lines. The use of the woodwind in the trio of the scherzo is masterly, and the march theme in the finale is not only as appropriate to the wind as the opening subject is to the strings, but supplies a telling contrast.

The recently published Overture in A minor-major probably belongs to the same period as the Symphony. Though less finely wrought, it has many of the same qualities and deserves to be heard. It is scored for larger orchestra, including piccolo, trombones and ophicleide. The form is somewhat lop-sided; Bizet may have been thinking of the overture to *William Tell*. There are four sections: *andante ma non troppo* in A minor, *allegro vivace* in the manner of romantic storm music, a very Italian *andante espressivo* in E major and an energetic *allegro vivace* (A major) in condensed sonata form. The themes are not original, but their treatment is lively, and the bridge-passage in the final section is characteristic:

The unpublished[1] *Marche funèbre* of 1861 is more ambitious but weaker. Rome had made Bizet self-conscious, and nothing could illustrate better than this march how unfitted he was for the expression of solemnity. Even his customary felicity in scoring deserted him. He adds English horn, trombones, ophicleide, tenor drum and two harps to the orchestra of the Symphony, but this inflation of the currency only draws attention to a depreciation in the value of the goods. Neither the fanfares of the opening nor the would-be pathos of the broken second theme ring true. The main theme was later used for Leila's entrance in Act III, Scene ii, of *Les Pêcheurs de perles*.

Bizet's first Symphony was written in a month. His second occupied him on and off for eleven years. For the work we know as *Roma* was to Bizet always 'my symphony'. The history of its composition is chequered and in places obscure. Whether it incorporates anything from the Italian symphony with movements entitled *Rome*, *Venice* (*andante*), *Florence* (scherzo) and *Naples*, which Bizet outlined to his mother in August 1860 (before he had seen Venice), we cannot tell. The earliest identifiable part is the scherzo, taken over with little change from his third Rome *envoi*. The first version was finished (though apparently not scored) by July 1866. In the early summer of 1868 the first movement, which had been a set of variations, was

[1] For the published (and mistitled) *Marche funèbre* see pp. 186–8.

completely rewritten, only the theme being preserved (with modifications), and the *Andante* also underwent alteration; it was at this time that Bizet inserted the C major theme from the finale, remarking how wonderfully it fitted. This second version was finished in June. In October Bizet expressed dissatisfaction with the finale. On 28th February 1869 Pasdeloup conducted three movements (omitting the scherzo) as *Fantasie symphonique, Souvenirs de Rome*. They carried the titles *Une Chasse dans la forêt d'Ostie,*[1] *Une Procession* and *Carnaval à Rome*, which may not have been Bizet's. He continued to call it a symphony, and revised it a third time in the summer of 1871. It was not performed complete till October 1880, when Pasdeloup reintroduced it as *Roma, Symphonie en quatre parties*; in the same year it was published by Choudens [2] as *Roma, troisième suite de concert* (the first two suites presumably being those from *L'Arlésienne*). The descriptive titles were dropped, except for the finale, which is headed *Carnaval* and alone shows any sign of Italian inspiration. In view of the disappearance of the autograph and the corruption of other works published at this period, it is possible that the score has been doctored. On internal evidence the *Andante* is a patched-up affair. The long opening melody and its codetta, the four-bar phrase with triplets that precedes the change to 12–8 time, were lifted bodily from a song (possibly an operatic fragment) called *Le Doute*. This was published posthumously in *Seize Mélodies*, and though the date of composition is unknown the song version is undoubtedly the original. Whether it was adapted by Bizet himself is another matter, especially as the 1869 title *Une Procession* seems quite inappropriate.

Whatever its original inspiration, Bizet wished *Roma* to stand on its own feet as absolute music. In this respect it compares very badly with the Symphony of 1855. It is too haphazard in form, too loosely articulated, especially the first and last movements, and contains too much that is at once pretentious and feeble. There are things beyond the boy of seventeen, but there is plenty that the boy of seventeen

[1] Attempts to identify this with the lost overture *La Chasse d'Ossian* fall to the ground. Halévy, who mentions the latter in his report of 1861, would hardly have accepted a set of variations as an overture without comment. The *Roma* movement did not receive its title till 1869.

[2] Choudens began to engrave a score in 1869, before Bizet's last revision.

instinctively and rightly avoided. Much of the freshness has gone; the vitality has suffered a Mendelssohnian dilution, and the faint exotic charm, neatly executed, has yielded to a surge of sanctimoniousness laid on with a trowel—or whatever is the equivalent ecclesiastical implement. The hand of Gounod lies heavy on this score, not the modest Gounod of *Mireille*, but the pretentiousness of the last scene of *Faust*. Bizet's concessions were, indeed, chiefly made, not to any outside influence, but to this artistic fifth column for long entrenched within himself. Only in its orchestration, a point of technique in which he seldom failed, is *Roma* consistently successful. Whether he could have written a mature symphony we cannot judge; *Roma* is too obviously a misfire. But it may be doubted: he was too much the musical dramatist, and of all composers with a genius for the stage only Mozart has achieved equal distinction in the symphony.

The opening theme on four horns owes something to Weber's *Freischütz* as well as to Gounod. Bizet wrote worse tunes, but there is no mistaking the flavour of insipid solemnity. The motive (*a*) introduced by solo trumpet supplies the germ from which the main theme of the *allegro agitato ma non troppo* springs, following a conventional boil-over on diminished sevenths. This is quoted (*b*) in its original form, from a letter of June 1868, and (*c*) as it appears (with improvements) in the published score:

It is somewhat Mendelssohnian in character (compare the scoring—strings in octaves with staccato wind chords—with the opening of the 'Italian' Symphony) and has that composer's tendency to amble when setting out to gallop. One passage of stormy suspense is very reminiscent of *Der Freischütz*. The wind instruments are charmingly used, and the quiet (*ppp*) division of the strings into many parts in the coda is a happy touch. The figure (*a*), especially when given to the horn, looks forward to the accompaniment of Micaela's 'Je dis que rien ne m'épouvante'.

The scherzo is by far the best movement, and significantly is much closer to the 1855 Symphony in spirit and date. It is less self-conscious, less inflated than the rest. It opens with a fugato on an admirable subject:

The little figure (*a*) pervades the whole movement and is woven into the accompaniment of the broader second theme and of the trio. This again recalls the Symphony, though here the main theme of the trio is new—or as new as the spirit of Gounod will allow. It is however saved from banality by the jostling of figure (*a*) and the fascination of the two-against-three rhythm. The whole movement, as Martin Cooper remarked, owes something to the *Menuetto capriccioso* of Weber's A flat piano Sonata. Two harps are employed in the orchestra.

The main theme of the *Andante* is an obvious though inferior foretaste of the *Adagietto* in *L'Arlésienne*. There is less concentration, less refinement here, but the shape and style of the melody and the layout (strings in four parts) are the same. The effect is not unpleasing, especially when the tune returns on the wind with violin arabesques. The great blot is the C major tune in 12–8 time, one of Bizet's very worst, scored after the manner of Meyerbeer for a mounting aggregate of wind octaves against arpeggios on the harp. It is a sad comment on his taste at this period that, having used it to spoil his finale, he should have chosen to deal a similar blow at the *Andante*. This movement uses bigger orchestral forces than the rest of the work.

The finale comes nearest to programme music. In form it is little more than a string of tunes, based in great part on an *ostinato* of alternate dominant and diminished sevenths. There are four main themes: the first, a brilliant and elastic affair on the flute:

brings a hint of the *Carmen* quintet; the second is a lilting Italian tune in thirds; the third with its distinctive rhythm echoes the finale of Mendelssohn's violin Concerto; while the fourth is the C major tune of the *Andante* taken at a brisk trot. The movement is brilliantly scored, and there are excellent pages, especially where the third theme disappears in fragments on individual instruments (a device put to admirable use in *Carmen*), to be revived at once in stimulating counterpoint with the flute melody; but, as is the way of the world, the most blatant element comes more and more to the front, and the coda, in which it is twice directed to be played *plus vite* and ends *fff*, only emphasizes its essential complacency. There is no balance of keys or regular recapitulation, the fourth tune being left to assert the tonic, which it does in no uncertain fashion.

The overture *Patrie* is the one thoroughly poor production of Bizet's maturity. Inspired by the recent memory of the Franco-Prussian War, it is an awful warning of the danger of confusing art with patriotism. Formally it is unorthodox and not uninteresting, but the extreme poverty of the ideas damps all enthusiasm. The opening theme, a sufficiently noisy affair in C minor,[1] repeated in C major and briefly developed, is succeeded by one of those weak sequential melodies, narrow in compass and limp in rhythm, of which Gounod so well knew the secret. This tune (*un peu animé*, F major), first cousin to that which disfigures the last two movements of *Roma*, is introduced by

[1] Some critics have discovered an echo of the Rakóczy March, but the similarity is so remote and so obviously fortuitous that much subtlety is required in order to perceive it.

clarinets, bassoons and violas in unison and presently pounded out *fortissimo* in full orchestral dress. Two more episodes follow, a species of funeral march on violas and cellos (*andante molto*, A minor, marked *piano mais sonore* like the opening theme of *Roma*), and a bucolically good-humoured tune in 3–4 time on first clarinet, English horn and violas against muted violin arpeggios (*andantino*, A major), that sounds as if it had strayed into the wrong work. The opening subject returns *ppp* on a single flute over chromatic *tremolando* cellos and basses, with deft touches from the percussion—one of the few characteristic passages in the overture. It is contrapuntally combined in a long *crescendo* with the F major theme, which at length, as the *Roma* precedent leads us to fear, rises in full state-robes—C major, *moderato maestoso*, *tutta forza*, 6–8 time—to declare the proceedings closed. Perhaps the most effective touch is the unexpected appearance of the A major tune in the final bars.

Bizet uses a large orchestra including, besides harps and a heavy battery of percussion, cornets and trumpets and an ophicleide. The appearance of the ophicleide at this late date is not a conscious archaism, but indicates a preference, shared by other French composers, over the more German and specifically Wagnerian tuba.[1] In the same way his inclination throughout his life—even in *Carmen*—for natural rather than valve horns need not be attributed to backwardness: he could employ modern developments when he wanted them, as he showed with the E flat saxophone in *L'Arlésienne*. The use of trumpets as well as cornets—the former for fanfares and solemn moments, the latter for melodic passages—was also a French habit. In *Patrie* these lavish forces, though well handled, hardly suit Bizet's orchestral style, which loses much of its delicacy; there is more doubling than usual, and the contrasts are uncharacteristically crude.

[1] He seems, however, to have had difficulty in making up his mind about the bass of the brass family. He uses an ophicleide in the early Overture, *Te Deum*, *Vasco de Gama*, *Marche funèbre* (1861) and *Don Rodrigue* as well as *Patrie*; bass trombone in various early works; contrabass trombone in *La Coupe du Roi du Thulé* and *Noé*; and bass and contrabass saxhorns in *Ivan IV* and *Don Rodrigue*. One movement in the published score of *Les Pêcheurs de perles* has a tuba, but this is not by Bizet. *See* p. 290.

Perils of Patriotism

Patrie marks Bizet's last attempt to chase the wrong hare. Like most French composers of all ages he was constitutionally unfit to thump a tub. But a lapse of this kind need not be dwelt upon: *Patrie* should be consigned to that limbo which houses Beethoven's *Battle Symphony*, Tchaikovsky's *1812 Overture* and other aberrations of the loftiest public spirit.

CHAPTER VIII

KEYBOARD AND NON-DRAMATIC VOCAL MUSIC

IT IS curious that a composer with Bizet's gifts as a pianist should have written so little for the instrument, and that much of his small output should be unsuited to it. The reason may be that, though he loved to play genuine keyboard music like Bach's preludes and fugues, his greatest interest in the piano lay in its power beneath his fingers to evoke the different colours of the orchestra. It was as a score-reader that he was most renowned, and no doubt his countless operatic and orchestral transcriptions affected his style (though the unpublished early works are as unpianistic as the later). Most of his original music for the piano suffers from a double disadvantage: it is too clumsy to reward the concert pianist and too difficult for the amateur. But not all of it is musically negligible.

Little need be said of the unpublished pieces written before the age of sixteen. Some have a flashy brilliance borrowed from the pyrotechnical school of Liszt and Thalberg; a curiosity is the *Thème brillant*, written on three staves with an orgy of tremolos and rapid repeated notes. The *Nocturne* in F major has Chopin's mannerisms without anything else of Chopin. The most interesting is the *Romance sans paroles*, whose middle section foreshadows a rhythm and lay-out characteristic of the later Bizet (compare the prelude to *La Coupe du Roi de Thulé* and the Frédéri theme in *L'Arlésienne*):

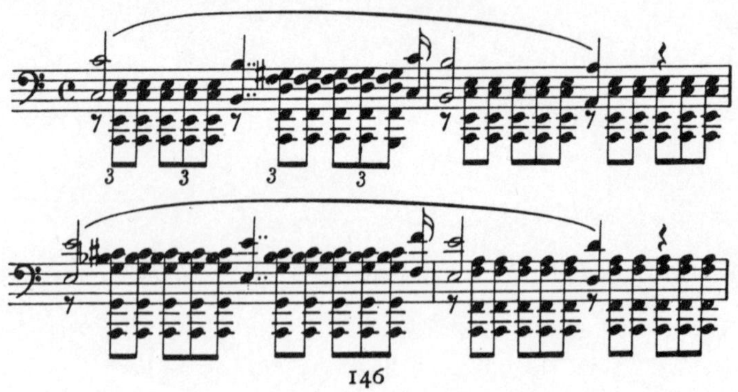

The *Trois Esquisses musicales* for harmonium (a piano adaptation appeared later, as well as an emasculated arrangement by Isidor Philipp), published in 1858, confirm the evidence of the Symphony on the youthful Bizet's freshness of invention and certainty of technique. This is light music in the best French style, polished, virile and neatly constructed. *Ronde turque* is an excellent specimen of Bizet's exoticism on a small scale, full of sap and well sustained by rhythmic and harmonic tension. The bare opening, ineffective on the piano, would be vindicated in an orchestral transcription, a procedure justified by the need to compensate for the sustaining power of the harmonium and (in this and other works) by the nature of the keyboard-writing. The two later themes look forward to the chorus of the Watch in *La Jolie Fille de Perth*; indeed *Ronde turque* has much of the epigrammatic skill of that little masterpiece, while pointing the way to *Trompette et tambour* in *Jeux d'enfants*. *Sérénade* is as remarkable for neat construction as for charm. It is in simple A B A form, A being in D flat major and 3–4 time, B in A major and 3–8. The two sections are well contrasted and cleverly bound together: in B the sudden incursions of the chord of C sharp major remind us enharmonically of the opening, and the little rhythm ♫♩♩, characteristic of B,[1] persists throughout the reprise of A and finally takes complete control. The tune of B:

is a Bizet fingerprint (*see* page 249). *Caprice*, almost in sonata form, is the least original movement. The polka-like tune in the middle proclaims Bizet's debt to Weber.

There is nothing fantastic about the inaptly named *Chasse fantastique* (? 1865) except its badness. It is a long, flashy and insipid production that looks like a Liszt transcription of Mendelssohn at his worst, with a dash of Weber thrown in. The six *Chants du Rhin*

[1] Compare the accompaniment to the second stanza of the song *Douce Mer*.

(1865), described as 'Lieder sans paroles' and based on trashy poems of the Christmas-card type by Méry (at this date the French could still be wistfully romantic about the Rhine), are uneven in quality. Here Bizet pays tribute to Mendelssohn and Schumann; the main theme of *Le Retour* is a half-sister of the opening of the former's B flat major cello Sonata. This was the period when Bizet was declaring himself a German heart and soul. Of the six pieces, the first has little character and the last two are poor; but the other three are worth occasional performance. *Le Départ* is lively and charming, with nicely extended rhythms; an odd feature is the outburst of Puccini octaves. The opening of *Les Rêves* with its long double pedal in seconds is striking for its date and brings to mind Borodin's song *The Sleeping Princess*. The main theme is cleverly reintroduced at intervals in the inner parts, and the mood faintly foreshadows that of *Colin-Maillard* in *Jeux d'enfants*. But the best is No. 4, *La Bohémienne*: already there was something about a gypsy that touched hidden depths in Bizet. The piece is full of character and shows great freedom of modulation. It is the most operatic of the set: some nameless José courts the gypsy throughout the last two pages.

Three piano works date from 1868. *Marine* is insignificant. The *Nocturne* in D major (called No. 1, though it had no successors) is marred by melodic feebleness and inorganic flourishes, but has a certain harmonic interest, particularly in its avoidance of the tonic chord for the first page and a half. It is the most Lisztian of Bizet's works. Of much greater significance are the *Variations chromatiques*. The theme itself is memorable, consisting of a rising and descending chromatic scale in 3-4 time over a pedal C. The combination of chromatic scales with pedal-note had interested Bizet since the Symphony of 1855. He had used it dramatically to characterize Zurga's jealousy in *Les Pêcheurs de perles*, and was to repeat it for the entrance of Mitifio and Frédéri's fatal leap in *L'Arlésienne*. In the variations he explores its possibilities in pure music. The result, though not a masterpiece, is so striking that its complete neglect is difficult to explain. There are fourteen variations, seven in C minor, seven in C major, and a coda ending in the minor. Bizet draws a variety of mood and suggestion from the theme, while never abandoning the framework. There are glimpses of old friends, past and to come: Catherine

Glover in the tenth variation (a great improvement on her polonaise 'Vive l'hiver,' which it so much resembles), Micaela in the eleventh, Frédéri in the fourteenth. The fifth and sixth are full of fire, while the seventh, in which the theme appears in contrary motion against a four-octave pedal in a mighty *crescendo* from *ppp* to *fff*, produces some remarkable harmonies for its date:

Unfortunately the double tremolo is not the way to the pianist's heart. The weak spot is the coda, where Bizet, having said all he has to say, seems unable to make an end. Instead of a cogent summing-up we are given a mixture of fireworks and recitative, and the return of the theme in the last bars hardly makes up for lost ground. This is a pity, for throughout the variations interest has been sustained in mounting tension. The conception was probably influenced by Beethoven's thirty-two Variations in C minor, which Bizet much admired. Two recently discovered miniatures, *Promenade au clair de lune* and *Causerie sentimentale*, are the third and fifth of a set of *genre* pieces of which no other record is known. Both possess considerable charm and character. The former, headed by two lines from Verlaine's *Clair de lune* and perhaps the first music inspired by a poem later associated with Fauré and Debussy, is a haunting dreamy piece that neatly interposes irregular 9–8 bars into a 12–8 fabric and is unexpectedly well written for the instrument. *Causerie sentimentale*, in mazurka rhythm, has some striking harmony with a flavour of Grieg and the whole-tone scale. Was Bizet thinking of Verlaine's *Colloque sentimental*? And if so, did he write a whole set of piano pieces inspired by the poet's *Fêtes galantes* of 1869? A third piece belonging to this set (No. 6, *Troisième danse*) has since turned up, and others may be in existence.

One keyboard work remains, the suite of twelve pieces for piano duet called *Jeux d'enfants*. Composed in 1871, this was his most perfect work to date and reveals a fresh brand of talent. Certain episodes in the operas, such as the chorus of the Watch in *La Jolie Fille de Perth*, had shown a power of concentrating atmosphere within a small compass; but the miniaturist's skill of *Jeux d'enfants* comes with all the surprise of a new departure. Music in this form is usually called into being by special circumstances, and appeals to the domestic rather than the public consumer. But it need lose nothing in musical value on this account, and Bizet's suite, having (even in the shortened orchestral form which the composer gave it) no headline appeal, has not always been rated as the little masterpiece it is. In France it was the forerunner of a number of similar works: Debussy's *Petite Suite* (1888), Fauré's *Dolly* (1893) and Ravel's *Ma Mère l'Oye* (1908) owe it a debt, though none has quite the freshness and perfection of Bizet's original.

The names of the movements speak for themselves: *L'Escarpolette* (Rêverie), *La Toupie* (Impromptu), *La Poupée* (Berceuse), *Les Chevaux de bois* (Scherzo), *Le Volant* (Fantasie), *Trompette et tambour* (Marche), *Les Bulles de savon* (Rondino), *Les Quatre Coins* (Esquisse), *Colin-Maillard* (Nocturne), *Saute-Mouton* (Caprice), *Petit Mari, petite femme* (Duo) and *Le Bal* (Galop).[1] Each evokes a facet of childhood, but there is not a trace of triviality, self-consciousness or false sentiment. Their quality is essentially musical; and their forms, though slight, are turned with a neatness that leaves no loophole for criticism. Here is a typically French wit and detachment combined with a warmth and a sympathy that recall Schumann, but without the adult nostalgia of the *Kinderscenen*. *L'Escarpolette* left its mark on Debussy's *En Bateau*. The last fifteen bars of *La Poupée* illustrate Bizet's power both of extending a melody (a particularly beautiful one) and rounding off the whole in an exquisite coda. The vivacity and elastic rhythm of *Trompette et tambour* is contrasted with the simple charm of *Colin-Maillard*, and the delicate part-writing of *Petit Mari, petite femme* with the busy gallantry and Haydnish capriciousness of *Le Bal*. The modulations in this finale are enchanting in their unexpectedness.

[1] *The Swing, The Top, The Doll, Wooden Horses, Battledore and Shuttlecock, Trumpet and Drum, Soap Bubbles, Puss in the Corner, Blind-Man's Buff, Leap-Frog, Little Husband, Little Wife, The Ball.*

For the bogus return of the main theme in the submediant, followed after four bars by an exhilarating plunge back into the tonic, there is

precedent in Beethoven and Schubert, but the effect remains fresh and brilliant. The piece ends with true childlike exuberance, marked *fff*, *furioso*. Bizet's harmonic resource is particularly evident in these pieces, many of which show signs of an impressionism that was to achieve ripeness in Debussy's Preludes a generation later. And the experiments with pedals and chromatic scales reach forward to a composer not yet born—Maurice Ravel (*see* page 151). It is notable how often such passages are marked *p* or *pp*. Doubtless Bizet would have stood better with posterity had he made a clamour of his harmonic audacities.

Six or seven of these pieces—*La Toupie, La Poupée, Trompette et tambour, Petit Mari, petite femme, Le Bal, Les Quatre Coins* and probably *Les Chevaux de bois*—were scored by Bizet himself, who published the first five under the title *Petite Suite d'orchestre*. It is strange that this version is not more popular today, especially as the scoring is executed with Bizet's usual aptness and includes certain details, such as the gay trumpet flourish in the last bars of *Trompette et tambour* [1] that do not appear in the duet version. His orchestration of *Les Quatre Coins*, still unperformed, contains forty-eight additional bars before the fugato in the middle, with a new theme on the violins used as a counterpoint.

Bizet was not a great song-writer, but he left some attractive music in this form, including one or two neglected gems. The French song before Fauré and Debussy did not, as has been too readily assumed, consist solely of faded romances for fashionable drawing-rooms. There was of course much rubbish of that kind, but Gounod was a charming song-writer in his own right: his lyrical gifts were at home in this small form, and he often found the perfect musical dress for poems of a pastoral or amorous lyricism. Bizet was for the most part content to follow Gounod, though his emotional range was wider. The weaknesses of his songs are uncritical repetition of the same music to every stanza, accompaniments conceived in terms of the orchestra and a resort to padding when inspiration fails. Their good qualities

[1] Most of the differences occur in this piece, which originally appeared in *Ivan IV*. The orchestral version is the more brilliant, and one of the themes is slightly altered. There is also a curious variant at bar 10 of *Petit Mari, petite femme*, in the cello counter-melody.

are charm of melody, happy modulation and the occasional capture of the essentials of a situation and their translation into an inevitably right musical setting. It is disappointing to find so little of the miniaturist of *Jeux d'enfants*, but the great majority of the songs belong to the early years; indeed he seems almost to have given up song-writing after 1868. He himself held a low opinion of them, and on the whole their chief interest lies in the light they throw on his dramatic powers; they show him instinctively responsive to character and atmosphere, but not always able to epitomize a mood or transcend a mediocre text. He was less sensitive to words themselves than to the human emotions behind them, and like many French composers he paid little attention to prosody in his songs and stage works. The verbal distortions are, however, a light fault to be set against the dramatic truth of his best vocal writing, and they are far less offensive in French, which is not a strongly accented language, than in English.

Bizet's first published works were two songs, *Petite Marguerite* and *La Rose et l'abeille*, issued (together with a very inferior song by Bizet *père*) in 1854, when he was barely sixteen. The words are the sorriest drivel (when Choudens reissued the songs in 1888 new poems were supplied by Armand Silvestre), but the music has charm and promise, marred only by a lapse into Gounodesque uplift in the major-key refrain of *Petite Marguerite*. *La Rose et l'abeille* anticipates *Chanson d'avril* in its effective modulation to the flattened submediant.

Bizet published two sets of songs in his lifetime. The six *Feuilles d'album* of 1866, undertaken during the composition of *La Jolie Fille de Perth*, include three of some merit. *Adieux à Suzon* is a delightful setting of a half-tender, half-mocking love poem by Musset. The Ronsard *Sonnet* with its happy modulations and irregular lengths of phrase might almost be by Schubert. *Guitare* shows Bizet responsive as ever to bolero rhythm; the return of the piano ritornello for the second stanza before the voice has finished with the first adds a characteristic thrust.

The *Vingt Mélodies* of 1873 (the date is misleading, for nearly all had been published separately some years earlier) are very uneven in quality. It would have been better for Bizet had the last two never seen the light, and some of the others are negligible; but about half a dozen are well worth preservation. *Chanson d'avril* and *Vieille*

Chanson, though in the Gounod tradition, have a refinement peculiarly Bizet's own. The modulation from E flat to C flat in the refrain of the former is happily characteristic, and the touch of archaism in the latter never degenerates into pastiche. *Pastorale* exploits the age-old device of a strophe in the minor key followed by a refrain in the major with a wayward charm that keeps it fresh. *Berceuse*, of which the accompaniment is based on a folk-tune used by Fauré in *Dolly* and Debussy in *Jardins sous la pluie* (and earlier by Couperin), beats Gounod at his own game. Melodic charm is combined with a clever use of the traditional tune (note the bass of the last bars) and neat harmonic touches, such as the repetition of the opening in F on an E flat (tonic) pedal, to produce a veritable little masterpiece. In complete contrast is *Vous ne priez pas*, a passionate C minor song whose one weakness is the employment of the same music for three stanzas, with only the pace indication altered. Reyer, reviewing *Vingt Mélodies* in the *Journal des Débats* (25th January 1874), singled out *Vous ne priez pas* as an inspiration worthy of Schubert.

The best of Bizet's songs is the intensely dramatic *Adieux de l'hôtesse arabe*, which owes nothing to Gounod or anyone else. Composed as early as 1866, this is a worthy ancestor of the Ghazel in *Djamileh*. Here again [1] we find the exotic and dramatic elements leading Bizet into harmonic experiment:

The rhythmic accompaniment figure persists throughout in an ever-varying harmonic colour, often enriched by pedals, that reflects

[1] *See* p. 173.

the rise and fall of the singer's passion. This is not a rigidly strophic song: the scheme—first stanza E minor ending in A major, second stanza E major ending in A minor—solves the musical and the literary-dramatic problem at one blow. For the rest *Chant d'amour* has the triumphant succulence of parts of *Samson et Dalila*, *Rêve de la bien-aimée* spoils an attractive start with the old diminished seventh lapse at the end of each stanza, and *Ma vie a son secret* redeems a dullish vocal line by a striking ritornello prophetic of José's flower song:

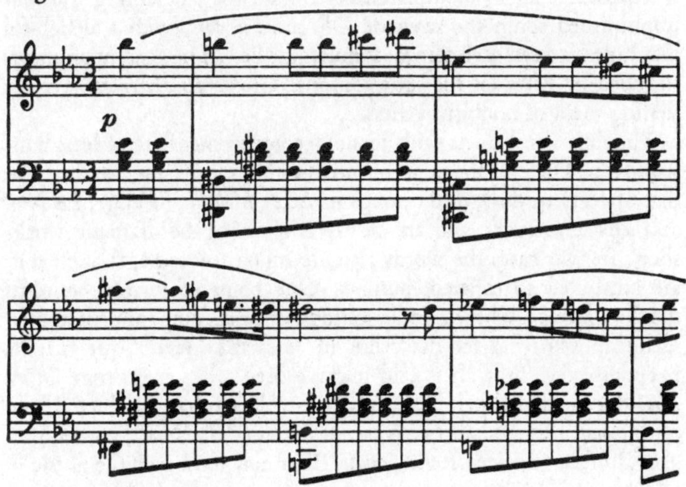

The posthumous *Seize Mélodies* (1886) consist largely of dramatic fragments with new words commissioned by the publisher.[1] With one or two exceptions the musical quality is not high; several are the merest sketches torn from a context we cannot even assess. Two come from *Noé*, one from *Vasco de Gama*, and at least three (perhaps six) from *La Coupe du Roi de Thulé*.[2] *Le Gascon*, a humorous character-study turned with exquisite grace:

[1] *See* Appendix F, p. 288.
[2] *See* p. 186.

does not read like a fragment: if the lilting tune was not originally set to these words, then Catulle Mendès was visited by genius when he put them to it. Seldom has a musical moustache been worn at a more gallant angle. *Aubade* has a deft charm that would be underlined by the scoring Bizet no doubt had in mind, and *La Chanson de la rose* is remarkable for its modulations and neat two-part writing. Of four unpublished songs the serenade *Oh, quand je dors*, with a delightful interlude between each stanza, is much the best. The accompaniments supplied by Bizet for the six traditional *Chants des Pyrénées* have the sterling merit of unobtrusiveness.

The four vocal duets with piano accompaniment are of little consequence. Three of them, published posthumously, include material that appears in three of the songs in *Seize Mélodies* (*Voyage*, *La Nuit* and *Aimons, rêvons*), and are clearly chips from the dramatic workshop. In two cases the words also are much the same, though they are attributed to different authors. One point of interest concerns the duet *Rêvons*, whose middle section has an accompaniment figure [1] identical with that for the cellos in Micaela's 'Je dis que rien ne m'épouvante'. This air is said to have been taken over from *Grisélidis*, but it seems likely from internal evidence that the duet *Rêvons* (+*Aimons, rêvons*), like *Les Nymphes de bois* (+*La Nuit*), comes from Act II of *La Coupe du Roi de Thulé*. Bizet may have used the music in all three operas. The fourth duet, *La Fuite*, was published in 1872, the same year as the song *Absence*. Both have words by Gautier, both amble along with repeated chords in triplets and rising scales in the bass, and both show Bizet's lyricism not at its best.

Still less important are the four so-called *Motets et hymnes*. Apart from *L'Esprit Saint*, published as a song with piano and optional harmonium accompaniment (the latter on a separate leaf) and subsequently included in *Vingt Mélodies*, Bizet was not responsible for the sins here inflicted on the long-suffering church. He certainly had no hand in *Regina Coeli*, a dreadful arrangement by one Flégier of the

[1] This does not appear in the version for solo voice.

original duet[1] in the last scene of *Les Pêcheurs de perles*. Nor is it credible that he perpetrated the *Ave Maria* and *Agnus Dei*, carved from the Prelude and E flat Intermezzo of *L'Arlésienne*. The *Agnus Dei* was sung at his funeral, together with a *Pie Jesu* fashioned by Guiraud from the duet for Nadir and Zurga—a classic example of double sacrilege. The male-voice part-song *Saint Jean de Pathmos,* composed for a Belgian choral festival, equally deserves its oblivion. It is notable for appalling prosody, a second bass part reminiscent of a military band which it must be difficult to sing with a straight face, and the only complete fugue that Bizet published—an ingenious but barren monument to his Conservatoire training.

There are a number of miscellaneous vocal works on a larger scale, mostly unpublished. The early cantatas and choruses are of poor quality. *Clovis et Clotilde*, which won Bizet the Prix de Rome, is able but colourless. The influence of Weber is very marked, especially in the themes used (without any idea of development) to distinguish the three characters. The music of Leila's 'O courageuse enfant' in Act II of *Les Pêcheurs de perles* (page 94 of vocal score) first appears here. The *Te Deum*, with the exception of the *Judex crederis* section, is a wretched work; most of the music is of the kind that seems to presuppose Blackpool pier and somebody's silver tuba band. 'Rex gloriae' begins with a trombone solo accompanied by the strings in a rhythm rendered notorious by misuse in Italian opera and frequently parodied by Sullivan. It is pleasant to record that part of 'Pleni sunt coeli' was afterwards fitted to the words 'O Brahma divin' (*Les Pêcheurs de perles*, page 60). The expected four-square fugue appears at 'Fiat misericordia'. Another work that illustrates Bizet's unfitness to compose religious music is *La Mort s'avance*, for four-part chorus and large orchestra with two English horns taking the place of the oboes. This is based on two Studies by Chopin, in C minor (Op. 25, No. 12) and C major (Op. 10, No. 1); but the ingenuity with which Chopin's themes are worked into the texture—the former, without its distinctive arpeggios, is turned into the Frédéri rhythm—does not atone for the flatulence of the conception as a whole.

Two early works for solo voice, mixed chorus and piano, *Le Golfe*

[1] This appears only in the 1863 and 1975 vocal scores.

de Baïa (Lamartine) and *La Chanson du rouet* (Leconte de Lisle), were among the posthumous pieces published in 1880, the latter with altered words. They were composed for the Prix de Rome competitions in 1856 and 1857. *Le Golfe de Baïa*, a barcarolle with an attractive syncopated refrain (which bears a characteristic fingerprint: *see* page 249), also exists in a shortened version for piano solo. Here the refrain supplies the main theme, the music of the second verse—that of the first is quite distinct—forming a kind of trio. Bizet re-used the material with striking effect in Act IV of *Ivan IV*. *La Chanson du rouet* is a spinning-chorus in G major with three stanzas, the first and third choral, the second a soprano solo in E minor. The music is charming, with a hint of Weber but one wholly individual passage:

CHAPTER IX

THE EARLY OPERAS

BIZET's first dramatic work, the one-act *opera-comique La Maison du docteur* with words by Henry Boisseaux, was probably designed for private performance among a circle of friends. The autograph contains a list of his teachers and colleagues at the Conservatoire. It dates from about 1855, and was never scored. In the absence of the spoken dialogue it is difficult to grasp the plot, though the appearance of a *buffo* bass called Lord Harley suggests an appropriate situation for the doctor's house. The music displays an easy flow of melody influenced by Weber and the Italians, and a native knack of extending a tune a bar or two longer than the ear expects.

The libretto of *Le Docteur Miracle* conforms to a familiar type. It concerns a young officer in love with the daughter of a magistrate who loathes soldiers. The officer disguises himself as a cook and serves the magistrate an omelette so bad that he believes himself poisoned. A doctor (the officer again disguised) is hastily summoned and promises to cure the magistrate in return for the hand of his daughter. The music is a trifle, but a very engaging one. It shows the eighteen-year-old Bizet in complete command of the light Italian style before he went to Rome. Nothing is original, but nearly everything sparkles with wit and vivacity, and the scoring too is that of Rossini. After a tripping overture an off-stage band comprising clarinet, tenor trombone, big drum and cymbals strikes up a gay tune, leading to a trio in which Bizet takes a naïve delight in playing with words like 'un charlatan'. The romance for soprano and the tenor *couplets* are pretty, but the high light is the 'Quatuor de l'omelette'. The dish is acclaimed by all the characters in turn—by the magistrate 'avec émotion', by his daughter 'avec indifférence'—to the words 'Voici l'omelette', which are then worked into an elaborate mock-heroic *ensemble*. After a flute cadenza the magistrate sits down to eat in commodious 6–8 time, interrupted by the statutory diminished seventh at the words 'Quel goût bizarre et singulier!' An admirably important *mélodrame* introduces the doctor, and the 6–8 finale echoes that of *Don Pasquale*.

Don Procopio comes still closer to *Don Pasquale*, for the two plots are almost identical. An old man, Don Andronico, wants to marry his niece Bettina to a fellow miser, Don Procopio, because he thinks a young man will run through her money. Bettina, however, is attracted to a gallant colonel, Odoardo, and with the help of her aunt Eusebia and her brother Ernesto a plot is hatched to teach the old men a lesson. Procopio, threatened with the dissipated minx which Bettina makes herself out to be, takes fright and tries to get out of the marriage; faced with her insistence, he insults her, abandons his contract and flees, thereby converting Andronico to the side of the lovers, as they had planned.

Bizet set the libretto in Italian; in consciously writing Italian music he was supplying an artistic requirement. Again his score is largely an imitation, but by no means a shoddy one; it is surprising how much of the vitality of his model he contrives to reproduce, an achievement to which natural high spirits and technical accomplishment equally contribute. In places the music bubbles and sparkles as if it were a genuine scion of the *Don Pasquale* stock. The *ensembles* in particular, which employ all the stock devices, voices in thirds, staccato chord accompaniment, endless repetition of words, show a very light touch, and some of the arias and duets, such as the love scene in Act II, 'Per me beato', and Ernesto's cavatina 'Non v'è, signor', an obvious descendant of Malatesta's 'Bella siccome un angelo' (an exact parallel: in each case the baritone describes his sister's charms to the miser-bridegroom in the key of D flat), are also purely Italian. There is little room for other influences, though Mozart and Weber (e.g. in Bettina's 'Voler che sposi') both left their mark. Flashes of genuine originality are few and far between—fewer than in the C major Symphony. One cadential figure in 'Voler che sposi':

bears witness to that lyrical exuberance that overflows from Bizet's best scores, and the expressive phrase that heralds Bettina's entry in the middle of the first finale at once stamps the composer:

There is little attempt at characterization beyond a generalized definition of the old *opera buffa* types, and no use of leading themes. The *entr'acte* and recitatives, which do employ certain phrases in this way, were added by Malherbe,[1] who made the mistake of imitating the self-conscious Bizet of a few years later and falsified this spontaneous little opera.

Several episodes in *Don Procopio* are familiar elsewhere. Odoardo's

[1] *See* Appendix F, p. 289.

entry at the head of his regiment is signalized by the march theme that forms the bridge-passage in the finale of the Symphony (page 137), but without the attractive modulations that follow. The three themes of the initial 2–4 section of the first finale reappear in the Carnival chorus in Act II of *La Jolie Fille de Perth*, and that of the chorus 'Cheti piano!' [1] in Act I of *Les Pêcheurs de perles* (to the words 'Ah! chante, chante encore'); in each case the unpretentious original is weakened by translation to a grander sphere. More interesting is the fate of Odoardo's serenade, 'Sulle piume', the main theme of which is well known as that of Smith's serenade in *La Jolie Fille de Perth*. In *Don Procopio* Odoardo sings two stanzas, the second of which has an added counterpoint on the mandoline with an attractive cross-rhythm, omitted in the later work but worth preservation:

Bettina replies in the tonic major (an effect reserved for the last act of *La Jolie Fille*); both then sing a passage for which Bizet later substituted the tune in F major known in the Beecham arrangement as 'Aubade'; and the piece ends with a remarkable cadence that sounds like a faint striving after some such effect as he achieved in the flower song in *Carmen*:

[1] There is a curious discrepancy here between the autograph and the 1905 vocal score of *Don Procopio*. In the former the tune is exactly the same as in *Les Pêcheurs de perles*; in the latter it has been modified, presumably by Malherbe. The full score is correct.

If the later serenade is more effective from the dramatic point of view, this earlier version can claim an equal if not greater musical interest, and the scoring, with two English horns, mandoline and guitar, is more unusual.

In *Don Procopio* Bizet does not seem to have allowed his creative (as opposed to his imitative) faculty free rein, and to that extent it is disappointing. Yet he has certainly matched the libretto with appropriate music, and its high spirits are so genuine that if well sung the opera (and *Le Docteur Miracle* as well) might still be worth occasional revival.[1]

The symphonic ode *Vasco de Gama*, though not a stage work, may be conveniently discussed here. Written a year later than *Don Procopio*, it is more ambitious, more uneven and in some ways more interesting. It was modelled on David's *Le Désert*, the prototype of a bastard form that was neither dramatic nor symphonic nor oratorio, but somewhere between the three. It would take a mature genius to fashion such a piece into a coherent work of art, and in addition to his immaturity Bizet was hampered by a text frigid in conception and comically inept in execution. It is not surprising that much of the music is perfunctory; the interest lies in observing how the appeal of local colour or the slightest opportunity for dramatic treatment at once fired Bizet's imagination. There is little enough to justify Halévy's strictures on the harmony, though a few modulations do hint at future development.

The text deals with Vasco da Gama's voyage of exploration to Asia; it takes the ship's company from the Tagus, through a calm

[1] Since these words were written both works have enjoyed several productions in England and elsewhere. *Le Docteur Miracle* was first revived at the Paris Conservatoire on 12th May 1951, the programme announcing (with an inaccuracy all too typical of French dealings with Bizet) that there was no evidence of a performance in 1857. In February 1954 the B.B.C. had the happy idea of broadcasting Bizet's and Lecocq's settings in the same programme. Both operettas came up well; but Bizet's greater resource in developing his ideas, in scoring, modulation and parody (where he picked up some hints from Offenbach), left the impression that Lecocq was lucky to share the prize. There have been at least three English stage productions of *Don Procopio* since 1955.

and a storm stirred up by the giant Adamastor (sung by six basses), to their rescue through prayer and first glimpse of the promised land.[1] There is little attempt at characterization, either of the principals (of whom Vasco has a most ungrateful part) or of the expedition as a whole. But Bizet does try to promote unity by means of a rocking figure in 6–8 time to denote the sea. The introduction follows David in its use of declamation against a slowly shifting harmonic background over a pedal.[2] The sailors' chorus is simple Gounod, the soldiers' chorus almost as square and banal as Gounod's notorious prototype (composed for his *Ivan IV* before Bizet left for Rome); the combination of the two is a very academic piece of counterpoint. There follows something much better, though it has nothing to do with the story. Léonard, a young officer with the rare gift of a soprano voice, offers to amuse the becalmed company with the 'joyful love-song which Ines with her gentle voice used to sing me every day'. The hint of local colour was enough for Bizet: this bolero might have been written at any period in his life. With its lively melody and *ostinato* rhythm it is the ancestor of the song *Adieux de l'hôtesse arabe*, the Almée and Ghazel in *Djamileh* and the *chanson bohème* in *Carmen*.[3] The first phrase:

is a fingerprint that constantly reappears, notably in the F sharp minor chorus in *L'Arlésienne* (where it is combined with a similar rhythmic figure). A storm follows, conventionally rendered by diminished sevenths, and the chorus describes it in music that looks forward to

[1] Meyerbeer's version of these events in *L'Africaine* was not performed till 1865.

[2] Ten years later Bizet used the same music to indicate the desert in *Noé*.

[3] The first seven notes of the oboe counterpoint in the second verse of the bolero are identical with Carmen's opening phrase, 'Les tringles des sistres tintaient'.

the first movement of *Roma* and backward to almost any movement of Mendelssohn marked *agitato* in 6–8 time (for instance, the opening of the 'Scottish' Symphony). Adamastor, however, though he has to utter such remarks as 'Respectez cette barrière, Retournez vite en arrière', evokes Bizet's talent for the dramatic, and the music rises to a higher plane. One recurring phrase with a distinctive harmonic twist which seems to depict the giant:

may have worried Halévy. The prayer is conventional, except for a chromatic passage at the end over a long tonic pedal, and the final chorus dreadfully square and empty. But between the two comes a beautiful moment when the look-out sights land:

The five-act grand opera *Ivan IV*, of which the surviving score probably dates from 1862–3, shows Bizet still worshipping false gods. The libretto is an extreme specimen of the grand-historical-dynastic type conceived for Spontini and solidified in Scribe's edifices for Meyerbeer and Auber. It presents a series of manufactured situations involving half a dozen characters in a perpetual clash of loyalties based on love, patriotism, religion, class, party, family ties and self-interest. There are numerous openings for spectacle, ballet and local colour, but no concessions to common sense. Incident follows incident in lurid profusion—pillage, rape, conspiracy, arson, usurpation, execution; everyone utters the loftiest sentiments but nobody stops to think. Act IV begins with a nuptial journey by gondola and continues with a series of murder-plots, the cremation of the Kremlin, the condemnation of the heroine and her brother to summary execution and the collapse of the tsar in a fit so apoplectic that he is given up for dead.

The music is very uneven and has all the faults that might be expected from Bizet's grappling with such a subject. The heroic parts tend to flatulence, and religion as usual proves the composer's downfall: the nuns' prayer to the Virgin in Act II is laughably like the hymn to Brahma in *Les Pêcheurs de perles*, with the harmony rendered more palatable to Christian ears by copious dominant thirteenths. The orchestration is formidable. The march in Act III —one of Bizet's worst lapses—employs a brass band on the stage composed of two cornets, two trumpets, three trombones and three saxhorns (soprano, bass and contrabass), an assembly calculated to gratify the eye rather than the ear. This is in addition to a very large orchestra in the normal place, including a heavy battery of percussion, bells and organ. The influence of Verdi and Meyerbeer appears in the *ensembles,* which are frequent and elephantine. While each act begins well—the second, fourth and fifth outstandingly so—all but the fourth are let down by their finales, where Bizet, instead of bringing the music to a satisfactory climax, merely repeats and inflates pedestrian material. The shade of the prelude to Act III of *Lohengrin* strays momentarily across the finale of Act I.

Although none of the chief characters comes to life—Ivan himself is frankly incredible—Bizet often succeeds with secondary persons and incidents. The gondola scene (a variant of the chorus *Le Golfe de Baïa)* is charming, and the episode of the two sentries on the Kremlin wall at the beginning of Act V, the music of which later became the march *Trompette et tambour* in *Jeux d'enfants,* is one of those perfect little vignettes that crop up from time to time in Bizet's operas. Several long billowing tunes with a wide compass and leaps of a seventh or ninth, generally introduced *espressivo* by flute or clarinet, also proclaim their composer. The exotic moments are fewer than might have been expected. The opening of Act III:

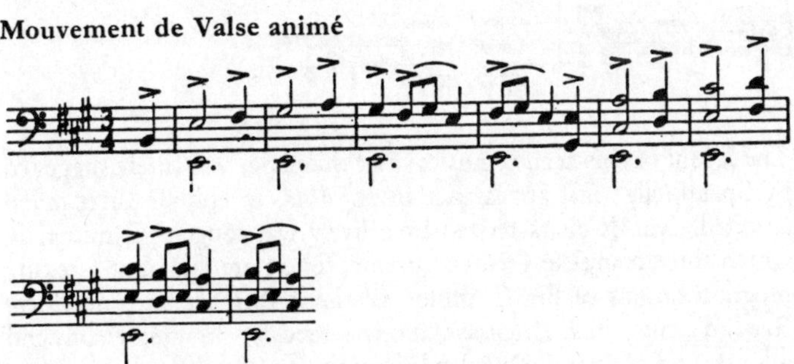

has a faintly Russian tinge, though the subsequent chorus reverts sharply to the fashionable ballrooms of the Second Empire, and it is perhaps significant that the young Bulgarian's serenade, given in response to the tsar's request for a national song, is no other than the bolero from *Vasco de Gama* with the words slightly modified. Essentially Bizet had only one type of local colour. Leading themes are used much as in the later operas, and one or two of them reveal a vivid sense of character. The motive of the double traitor Yorloff, betrayer of his sovereign and his fellow conspirators, which appears first on violas and cellos when he is trying to ingratiate himself with the wronged Caucasians, is full of possibilities:

The layout of this scene, musical and dramatic, was surely suggested by Sparafucile's first appearance in *Rigoletto*, an episode Bizet much admired. Ivan is characterized by a lively war-song in C minor, of which three complete versions survive. There are faint but arresting prognostications of the C minor *mélodrame* that accompanies Mère Renaud's entry in *L'Arlésienne*, nicely scored for the four woodwind soloists, and of José's 'Dût-il m'en coûter la vie'.

Several further passages turn up in other contexts. The duet in Act I for Marie and the young Bulgarian (who is both Ivan's secret agent and a vehicle for local colour) reappears as the flute theme at bar 28 of the prelude to *La Jolie Fille de Perth*, a transformation as successful as it is unexpected. There are four borrowings from *Ivan* in *Les Pêcheurs de perles*, though only one, the chromatic *ostinato* figure accompanying the first entries of Ivan and Leila (in the same key and tempo), can be detected from current scores. The others are four bars from the duet for Marie and Igor in Act IV (identical with Zurga's 'Et nul ne doit la voir, nul ne doit l'approcher' in Act I of *Les Pêcheurs de perles*) and a theme that occurs in Marie's Act I air and again in her Act V duet with Igor (page 328 of vocal score); this, with a slight change of rhythm, became the main theme of the similarly placed duet 'O lumière sainte' at the end of *Les Pêcheurs de perles*. The first two of these parallels are omitted from the vocal score of *Ivan*; the last was dropped from all scores of *Les Pêcheurs de perles* between 1863 and 1975. Several substantial episodes from *Ivan* were transferred to *Noé*. *Ivan IV* was first performed in 1946 and published in 1951; for further particulars, *see* Appendix F, page 289.

The libretto of *Les Pêcheurs de perles*, by Carré and Cormon, is also typical of its era. The scene is laid in Ceylon and concerns the love of two men, Zurga king of the pearl fishers and his friend Nadir, for the same woman, the priestess Leila. They saw her first in Candy and vowed to part from her and each other. In Act I they meet again, apparently recovered from their passion; but in the veiled priestess, who under a strict oath of chastity is appointed by the pearl fishers to ward off the wrath of Brahma during the fishing season, Nadir recognizes Leila, and mutual love springs up between them. Nadir is caught with her in the sanctuary; the high priest Nourabad tears off her veil, and Zurga, recognizing her in his turn, in jealous fury condemns them both to death. Meanwhile it has transpired that Zurga was once beset by robbers and rescued by a girl, to whom he gave a necklace in gratitude. When Leila takes off her necklace before execution and asks for it to be sent to her mother, Zurga recognizes his gift. At the last minute he starts a fire in the pearl-fishers' tents and releases the prisoners, who despite the denunciations of the fanatic Nourabad make good their escape.[1]

[1] In later scores (except that of 1975) Zurga is killed. There is nothing about this in the printed libretto or the 1863 vocal score, the only one published during Bizet's life. *See* Appendix F, p. 290.

The weaknesses of this plot are obvious: it depends too much on coincidence, and the necklace episode puts Zurga's noble action on a *quid pro quo* basis worthy only of Hollywood. Moreover, the whole background is false. It is impossible to believe in these 'Indians' and their worship of Brahma and 'blanche Siva'.[1] They are the regulation sopranos, tenors, etc., with their faces blacked. Consequently no illusion is established, and none of the characters comes to life. There are some effective stage situations of the conventional sort, and the 'exotic' setting, bogus as it is, does draw sparks from a composer uniquely gifted for the evocation of atmosphere; but that is little credit to the librettists. They were aware of the shortcomings of their work; after the first night Cormon is reported to have said: 'If we had realized M. Bizet's talent we should never have given him *cet ours infâme*.'

If in *Don Procopio* Bizet looks musically backwards, and in *Ivan IV* goes out of his way to challenge Meyerbeer, with *Les Pêcheurs de perles* he is at the crossroads. It is a very uneven opera both in style and quality. Contemporary critics discovered the influence of Gounod, Félicien David, Verdi and Wagner; and, if for Wagner we substitute Meyerbeer, they were right. The libretto, though much less pretentious than that of *Ivan*, still emphasized situation at the expense of character; hence it tended to lead Bizet away from the true bent of his genius, which lay in the interpretation of human emotion, dramatic conflict and atmosphere. He did his best to bring the four characters to life, but the result is not very convincing. Leila remains the typical suffering soprano, Nadir the aspiring tenor who is all emotion, no brain and little brawn (it is hard to imagine him stalking, 'le poignard aux dents', the various wild beasts to which he lays claim), while Zurga, like other stage baritones, is required to veer between ferocity and magnanimity as the situation demands. The conflicts between love and religious vows (Leila), love and friendship (Nadir) and love, jealousy and kingly obligation (Zurga) are

[1] Originally they were American Indians; Bizet told Gounod that the scene was laid in Mexico. The librettists themselves seem to have taken a somewhat cynical view, for all their sympathy is on the side of Leila's perjury. The sacred virgin who yields to love was a favourite theme of romantic opera: e.g. *La Vestale* and *Norma.*

not well dramatized; Bizet, besides being hindered by his libretto, was not yet equipped to deal with them. But he clearly recognized the existence of the problem and tried to solve it by the use of leading themes. Thus the beautiful tune of the Prelude with its characteristic *ostinato* figure:

symbolizes Leila the virgin priestess, and of several other recurring motives the most prominent is that of the duet for Nadir and Zurga, 'Au fond du temple saint'. This is brought back repeatedly whenever the friendship of the two men is in question. The stroke is often dramatically effective, but the tune itself, a fair specimen of the Gounodesque type, is not strong enough to bear the weight put upon it, especially as it is never developed. Bizet had not yet learned that leading themes must have a musical as well as a dramatic aptness: if they are to be used repeatedly without development they must be of a type, preferably brief and epigrammatic, that will fit naturally into varied contexts. The principal motive in *Carmen* answers these requirements, but not the duet in *Les Pêcheurs de perles*.

That theme illustrates another of the opera's weaknesses: most of the solo music is derivative (usually from Gounod) and some of it insipid. But here a distinction must be made. Where the Gounod influence is primarily melodic (and Gounod was most successful as a melodist), as in the Prelude or Nadir's 'Je crois entendre encore' or Leila's cavatina 'Comme autrefois', Bizet's music retains a considerable charm. Leila's cavatina, with its 9–8 time, more agitated middle section [1] and accompanying horns and cellos, strikingly

[1] The resemblance here to a tune in the duet 'La brise est douce' in Gounod's *Mireille* is deceptive, for Bizet's work was written first.

anticipates Micaela's 'Je dis que rien ne m'épouvante'. It is where Bizet follows Gounod's worst feature, his rhythmic ineptitude, as in the choruses 'Voilà notre domaine', 'Sois la bienvenue', 'Brahma, divin Brahma' and 'Ah! chante, chante encore' (taken over from *Don Procopio*), that he writes really bad music. It is notable that whereas the solo music is fairly even in quality, if not very individual, nearly all the best and the worst passages occur in the choruses and concerted numbers. Verdi is still a potent influence; the accompaniment figure in the final pages of the duet 'Je frémis, je chancelle' is the clearest of many hints of *Il Trovatore*. This eclecticism of style, though of course a defect, is not to be confused with the notorious eclecticism of Meyerbeer. Bizet did not, as it were, put into his shop-window all the devices he could pick up here and there from his intercourse with the world. On the contrary, a multiplicity of influences in a young composer is a healthy sign: it shows him prepared to found his style on the widest basis. It is as a rule easier to eliminate alien influences than to generate a creative originality out of a vacuum—a lesson often forgotten in the present century.

Most of the genuinely original music in *Les Pêcheurs de perles* is concerned with the exotic element. It is here that the influence of David's *Le Désert* has been detected; but though no doubt Bizet did owe something to that rather frigid work, an immediate difference is apparent. Whereas with David exoticism was an end in itself, an attempt to paint coloured pictures because the colour was strange and exciting, Bizet is already using it as a vehicle to convey character and dramatic atmosphere. The opening choral dance conjures up a more vivid picture than a reader of the text could believe possible; with its incisive rhythms, sharp modulations and touches of chromaticism it launches us well into the story, and a discerning listener in 1863 might have seen (as Berlioz did) that a new and genuinely dramatic composer had arisen. The neat coda, with the tune dying into the distance in fragments over a long tonic pedal, is prophetic of *Carmen*. Equally fine is the bloodthirsty C minor chorus 'Dès que le soleil' in the last scene, which adds to its fire something of the nimbleness of a Mendelssohn scherzo. The exotic touch is apparent too in the finest of the solo numbers, Nadir's 'De mon amie', which with its subtle rhythms (12–8 with occasional bars of 9–8), alternating major and minor key and harp accompaniment has a haunting beauty. The introductory phrase:

recalls the oboe theme in the slow movement of the Symphony.

Harmonically too Bizet's exoticism is more enterprising than David's. Most of the latter's special effects are based on long pedals or *ostinato* rhythms such as or both together. But he runs both devices to death and is careful to avoid serious clashes. His contribution lay in opening a new door; he had not the genius to enter and take possession of the territory that lay beyond it. Bizet was perhaps the first to do this, and if the ground has since been trampled by many feet, his contributions often retain their freshness where much exotic music of a later date has tarnished. The reason lies of course in their musical quality. Bizet shared David's fondness for long pedal notes, which were in any case a commonplace, but by using them as a basis for patches of chromatic harmony he extended their functional possibilities and evolved one of the most fertile elements of his style. So far from avoiding clashes, he used the novel effects thus derived to add a new range to his powers of expression. It seems to have been experiments of this kind that provoked the censure of Halévy and his other teachers. They sound mild enough today, but taken in their context they can still strike the listener with the force of a fresh sensation.

Bizet used his chromatic pedal-passages for three main purposes: (*a*) as an element of variety in absolute music; (*b*) to express 'exotic' colour or atmosphere, nearly always for a dramatic purpose; (*c*) to heighten tension at moments of crisis. Examples of (*a*) have been quoted from the early Symphony and the *Variations chromatiques* for piano. The second purpose is much in evidence in *Les Pêcheurs de perles* (e.g. in the opening chorus) and of course still more so in *Djamileh* and *Carmen*. But it is the third method that he uses most potently. *Les Pêcheurs de perles* abounds in such touches. In Act II Nourabad, after reminding Leila of her oath, the spirit of which she has already half broken, goes out, leaving her troubled and afraid, while the orchestra plays this:

The effect is extraordinarily impressive. The jealous Zurga's entrance at the beginning of Act III is depicted by quiet chromatic scales in contrary motion over a tonic pedal—a stroke repeated at Mitifio's entrance in *L'Arlésienne*. We are again reminded of *L'Arlésienne* in the opening chorus of Act II, 'L'ombre descend', sung behind the scenes. The bass voices in fifths together with a tambourine keep up their thrumming rhythm throughout, and the only other instruments used (very sparingly) are two piccolos, whose trills and arpeggios give the scene a remote magic very characteristic of Bizet:

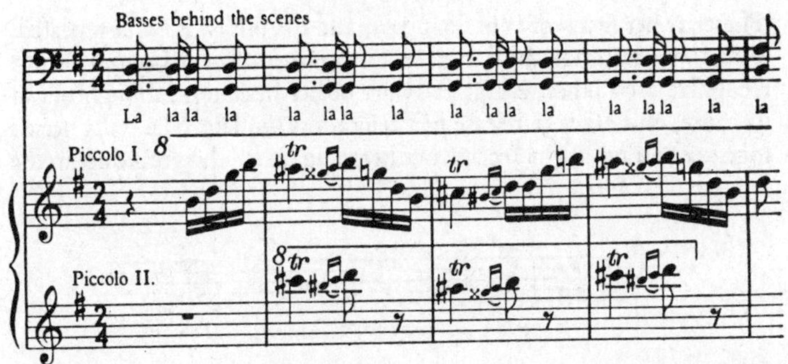

There is already ample evidence of Bizet's musical and dramatic gifts; but they are inconstant (especially the former) and insufficiently fused. He is apt at climaxes to take refuge in the diminished seventh or the tremolo, and a certain rhythmic deficiency is apparent in some of the choruses, notably in the excessive use of an ambling 6–8 time. In the last act his inspiration flags: except for one chorus and one or two passages, such as Zurga's entry mentioned above, the music is very weak. In the duet for Zurga and Leila, where she comes to beg for Nadir's life, unaware that Zurga also loves her, Bizet misses a great operatic opportunity. This is exceptional, however. In general his dramatic sense is surer than his musical style. The finale of Act II, with its piled-up climaxes as the chorus demand the culprits' death—especially the passage in dotted rhythm 'Ni pitié, ni merci'—is very good theatrical music, though not yet mature Bizet. Here and there he hits on the musical *mot juste* that sums up the situation in the most economical way—which is after all the aim of the dramatic composer. Such a stroke is Leila's oath of chastity in Act I:

These are her first words in the opera, and the phrase is twice repeated, each time a minor third higher. A moment later she and Nadir recognize each other. Zurga is aware of her hesitation, though not of its cause, and offers to release her before it is too late. She pulls herself together and replies in accents not heard again till the great duet in the last act of *Carmen.*[1]

Here is the first hint of that flexible melodic recitative that Bizet used so subtly in *Carmen* (Seguidilla, card scene, final duet) and which he would surely have further extended had he lived.

One of the features that troubled contemporary critics was the scoring. They found it painfully noisy and overloaded (one referred to the opera as a 'fortissimo in three acts'), and it may well have offended an ear attuned to Auber. The more grandiose passages, which are the least typical of Bizet, owe not a little to Meyerbeer and Gounod, whose scores then seemed the height of romantic extravagance (Berlioz's were regarded as merely eccentric). Nadir's 'Des savanes et des forêts', where the voice is doubled by cellos and bassoons beneath a long string tremolo, reflects the practice of Meyerbeer as well as early Wagner. Certainly *Les Pêcheurs de perles* is (with the exception of *Ivan IV*) the most massive of Bizet's operatic scores and the least rich in subtlety. He is more sparing than later in the use of solo instruments and groups, but already shows an eye for colour and the combination of timbres. The exotic parts, as we should expect, are scored with most skill. The dance in the opening chorus (page 12 of vocal score), in which melody and harmony are entrusted to three solo wind instruments while violas, cellos, tambourine and triangle keep up a rhythmic drone in open fifths, admirably suits colour to action. Already the flute and harp, instruments he used with

[1] Compare Carmen's 'Mais que je vive ou que je meure, Non, je ne te céderai pas!' (p. 349 of the Choudens vocal score), where the same sentiments are expressed in almost the same striking phrase.

special understanding, take a prominent part. Together they introduce the theme of the duet 'Au fond du temple saint', over whose later appearances one or both of the flutes, supported by tremolo strings, exercise almost a prescriptive right. The English horn, whose first appearance in Nadir's charmingly scored romance is most effective, and the percussion are used sparingly. If parts of the score pay service to current convention, there are clear signs of the piquancy, suppleness and economy that distinguish Bizet's later practice.

In later years Bizet thought little of *Les Pêcheurs de perles*, judging it quite as severely as the critics. It remains, however, an opera of interest and promise, justifying perhaps more than *Djamileh* Reyer's wise words: 'The composer who stumbles in taking a step forward is worth more attention than the composer who shows us how easily he can step backwards.' Here we see in embryo, intermingled with much dross, many of the qualities that were to make Bizet the foremost dramatic composer in France.

The development shown in *La Jolie Fille de Perth* is in some ways negative rather than positive: Bizet has eliminated many of the weaknesses of the two previous operas, but not pursued his advances, particularly in the harmonic sphere. It is a less arresting and a less uneven opera, and consequently has been underrated. For much of its apparent tameness the libretto is responsible. This extremely remote adaptation from Scott, by Saint-Georges and Adenis, is nothing but a receptacle for age-old operatic devices. The construction is poor, the characterization standardized, the verse execrable. On the other hand there is no attempt at the monumental; the characters are, in intention at least, ordinary human beings. We are closer to *opéra-comique*, and in this sense there is an advance: Bizet was heading for the right goal along the right road, and needed only time in order to reach it. The weakest points in the music (which include most of Act IV) invariably correspond to those of the libretto.

The opening of Act I finds Smith in his workshop, lamenting the fact that Catherine Glover will not take her father's advice and consent to be his Valentine. He hears a noise familiar to operatic audiences: 'Je crois qu'on insulte une femme!' Mab, queen of the gypsies, rushes in and is given shelter, but has to be hurriedly hidden when Glover, Catherine and the apprentice Ralph appear, ready to celebrate the carnival with 'un peu de venaison, un superbe pâté, du vieux Wisky [*sic*] d'Écosse, un succulent pudding'.[1] Smith gives the flirtatious Catherine a gold-enamelled flower, while Ralph growls out his jealousy. Presently a stranger, who turns out to be the Duke of Rothsay, comes in with a request to Smith to straighten his dagger; his real quarry of course is Catherine, who thinks a little flirtation with him in Smith's presence will do Smith good. Only the intervention of Mab prevents a fight between the two men, but her appearance from behind the arras gives rise to the usual recriminations, and Catherine throws away Smith's flower, which is retrieved by Mab. The duke departs, having invited Catherine to a midnight ball in his palace. In Act II amid the carnival revels the duke asks for Mab's assistance in abducting Catherine, who has refused him. Mab, a cast-off mistress of the duke, substitutes herself for Catherine and enters the palace. Ralph, the worse for drink, thinks he sees Catherine being abducted and rouses Smith, who has been vainly serenading her. As they rush off, the real Catherine appears at her window to answer Smith's serenade.

In Act III the duke woos the veiled Mab while the courtiers dance a minuet off-stage, and in the process takes the gold flower. Presently Glover and the real Catherine appear, and to the astonishment of the duke and his courtiers ask for his consent to her marriage with Smith. Smith indignantly rejects her, and his resolution hardens when he sees the flower in the duke's hand; Catherine finds herself disbelieved by both parties. In Act IV Ralph has taken Catherine's part and is to fight a duel with Smith for her honour (on the banks of the Tweed—the librettists were weak at Scottish geography). She and Smith while away the time by sentimentalizing over their past love. The duke at Mab's instance stops the fight, but meanwhile Catherine has gone mad. She is cured by the sight of Smith serenading Mab at her (Catherine's) window, and all ends happily.

[1] These viands vary with each edition of the text. For Germany and Italy in 1883 they were reduced to meat and wine. In the 1888 libretto the venison is in the *pâté* and the pudding replaced by 'un rôti succulent'. All this, including the 'Wisky', then disappears in favour of 'quelques paniers, bons vins et chère fine'. The latest vocal score restores the 'Wisky' but not the rest. The full score transfers the epithet and offers 'un vieux repas de noce'.

A Travesty of Scott

It is difficult to see how a worse libretto[1] could be founded on Scott's novel. The story bristles with improbabilities that would be tolerated nowhere but in an opera-house, and the last act, in which the duke does not appear at all, is appallingly weak. It seems to have been constructed solely for the purpose of introducing a mad scene,[2] a device as popular then (witness Donizetti's *Lucia di Lammermoor*, Meyerbeer's *L'Étoile du Nord*[3] and Thomas's *Hamlet*) as a display of tap-dancing in a film of the 1930s. It is not surprising that Bizet could do little with the characters. Scott's mettlesome Smith becomes a typical asinine tenor, while his Duke of Rothsay, a memorable compound of vacillation, daring, charm and complete recklessness of other people's interests and his own, is turned into the traditional operatic seducer—and not a very efficient one at that. Catherine, a somewhat mawkish character in the original, is here the complete opposite—a frivolous coquette who deserves all that comes to her. Glover is turned from a hard-boiled burgess into a *buffo* bass *manqué*. Mab, presumably based on the Glee-maiden Louise, has flashes of vitality, though her part is very much that of the conventional *seconda donna*. The one success is Ralph, who bears not the remotest resemblance to Scott's Conachar, the disguised Highlander with a sharp tongue but a lamb's courage. Bizet makes him a real man; his drinking-song in Act II with its fuddled accompaniment figure:

[1] Except perhaps the original draft, Act III of which survives. Bizet was responsible for the words of the duke's cavatina and Smith's air (not those in the current vocal score) and the structure of the finale. Saint-Georges placed a big static *ensemble after* Smith has seen Catherine wearing the duke's flower. He spelt the name Schmitt throughout.

[2] There is no justification for this in Scott, whose heroine remains almost too level-headed.

[3] In this opera (1854) the heroine, also called Catherine, is likewise restored to sanity by the re-enactment of a scene from the past.

is a brilliant piece of characterization, piercing the comic façade of drunkenness to reveal the underlying tragedy. Nor does the libretto give the composer much chance to bring the background to life. The chorus of the Watch admirably sets the atmosphere for Act II, but the smiths at the anvil and the carnival (including the St Valentine chorus) had long been stock devices of French and Italian opera. The absence of local colour may be due to Bizet's inability to find a musical equivalent for Scotland; but even if he had one, it is difficult to see how he could have made use of it. The one opportunity for exploiting the exotic he seized with both hands. This is the justly famous Gypsy Dance, the best thing in the opera. It is no doubt due to the lack of such opportunities that the harmonic style of *La Jolie Fille de Perth* seems comparatively tame after *Les Pêcheurs de perles*.

These deficiencies in the libretto are particularly to be regretted, for Bizet does show signs of an increasing mastery of the dramatic style. His use of leading themes is less frequent than in *Les Pêcheurs de perles*, but far more effective. Glover's fussy little motive:[1]

which occurs in several related forms, nicely portrays that worthy as Bizet saw him. Smith's serenade (from *Don Procopio*) is put to a genuinely dramatic purpose in the finales of Acts II and IV. Best of all is Bizet's use of the theme that accompanies the duke's wooing of Catherine:

It comes three times in the trio 'De ce beau seigneur' (where the duke first approaches Catherine in Act I), in the orchestra in D major and G major, and then sung by the duke in C major to the words 'Que vous êtes jolie, quelle grâce accomplie'. Its later appearances are all in the orchestra: when the duke enlists Mab to assist his designs, very effectively (in the minor) in the finale of Act II when the majordomo takes off the supposed Catherine in a litter to the

[1] Compare the similar motive for Haroun's friends in *Djamileh*.

palace, and twice in Act III, at the approach of the litter and (in 6–8 time) when the duke announces that his victim has fled at the approach of dawn. On each occasion it binds the action together in a striking and economical manner. The finale of Act II, with this smooth tune accompanying the abduction of the wrong woman (its suave irony again recalls the cello theme in the duet for Rigoletto and Sparafucile), with its echoes of Ralph's drunken song and the real Catherine's appearance at her window singing Smith's serenade for the first time in the major key, is the finest piece of dramatic writing Bizet had yet achieved.

Almost equally good from the musico-dramatic point of view is the minuet (familiar from Guiraud's arrangement in the second *L'Arlésienne* suite) that accompanies the duke's wooing of the false Catherine in Act III.[1] Again dramatic irony redoubles the success of a charming piece of music. The trio 'De ce beau seigneur', where Smith tries to drown the duke's whispered advances to Catherine by his blows on the anvil, is effective in a more conventional way; so is the first finale, where Glover's tipsy song (he has been at the 'vieux Wisky d'Écosse') is ingeniously combined with the arguments of the other characters about the relative innocence of Mab and Smith. A sterner test is presented by the finale of Act III, the most substantial number in the opera; and Bizet comes out of it fairly well. It is perhaps a little stiff, but we need only glance at the contemporary operas of Gounod and Thomas to notice an advance in dramatic power. The contrasts are well managed and the characters differentiated with skill. Particularly fine is Catherine's protestation of innocence, 'Il veut vous le cacher', a long *crescendo* over a dominant pedal with the accompanying chords first halved in value and then halved again.[2] There is one dramatic failure: the duke's remarks in the opening chorus of Act III, and also a passage in the ensuing cavatina, 'Comme un rayon charmant', are marked 'avec fatuité', and there is little doubt that Bizet intended the music to portray the

[1] An operatic seduction seems to have been traditionally accompanied by a minuet, as in *Don Giovanni* and *Rigoletto*. Guiraud used a synthesis of the vocal parts as a counterpoint to the main theme at its return.

[2] pp. 168–9 of current Choudens vocal score; the passage is too long to quote.

triviality of the duke's character. Unfortunately the music is not a dramatic presentation of triviality; it is trivial itself. Bizet tried the same thing, this time triumphantly, with Escamillo, who is directed to sing the refrain of his famous song 'avec fatuité'.

The copious ornamentation of Catherine's part, which angered generations of French critics, may likewise have been designed to suggest the frivolity of her character, as well as to serve as a show-piece for Christine Nilsson. Certainly her polonaise 'Vive l'hiver', with its likeness to the polonaise from *Mignon* and also to one of Bizet's own *Variations chromatiques*, is feeble enough, and the mad scene *à la* Donizetti raises a critical blush; but they represent a marking of time rather than a backsliding. Gounod's *Roméo et Juliette*, produced the same year, contains equally absurd concessions to convention. But the love music as a whole lacks distinction. All through his life Bizet found difficulty in giving individual expression to the more conventional forms of love; it was here that Gounod's influence struck deepest. He was to startle the world with a novel and unrivalled depiction of consuming passion, but in every one of his dramatic works, including *L'Arlésienne* and *Carmen*, the straightforward love music, though seldom poor and often charming and appropriate, tends to be less original than the rest of the score. But if Catherine and Smith remain lay figures, there are the makings of more serious stuff in Mab. Her intervention when Smith attacks the duke in Act I is among several passages with a distinct flavour of *Carmen*, while the relationship of the Gypsy Dance to the *chanson bohème* is too striking to need comment. Mab's *couplets* in Act I, 'Catherine est coquette', which survive only in the 1868 vocal score,[1] are pure Bizet:

[1] *See* Appendix F, p. 291.

The little figure (*a*) almost amounts to a Bizet fingerprint: it occurs in the Glover motive quoted above, the scherzo of *Roma*, the *chanson bohème* and card scene in *Carmen* and many other places.

In *La Jolie Fille de Perth* Bizet has shaken off Meyerbeer. There are still signs of Weber, notably in the first chorus with its echoes of Ännchen's arietta in Act II of *Der Freischütz*; and of course Gounod. But there is much less of his rhythmic smugness (the duet with chorus that opens Act IV, especially Ralph's 'Moi, Ralph, simple artisan', is a painful exception), and more of the lyrical charm of *Mireille*, which left its mark on the attractive St Valentine chorus. Mab's 'Les seigneurs de la cour' in Act II clearly derives from Sganarelle's *couplets* 'Qu'ils sont doux' in *Le Médecin malgré lui*. More significant is the influence of Verdi on the style and the dramatic approach: the duke again and again reminds us of his more virile counterpart in *Rigoletto*, Mab is not unlike Maddalena, and a parallel to the Rigoletto-Sparafucile duet has already been noted. Stylistic resemblances are scattered through the opera, especially in the *ensembles*, whose compound of stiffness and energy is very much that of early middle Verdi. Bizet was a great admirer of *Rigoletto*, and Verdi's influence was no bad thing for him; his flexible melodies and vivid sense of drama, added to Bizet's native ability in those respects, helped to counterbalance the sugary seductions of Gounod.

There is much good music in *La Jolie Fille de Perth*, even if less strenuousness seems to have gone to its composition than into *Les Pêcheurs de perles* (a deceptive sign, especially with French music). The Gypsy Dance is a subtle miniature that repays attention and analysis. The variations in rhythm, the alternation of minor and major key, the gradations of pace (from *andantino molto* to *presto*) and dynamics (from *ppp* to *fff con furia*) are managed with the greatest skill; the sudden check (*fpp*) when the minor key returns at the beginning of the 6–8 section serves brilliantly to redouble the excitement. Together with the Watch chorus 'Bons citoyens', a vivid little scene possessing the rare ingredient of humour,[1] the Gypsy Dance illustrates one of Bizet's characteristic procedures. This is the melodic variation, the music being built up like a mosaic from repetitions of a single short

[1] The cut in the current vocal score spoils the effect of this.

theme, simply varied in rhythm, harmony, scoring or dynamics. The device is old as the hills, but Bizet's application of it to dramatic purposes is his own. The opening of the Watch chorus on the bassoons foreshadows the *entr'acte* before Act II of *Carmen*, while one of its cadence figures:

reappears most effectively at the end of Act III of the same opera.

In orchestration too there is progress. The second act in particular is beautifully scored, as Bizet himself noted. He ranges farther afield in his choice of colours and shows more finesse in their application. The scoring of the duke's love theme (page 180) on its several appearances is particularly happy. When the duke is enlisting Mab's support it appears on two solo violas, then on two violins, then on a single clarinet. In the ironical litter scene we hear it on two violas, two cellos and one clarinet very low down, with the harmony supplied by three more solo cellos and two basses. It dies away on the violas and clarinet echoed by a single horn. The solo clarinet is more prominent than in *Les Pêcheurs de perles*, with a certain emphasis on the chalumeau register; and the flute already receives that affectionate treatment that distinguishes the score of *Carmen*. The prelude shows the delicacy of Bizet's scoring and the clarity of his part-writing at their best. Its fine web of woodwind solos looks forward to the *entr'acte* before Act III of *Carmen*. In the Gypsy Dance, opening with the favourite combination of flute and harp, he obtains an exhilarating effect by ringing the changes on the groups of instruments that play the tune. The sparing but effective use of the percussion should be noted here. The serenade, which introduces the hitherto silent English horn, is scored with a nice blend of richness and restraint, plucked strings taking the place of the guitar. In happy contrast the accompaniment to Ralph's drunken song employs the lowest notes of violins and clarinets (often in thirds), with bassoons, cellos and horns prominent in staccato interjections. The scene ends on a *pppp* chord for three trombones. The closing scene of the act, with all the strings divided (the cellos in five parts), is a rich and dramatic piece of atmosphere painting. The first half of Act III has a second orchestra behind the scenes, consisting of first flute, second oboe, two solo violins, two cornets, third trombone, harp and triangle. It is this group that plays the minuet during the seduction scene. This too begins on flute and harp, but the flute is joined, one by one and in unison, by the two violins and the oboe.

The story of *La Coupe du Roi de Thulé* concerns a young fisherman, Yorick, who falls under the spell of Myrrha, a woman of the Arlésienne-Carmen type. The old King of Thule is dying of love for her, but she has become the mistress of Angus, his favourite and presumed successor. Only the royal jester Paddock remains, beneath his professional veneer of irony, devoted to his master. Angus and the corrupt court [1] are waiting impatiently for the king to die, but Myrrha reminds them of the legend of the golden cup, given to the first King of Thule by the siren Claribel, queen of the sea. This is the emblem of royalty, and each king on his deathbed summons his successor to bestow it on him. The dying monarch, who has no heir, summons not Angus but Paddock, who throws the cup into the sea. Myrrha offers her love to whosoever will bring it back, and Yorick, ignoring all appeals, plunges after it. In Act II we see Claribel in her turn possessed by vain love for Yorick; she offers him immortality, but he asks only for the cup and remains unshaken even by a vision of Myrrha in Angus's arms. So he brings back the cup to Myrrha, who thanks him politely and bestows herself and the throne on Angus. Yorick at last comes to his senses and invokes the siren; the sea rises, and the guilty couple and servile court are overwhelmed.

Given the romantic convention, the libretto is a good one, refreshingly free from the false sentiment and stilted diction customary

[1] Bizet's republican sympathies emerge in the letters to Galabert, where he refers to the courtiers by the names of Napoleon III's ministers. This was suppressed in the published text.

at the Opéra. The attraction for Bizet obviously lay in the Myrrha-Yorick relationship. We have seen how, in his letters to Galabert, he emphasized the fascination of Myrrha. The music, even the sad torso that remains, shows how profoundly he was stirred. The eighty-six surviving pages of autograph (417 bars in all) comprise fifteen fragments varying in length from four to eighty bars. Only one number is complete, though two others are very nearly so.[1] To these can be added at least five pieces published posthumously under false titles—the prelude (*Marche funèbre*), the duet *Les Nymphes des bois*, and the songs *La Sirène, N'oublions pas!* and *La Nuit* (all from *Seize Mélodies*)—and perhaps four more, the duet *Rêvons*, and the songs *Le Gascon, L'Abandonnée* and *Aimons, rêvons!* Owing to the disappearance of the autographs and the alteration of the words[2] it is not possible to be certain of this last group; but the others are positively identified by a unique feature of this opera, its interesting and elaborate *Leitmotive* system. Although only a fraction (perhaps a sixth) survives, at least eight motives recur on one or more occasions, and Bizet would almost certainly have introduced several others where the libretto harks back to earlier words or incidents. He spoke in a letter to Galabert of using a combination of three motives from Act I for Yorick's dazed arrival at Claribel's court. His music for this does not survive, and none of the three motives he mentions is among the eight that do recur. Some of these are subtly transformed. For example Yorick's love for Myrrha and Claribel's love for Yorick are expressed in variants of the same (Yorick) motive, one form of which is quoted below (page 187). Other themes appear to denote the cup itself, its efficacy, the legend attached to it, the characters of Myrrha and Paddock, and Claribel's pitying view of Yorick's love for Myrrha. Bizet used the last in *Djamileh*, at the words 'L'amour était ma vie' in the final duet.

The splendid prelude begins with the motive of the legend on full orchestra:

---

[1] These three pieces, together with the prelude, were played for the first time in the B.B.C. Third Programme under Stanford Robinson on 12th July 1955.

[2] *See* Appendix F, p. 288.

The sombre main theme follows on bassoons and cellos and is twice repeated, each time an octave higher. Perhaps 'repeat' is the wrong word, for only the opening bars are the same; the continuation develops an expanding vitality till it reaches a big climax that very strikingly foreshadows, in melody, rhythm and accompaniment, the Frédéri theme in *L'Arlésienne*:

This is something more than coincidence; clearly this type of phrase came to symbolize for Bizet the emotional state of a young man in the grip of a passion he cannot shake off or control. There are affinities too with phrases in José's flower song. After the climax, on which all the strings in octaves play the little rhythmic figure associated with the cup, the opening returns and modulates to E flat, the key of the central section. This depicts Claribel. It begins with a melody for flute and English horn in octaves with harp accompaniment and a long inner pedal on the horn; as it proceeds the relationship with Yorick's motive emerges more and more clearly. In the coda, after a shortened return of the main theme, the second half of the E flat section, its link with Yorick now explicit, bursts out *fff* in B major. A sinister chromatic passage with clashing major sevenths and the cup motive sounding distantly on solo woodwind leads to a gloomy end: Bizet had the vision to close with the tragic Myrrha element instead of the conventional happiness of Yorick's union with Claribel. The whole prelude may be seen as a portrait of Bizet's hero between the two women who decide his fate.

Act I contains the best of the surviving music. Paddock's air 'Quand la nuit te couvre' expresses with touching eloquence the love for his dying master that underlies the jester's professional manner. Yorick's first air is the striking song *N'oublions pas!* which uses two motives from the prelude. Myrrha's entry is accompanied by a beautiful melody for solo violin that winds its sinuous way through the following scene. Yorick offers her a pearl; Myrrha, thinking it comes from Angus, turns to thank him; Angus suspiciously watches Yorick disappear in the crowd:

This exquisite passage has something of the magic and suspense of the moment in Act IV of *Carmen* when Frasquita and Mercedes warn Carmen that José is waiting for her. Scarcely less fine is the Legend, in which Myrrha tells the story of the cup. This begins like the prelude and introduces several of the other motives, culminating in a splendid B major climax where the singer is joined by the chorus:

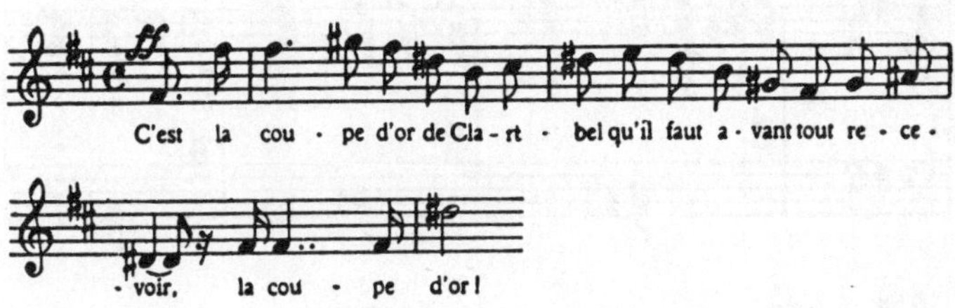

Two interesting fragments survive from the finale. For Paddock's entry with the cup we have a superb melodic paragraph based on a tune (*Maestoso avec noblesse*) nineteen bars long with a compass of two octaves:

The comments of the courtiers range from astonished salutation to mockery, the latter in music transferred to Haroun's friends in *Djamileh*. Later, when Paddock throws the cup over the cliff and Myrrha makes her vow, Yorick takes up the challenge in these terms:

Myr-rha ____ la brise est for - te et le flot ____ é-cu-

pp

mant ____ Si __ la mer me rap-por - te gar-de-moi ton ser-

etc.

- ment, _ Si __ la mer me rap-por te gar-de-moi ton ser-ment

This, with slight differences, is the melody of José's 'Dût-il m'en coûter la vie,' [1] the great climax in Act III of *Carmen*. What is more, after a stormy interlude in which Paddock begs Yorick not to go, there follows, as in *Carmen*, a repetition of the whole passage a semitone higher—this time as a duet for Myrrha and Yorick.[2] In

[1] Already foreshadowed—unconsciously no doubt—in Yorick's first air: see *N'oublions pas!* bar 5.

[2] Myrrha of course sings 'Je tiendrai mon serment'. This was an addition by Bizet, who rightly thought that the librettists had not tied Myrrha sufficiently to her oath.

Carmen Bizet improved the vocal line and the accompaniment, but the dramatic parallel is most illuminating. In both operas the victim leaves his betrayer on the climax of the finale, and the audience, on the stage and in the hall, know what she will do the moment his back is turned; in both operas, ignoring the advice of the spectators, he emphasizes his resolution by repeating his outburst a semitone higher; but whereas in *La Coupe* it is his departure that he proclaims, in *Carmen* it is his refusal to depart—overborne as this is by weightier considerations a moment or two later. The dramatic gain in the later opera, with José cornered between Carmen, Escamillo and Micaela, is enormous, but the seeds of that great scene lie in this unregarded manuscript of six years earlier.

Act II, in which Bizet used a second orchestra (with two harps) behind the scenes, begins with a chorus of sirens (*Les Nymphes des bois* and *La Nuit*) followed by an air for Claribel lamenting that even her immortality cannot win Yorick's love (*La Sirène*). This is almost identical with the E flat section of the prelude; its beautiful final cadence reflects the stage direction 'Elle pleure':

Three of the posthumous pieces mentioned above probably come from this act.

There are only three brief fragments from Act III, but each includes a motive heard earlier, and the last two bars of all, when Yorick falls into Claribel's arms, introduce the motive in 12–8 time later used to characterize Djamileh. This is sung to the words 'Vagues murmurantes', and is almost certainly a reminiscence of the siren music in Act II. It is also fairly clear that Bizet would have brought back the music of 'Myrrha, la brise est forte' in Act III. The orchestration of the opera is very rich, but much more subtle than that of any earlier work. Two English horns appear in the Legend, and the whole score uses three flutes (sometimes two piccolos), trumpets as well as cornets and four each of bassoons and trombones, including a contra-bass trombone which appears elsewhere only in *Noé*. In the prelude the timpani play chords with the trombones, a device no doubt derived from Berlioz.

There can be no doubt whatever of the importance of this opera in Bizet's development. The music still shows Gounod's influence but is quite free from the mistaken grandiosity of *Ivan*, even though it was intended for the Opéra. Above all, the characters are seen in the round. When he was writing it Bizet felt that a radical change was taking place within him; he spoke of changing his skin as man and artist. He may have been thinking of the manipulation of motives, which is certainly striking, but the emotional advance is quite as significant: here is the first unmistakable sign of a tragic power that was to culminate in *L'Arlésienne* and *Carmen*. From now on his progress to maturity was rapid; its acceleration should be dated, not from his marriage or his experiences in the war of 1870, but from the spiritual crisis he underwent while composing *La Coupe du Roi de Thulé*.

Bizet's completion of Halévy's *Noé* presents a problem. He wrote to Lacombe (about October 1869): 'Halévy left three acts nearly finished; but I've had to score it all—pretty well guess it all—and I have to compose a fourth act that is short enough.' It has always been assumed that this fourth act (actually the second scene of Act III) was the extent of his contribution. An examination of the score shows this to be far from the case. The final scene as printed in 1885 consists of two numbers, an orchestral Intermezzo (*L'Arc-en-ciel*) based on somewhat nondescript music that has occurred earlier in the opera, and a final 'Hymne à Dieu' that proves (most inappropriately) to be an arrangement of the solo song *Chant d'amour*. Bizet was not responsible for this: a note states that the finale and ballet music were lost and their places supplied by the publisher from other works by Bizet (the ballet is an arrangement of excerpts from *Djamileh* and the song *La Coccinelle*). If Bizet wrote any music for this scene it does not survive. On the other hand, his pen is recognizable in many other parts of the score. The posthumous volume of *Seize Mélodies* contains two excerpts from *Noé*, 'Pourquoi pleurer?' from Act I and 'Qui donc t'aimera mieux?' from Act III, Scene i. Each of these forms the middle section of a duet; the outer portions, in a more old-fashioned style, can be assigned with fair confidence to Halévy. Phrases from 'Pourquoi pleurer?' are used as a leading motive throughout the first two acts. Internal evidence proves that practically the whole of the long duet for Sarai and Ituriel in Act II is Bizet's work; it is a compound of several passages from *Ivan IV*, the last of them, at Sarai's 'Ah! c'est par trop d'outrage' (page 138 of vocal score), having a characteristic melody. The *entr'acte* before Act II must also have been put together by Bizet. Of its four themes the first stylistically suggests Bizet rather than Halévy, the second is taken from the preceding finale, the third from 'Pourquoi pleurer?'; while the fourth is no other than the opening of *Vasco de Gama*, written ten years earlier but not published. The curtain goes up to reveal 'an oasis in the desert', and the same phrase from *Vasco de Gama* is quoted later when the desert is mentioned in the text.

There is no doubt that Bizet's work on *Noé* was greater than is commonly supposed and is inextricably mingled with Halévy's;[1] it is difficult to say more, since in finishing another man's work he would presumably try to adapt his style and would not feel free to experiment. But certain other passages suggest his hand rather than Halévy's. Among them are the last ten bars of page 149, a typical Bizet coda (compare the end of the first chorus of *Les Pêcheurs de perles*, the departure of Escamillo in Act II and of the smugglers in Act III of *Carmen*); Sem's 'Reviens à toi' (page 161) with its strong lyrical impulse (never one of Halévy's strong points) and particularly the sudden modulation from D flat to C major; and the fine first finale based on a tune that at once suggests Bizet:

[1] Attempts to disentangle it proved vain owing to the disappearance (since 1938) of Halévy's unfinished autograph.

Not that it is fair to ascribe only the best music to Bizet; the smug religious stuff is only too much within his compass.

The question is perhaps academic, for *Noé* is unlikely to be revived. Apart from the uneven quality of the music, the libretto is among Saint-Georges's more fantastic efforts. The story, concerned with the sexual digressions of Noah's family and the fallen angel Ituriel (who loses his wings on the stage to an orgy of diminished sevenths), reads like a mixture of *Paradise Lost* and *The Country Wife* couched in the most inflated language of Scribe. The behaviour of the characters and the landscape is unpredictable in the extreme, and it is not clear who survives the flood which terminates the first scene of Act III. It is, however, unlikely that the loss of the finale deprived us of the chance of judging Bizet's powers of animal characterization.

The sketches for *Clarissa Harlowe* and *Grisélidis* are too fragmentary to permit any judgment, especially in the absence of the librettos. Often neither words nor notes are clear, and the latter are for the most part confined to snatches of melody with a spasmodic bass, sometimes figured. But one interesting point emerges about *Grisélidis*. It contains not only the theme of Paddock's entry with the cup from *La Coupe du Roi de Thulé* (page 189) but two melodies destined to become world-famous in later works. L'Innocent's saxophone theme in *L'Arlésienne*, with the accompaniment figure in thirds, the four-note *ostinato* and the bass all indicated, appears here in G flat, immediately followed by a tenor's cry of 'O surprise!' (which we may well echo) and a modulation to E flat; and the greater part of José's flower song—the first thirty-three bars without the very distinctive continuation—proves to have been conceived for a baritone in C major.

CHAPTER X

'DJAMILEH' AND 'L'ARLÉSIENNE'

THE libretto of *Djamileh* is based on *Namouna* by Alfred de Musset, a reflectively amorous poem after the manner of Byron's *Don Juan*; hence its dramatic weakness. There is not much story, and what there is has little of the dramatic. Haroun, a disillusioned voluptuary who proclaims his love for nothing except love itself, changes his mistress once a month: the old one is pensioned off with a gift of jewellery while a new candidate is bought by his servant Splendiano in the slave-market. The reigning mistress, Djamileh (she is a Spaniard in Musset's poem), has the misfortune to fall in love with Haroun, and when the day of dismissal arrives she makes a bargain with Splendiano: he is to admit her disguised as her successor, and if this proof of devotion fails to win Haroun, he can have her for himself. Splendiano thinks he is on a certainty, but Haroun's heart after a struggle capitulates to Djamileh.

There seems little for a theatre composer here. Haroun is a hopeless hero, being no more than an abstraction; there is almost no action, and one of the few incidents—Djamileh's bargain with Splendiano—takes place in spoken dialogue; with only one real character little conflict is possible. Yet *Djamileh*, Bizet's first *opéra-comique* proper, is not far short of a masterpiece. He contrives not only to cover up many of the defects of the libretto but to create a work of art that stands on its own feet. His power of evoking an atmosphere in which the characters move and have their being is at its highest; from the opening chorus of off-stage voices acclaiming the sunset on the Nile, accompanied by quiet chords and a persistent rhythm on the tambourine—a maturer version of the initial chorus of Act II of *Les Pêcheurs de perles*—the dramatic illusion is complete. Bizet achieves what he attempted with only partial success in *Les Pêcheurs de perles*—an exotic background that is interesting in itself and in complete harmony with the foreground.

In characterization too he does wonders. Nothing could vitalize Haroun, but his moods are musically portrayed. Splendiano is a clever study of the type immortalized in Mozart's Osmin: his *couplets*, 'Il faut pour éteindre ma fièvre', are turned with admirable wit. Haroun's gaming friends, with their fussy motive so reminiscent of Simon Glover and their brilliant little unaccompanied chorus behind the scenes, are surprisingly alive. But the great achievement is the character of Djamileh herself. In this portrait of a young girl in love Bizet surpasses anything in the earlier operas. The theme in the orchestra in 12–8 that heralds her silent appearance in the opening scene, though effective, has no exceptional merit (like at least two other passages in *Djamileh*, it came from *La Coupe du Roi de Thulé*), but the first music she sings, when she tells Haroun her alarming dream, reveals that combination of strength and tenderness that characterizes her throughout. It is based on the same chromatic *ostinato* figure on the dominant as the prelude to *Les Pêcheurs de perles*.[1] The Ghazel of Nour-Eddin, King of Lahore, the song of a girl's unrequited love, which she sings at Haroun's supper table, has an exquisite pathos. The irregular rise and fall of the vocal line, the varied phrase lengths, the monotonous rhythm of the accompaniment figure, the long pedals, above all the exquisite harmony, create a most individual and compelling atmosphere. We are nearer Ravel's world than Gounod's here. The harmony of the refrain:

[1] Note the Puccini octaves, as usual reserved for a special effect, as in José's 'Et moi, Carmen, je t'aime encore'. The heavily charged atmosphere too foreshadows Carmen's reading of the cards.

was too much for the critics of 1872, and half a century later the shifting tonality defeated Landormy's attempts at textbook analysis and reduced that schoolmasterly critic to puzzled mortification. Equally remarkable, both musically and in psychological understanding, is Djamileh's lament, when she has made her compact with Splendiano but is fearful of the outcome. Here again the harmony upset contemporaries, as well it might. Some writers have detected an echo of *Tristan und Isolde* in the opening bars:

The Phrygian mode tonality with the ending on the dominant and some remarkable chords towards the end with their hints of Scarlatti or Falla:

suggest that fate was already pointing Bizet's steps towards the Iberian peninsula. He seems to have divined by instinct the Moorish link between North Africa and Spain. Djamileh's dance (*Almée*), where the English horn makes its sole and striking appearance in the opera, is rhythmically reminiscent of the Gypsy Dance in *La Jolie Fille de Perth*; it is in the same melodic variation form, but the exotic colour is much more pronounced. Its strange melody, half in the major key, half in the minor, accompanied by a syncopated rhythm that produces characteristic pedal clashes, gives that effect of drowsiness and seductive languor that David no doubt intended in his corresponding dance in *Le Désert*:

Only at the very end does Bizet let down his heroine and his opera, and significantly this is the weakest moment of the libretto. We cannot believe in Haroun's conversion and feel that Djamileh's fate is only postponed. In a final plea she sings the third stanza of the Ghazel, in which the lovesick maiden dies of her despair; this is a beautiful stroke, but the rest of the duet is superficial. The C major chorus with which the opera originally ended (the first fifteen bars survive in the autograph) is no better. Bizet's imagination seems to have reacted instinctively to the falseness of the situation.

Musically *Djamileh* is his first really mature work. Gounod's influence is still perceptible in the music of the undramatic Haroun. His *couplets* in praise of love, 'Tu veux savoir', are conventional but not out of place; the equally derivative final duet, because it involves a previously individual character in Djamileh, does strike a false note. Bizet handles the exotic element with entire success. It is never obtrusive, never mere titillation of the ear, always subservient to the dramatic purpose. The *mélodrames* too are excellent. Though less finely chiselled than those in *L'Arlésienne*, they concentrate a world of feeling in a small space. The chorus of Haroun's friends behind the scenes, a mere twenty-two bars, has the shapeliness of the miniatures in *Jeux d'enfants*, which Bizet was composing about the same time. There is some exquisite detail in the scoring, especially of the exotic numbers. The strings, often divided, find rich employment; one of the *mélodrames* (No. 8b) has seven string soloists. A piano is introduced in the opening chorus, the only other instruments being the tambourine and the oboes, which double the languorous soprano melody. *Djamileh* is alone among Bizet's operas in having an extended overture, which, however, does not quite live up to its splendid opening. The main theme with its bold appoggiaturas:

and its suggestion of the barbaric is used in the opera as a march for the slave-dealer and his wares. It dominates the overture, suitably enough, but the two episodes are less interesting, and the second overbalances the whole by its disproportionate length. Bizet might have tightened up the work by introducing here the theme in 12–8 time that characterizes Djamileh herself.

Djamileh contains some of Bizet's most striking music. As with *L'Arlésienne*, he was obviously inspired by the lyrical intensity of his text, and created something which it is impossible to conceive as having come into existence without it. He is known to have been attracted by Musset's *Namouna*, especially the sufferings [1] of the heroine, before he saw Gallet's libretto or set about revolutionizing *opéra-comique*. It is perhaps not fanciful to suppose that his eye fell upon the words printed at the head of the first canto: 'Une femme est comme votre ombre: courez après, elle vous fuit; fuyez-la, elle court après vous.' Not long afterwards he was to come across this in the mouth of Mérimée's (and Meilhac and Halévy's) Don José: 'Suivant l'usage des femmes et des chats, qui ne viennent pas quand on les appelle et qui viennent quand on ne les appelle pas. . . .' It was this element in woman, and its effect on her victim, that Bizet has interpreted with greater dramatic penetration than any other musician.

The music to Daudet's play *L'Arlésienne* has become so popular in concert form that a mental effort is required to appreciate its original purpose. It is never easy to write incidental music for a straight play. The composer is restricted to small forms and must play second fiddle to the dramatist, to whom he is not a partner but a servant, a kind of extra effects man. He may be allowed a modified fling in the way of an overture and a few *entr'actes* (through which the audience is sure to talk), but when the curtain is up he is usually confined to what the French call *mélodrames* (i.e. background music to the dialogue) with perhaps a chorus or a dance here and there. He is at the mercy of both audience and stage characters. If he is too reticent, he will not have scope to express himself and his music will not survive or bring him credit; if he is too bold, he will be at odds with the dramatist and his subtleties will probably not be heard. The most he can do is to put the audience in the right humour for each act and underline the dramatic situation as best he can, while adding such musical elaborations as he chooses for the few able to appreciate them.

Bizet's answer to this problem is notable. He had proved himself a miniaturist in the *Jeux d'enfants* of a year before; he now transferred this talent to the stage and supported it with his mature dramatic powers. He composed twenty-seven numbers, none extended in form and many of them short *mélodrames* less than twenty bars long. Not a single one is musically or dramatically negligible. Except for a few

[1] He must have imagined them, for Musset, after endless Byronic reflections of his own, polishes her off with a few final stanzas not untouched by irony.

short choruses all the music is instrumental. When the play was first produced Daudet's friends were afraid that the music would kill it. Something like the opposite occurred: the play survives through the music, and it is impossible to appreciate the latter fully (so wonderfully is it integrated with the action) without going to the trouble of reviving the former. In one sense the music is too good: it exposes with painful vividness the drawbacks of the *mélodrame*. Nobody can listen with full attention to music and speech at once, and when the lovely *Adagietto*, for instance, is accompanied throughout by dialogue, the listener may applaud the psychological aptness of the music, but he curses the convention that ruins it in performance. A play with incidental music is a more misshapen hybrid than an opera, for its components cannot be evenly balanced. We thus reach the paradox that the only place where we can listen to the *Adagietto* in comfort is the concert hall.

In one respect Bizet was fortunate. Daudet's play is a far better piece of work than any of the composer's earlier libretti. It tells the story of two peasant brothers, Frédéri, the elder, who is bewitched by a girl from the neighbouring town of Arles, and Janet, known as 'L'Innocent' because of his arrested development. Frédéri discovers that his Arlésienne (whom the audience never sees) is the mistress of a shady character called Mitifio, and the shock nearly unsettles his reason; however, through his mother's influence he becomes engaged to Vivette, a girl from his own environment who has long loved him. A chance meeting with Mitifio on his wedding-eve revives his passion, and unable to withstand it he throws himself to his death. At this point 'L'Innocent', who in an obscure manner has understood his brother's sufferings, regains his wits, and so the mother, by the same blow that deprives her of one son, gains another. Two things are notable about this story. It is a drama of real life, and peasant life at that; and its potency depends not so much on the details of the plot as on its lyrical intensity, especially the depiction of the Provençal background. There is something inexorable in the landscape that reflects the lives of Daudet's peasants, with their mixture of drabness and colour, of protest and resignation. The human tragedy is one with the environment in which it is set, and both are presented in a strong, clear light, with a notable absence of sentimentality.

All this is re-created in Bizet's music with extraordinary subtlety. There is nothing synthetic about his local colour; [1] it *is* the Provence of Daudet's play (the qualification is important, for the standard must be artistic and not topographical).[2] But it is wrong to ascribe this to the use of traditional themes (a new feature in Bizet's work), or to the fact that he had visited Provence whereas he never set foot in Ceylon, Scotland or Spain. It is unquestionably due to the action of an evocative text upon his newly found creative maturity. The original music, especially the *Carillon*, *Pastorale* and the wordless female chorus that opens Act II, is quite as picturesque and apposite as that based on traditional tunes. There are three of these: [3] the *Marcho dei Rei*,[4] on which the first section of the prelude and two choruses in the last scene are based, the *Danse dei Chivau-Frus*, familiar as the *Farandole* in Act III, and the very beautiful *Er dou Guet*, which makes a solitary appearance when 'L'Innocent' tries sleepily to console his love-sick brother with a fairy story. The tunes are wholly assimilated to Bizet's style and treated in the manner of composed music: the *Marcho dei Rei* becomes the theme for a set of variations, and is later worked in canon and contrapuntally combined with the *Farandole*.

But the rarest qualities of the score are dramatic, and are of course lost when it is played in the concert hall. The advance even on *Djamileh* is considerable. The characters are distilled in music that

[1] To a northern Frenchman like Bizet, Provence would appear almost as much a foreign country as Egypt or Spain.

[2] If *L'Arlésienne* is more genuinely Provençal than *Carmen* is Spanish, as is commonly admitted, this is no reflection on the music; it is a comment, more or less relevant, on the insight into local conditions of Daudet on the one hand and Meilhac and Halévy on the other.

[3] He found the themes in a collection published in 1864 by the *tambourin* (Provençal tabor) player Vidal of Aix.

[4] This tune, known in the eighteenth century as the *Marche de Turenne*, was probably not of Provençal origin at all, but a military march by a composer of the Lully school which one of the Avignon *noëlistes* adapted to the Three Kings story. The music was first printed in 1759, but the words are found in a manuscript of 1742 with the indication 'sur l'air de la Marche de Turenne'. *See* J. Clamon, 'Bizet et le folklore provençal', in *Revue de Musicologie*, November 1938.

is all the more pregnant through being expressed of necessity in concentrated form. The themes of the two brothers, on which the second and third sections of the prelude are based, are beautiful and appropriate in themselves and admirably contrasted. 'L'Innocent's' theme, to which the timbre of the saxophone gives a strangely haunting quality, suggests at once the fuddled brain and the hidden serenity of spirit:[1]

The four-note clarinet figure (*a*)[2] is repeated eight times above the tune, persisting like an obsession throughout the changing harmonies

[1] Though we now know that it was composed for *Grisélidis*. In July 1872 Bizet told Carvalho that he had found the motives of 'L'Innocent' and the girl from Arles. The latter has no motive in the present score; did he mean Frédéri's? The choice of the saxophone may have been suggested by its use in the play scene of Ambroise Thomas's *Hamlet*, whose vocal score Bizet had arranged.

[2] Meyerbeer had made much of this phrase in the big duet for Valentine and Raoul in Act IV of *Les Huguenots*.

beneath it. This theme undergoes a number of later transformations (with or without figure *a*), mostly of a harmonic nature, before reappearing in its complete form in the last *entr'acte* and in the moving *mélodrame* (No. 25) when 'L'Innocent', as the old shepherd Balthazar had always prophesied, wakes up to his full mental stature. The harmonic turns Bizet gives to the incomplete melody are very telling in their dramatic effect: the suspense of the dominant and diminished sevenths in No. 2, the diatonic hopefulness of No. 4, when Balthazar detects an awakening in 'L'Innocent's' brain like the stirring of a silkworm in its cocoon, and the agitated modulations of Nos. 8 and 9. The transformation in No. 8 is so subtle as to convince Martin Cooper that he is hearing a totally new melody.

Frédéri's theme by contrast is wild and passionate. The dramatic situation and the music are prophetic of a later character torn by a similar passion—Don José. We see the simple countryman carried away, maddened and finally destroyed by his love for a worthless woman he cannot bring himself to forget; and in both stories he is thrown into relief by the homely but rather colourless girl who loves him and who is characterized (most appropriately) by music in the traditional style of Gounodesque sentiment. If the girl from Arles had appeared, her music would surely have shown some foreknowledge of Carmen. The *mélodrames* based on Frédéri's theme are even more remarkable than those based on 'L'Innocent's'. The chromaticism of No. 10, when Frédéri lies miserably in the barn, trying to get away from his mother and Vivette, has a flavour of Franck:

while at the end of No. 26 occur a few bars that illustrate with incomparable vividness Bizet's dramatic economy, here achieved, as so often, by a chromatic scale on a pedal bass. On the last chord Frédéri appears for the last time, to throw himself to his death:

Vivette's music is the least original part of the score, but (like Micaela's in *Carmen*) it is in character and valuable as contrast. Only when the E flat *entr'acte* (the *Intermezzo* of the second suite) is played out of its context does it approach banality; in the play this movement precedes the scene in which Frédéri consents to marry Vivette. The later appearances of the tune call for little comment; the version on tremolo strings in No. 16 recalls the similar treatment of a similar theme in *Les Pêcheurs de perles*. The music associated with Mitifio is of very different calibre. In the whole work he is given fewer than twenty bars, mostly in bare octaves, yet the effect is unforgettable. Seldom can so much have been suggested by so few notes; and once more we find the chromatic scale-pedal gambit employed with striking effect:

A third type of love-music, happily contrasted with Vivette's and Frédéri's and perhaps rarer than either, is that provided for Balthazar and Mère Renaud, who loved and parted in youth and now meet again after fifty years. The stage knows many a jealous tenor and simple soprano, but to portray such a love as this without lapsing into the sentimental or trivial is no mean feat. The *Adagietto* for muted strings in four-part harmony (it is marked simply *adagio* in the original score) is so simple and so perfect that it defies criticism. Here is the apotheosis of the Gounod element in Bizet, purged of all weakness and infused with a breadth and a serenity altogether beyond Gounod. The melody is beautifully extended and the harmony is full of quiet touches that strike home by just avoiding the commonplace, such as the exquisitely unexpected chord[1] (*x*) in the final cadence:

This economy of effort extends to movements of more complex structure. The finale of Act I is a miracle of compression: it comprises Mitifio's exit (five bars), an ironical echo of the drinking-chorus in the orchestra, while Frédéri bids Francet and Balthazar drink to his Arlésienne and they tell him to throw away his glass for the wine will poison him (six bars), four bars of accompaniment while Frédéri reads the fatal letters, the return of the drinking-chorus (nine bars) and a passionate restatement of the Frédéri theme in the orchestra as the curtain falls (seven bars). Every facet of the scene makes its mark in thirty-one bars. These vignettes are as rich in musical resource. The wordless chorus that opens Act II, after thrumming out its distinctive rhythm for some time on the simplest basis of repeated chords, plunges into a series of wild modulations towards the end and gets back to its key only just in time. This is a characteristic trick of Bizet's, and its almost unfailing success is a sufficient comment on his mastery of

[1] This chord is bowdlerized in the current (though not the original) piano score, B flat appearing for the A in the viola part.

form. The trio of the *Intermezzo* (the *Minuet* of the first Suite[1]) illustrates the ease with which he handled the difficult art of two-part counterpoint. Neither of the themes is in itself distinguished, and the saxophone and clarinet tune recalls the trio of the *Roma* scherzo; but its effortless combination with the violin melody (on a tonic and dominant pedal) and the felicity of the scoring lift the movement on to an altogether higher plane. Towards the end of this trio a phrase on the oboe:

looks back to the tune on the same instrument in the *adagio* of the early Symphony.

The orchestration is a remarkable *tour de force*. Owing to Carvalho's limited funds Bizet was allowed only twenty-six players, who were disposed on the following odd plan: 2 flutes, 1 oboe (taking English horn), 1 clarinet, 2 bassoons, 1 saxophone in E flat, 2 horns, timpani and tambourine (1 player), 7 violins, 1 viola, 5 cellos, 2 basses and a piano, besides a harmonium behind the scenes to accompany the choruses.[2] In the published full score the items used in the suites appear in their final form, not with the original orchestration. But the *mélodrames* show how Bizet went to work. Every one of them repays attention. The limitation, so far from hampering him, stimulated his invention, this time in a manner approaching that of chamber music. Several pieces are for solo string quartet, muted in the *Er dou Gouet* (No. 13) and *Adagietto*. Mère Renaud's entry (No. 19) employs two flutes, two violins and viola with enchanting effect. The solitary viola—an instrument accustomed to bewail its neglect by composers—has a most grateful part; twice it takes charge of 'L'Innocent's' theme—in No. 4 with the obsessional counterpoint (page 203 (*a*)) on the English horn and the repeated thirds low on the flutes, and in No. 25 with (*a*) on one flute and the thirds on two

[1] In Bizet's autograph it is entitled *Valse-Menuet*.

[2] A list of instruments scribbled by Bizet on the back of one of Daudet's letters includes a second clarinet and a third bass instead of the second bassoon and the timpanist. This seems to have been his first plan.

violins. The saxophone, presumably chosen to suggest the rare quality in the character of 'L'Innocent', adds a distinctive flavour to the whole score. Numerous alterations and corrections in the autograph, especially in the *Pastorale*, attest the trouble that Bizet took before he was satisfied with the layout.

The first Suite, put together by Bizet for a Pasdeloup concert a month after the performance of the play, consists of the *Prelude*, *Intermezzo* (with its title changed to *Minuet*), *Adagietto* and *Carillon*. The *Prelude* (except for the scoring) and *Adagietto* are unchanged; the latter of course gains by its separation from the dialogue; but the former, owing to its loose form, is unsatisfactory outside the theatre. To the *Intermezzo* Bizet added six bars of coda, a little duologue for strings and wind ending *pppp*, a neat touch that has escaped comment. As a middle section to the *Carillon* he used the *mélodrame* that accompanies the entrance of Mère Renaud, with its plaintive flute melody and exquisite discords, transposed up a semitone to C sharp minor, and followed it with a new and striking passage leading back to the opening: while flutes and strings persist with the 6–8 melody, two of the horns suddenly interject their original *ostinato* and drag the music back to 3–4 time. Bizet rescored this Suite for full orchestra, adding a second oboe, second clarinet, third and fourth horns, two trumpets, two cornets, three trombones and side-drum, besides a full complement of strings. With these resources he was able to widen the dynamic range. Frédéri's theme in the *Prelude* is introduced by the first two desks of the strings, the others entering gradually, till the complete theme appears on the full orchestra. This would have been impossible on the original orchestra with its few violins and solitary viola. Similarly in the string passage that ends the trio of the *Minuet* the desks drop out one by one at intervals of a bar, till the opening theme reappears *aussi pp que possible*.

The second Suite, arranged by Guiraud after Bizet's death, makes a less satisfactory whole. Guiraud improved the balance of the E flat *entr'acte* (now confusingly entitled *Intermezzo*) with twelve additional bars of recapitulation, and treated the *Pastorale* and ensuing chorus in the same way as Bizet had treated the *Carillon* (though less individually); but the *entr'acte* sounds weak when divorced from its context, and the second *Minuet*, imported from *La Jolie Fille de Perth*, is not happy in this company. Guiraud's version of the *Farandole*, a free arrangement of Bizet's material from Nos. 22–24, including the *Marcho dei Rei* in canon and the two tunes in combination, though effective, involves too much repetition. The transference of the choral parts to the orchestra brings a loss of contrast and damps the exhilaration of the climax. In his rescoring Guiraud used the same forces as Bizet in the first Suite, with additional percussion in the *Farandole*, but the effect is considerably more blatant, especially in the *Pastorale* and *Farandole*.

The unfinished *Don Rodrigue* of 1873 demands a few words. The autograph has the vocal parts complete, but little else, the accompaniment being indicated by occasional pencil sketches, though it is clear that Bizet had a very large orchestra in mind. It is of course impossible to judge an opera on these remains, but the themes have less character than we should expect from a work written at the same time as *Carmen*. The cause no doubt is the stiff, old-fashioned libretto. It is the story of a family feud, the hero and heroine springing from the rival clans, varied by external war and a strong religious element. The music bears no sign of Spanish colour, but only too much of the style of *Patrie*. The main theme of that overture turns up in Act V as an orchestral march, immediately followed by the dreadful wedding march from *Ivan IV* in all its saxophonic splendour (this is the one number Bizet wrote out in full). Another item from *Ivan*, Temrouk's (unpublished) air in Act I, reappears, slightly altered, in the first finale. The religious element, as we might expect, brings out all that is squarest and most sequential in Bizet's melodic invention. Some of the fragments suggest better things, such as a female chorus in the finale of Act II and this tune accompanying an air of Chimène, the much-loved and long-suffering heroine, in Act I:

The *ensembles*, especially two trios in Act II, are richer than usual in counterpoint and overlapping phrases, a feature that would soften the squareness of the themes. But this was not the right material for Bizet, and Guiraud and others were surely wrong in thinking the world has lost a masterpiece. It was a retrograde step over which no tears need be shed. Legendary heroes were beyond Bizet's grasp; besides, he was already at work on a portrait of real men and women that was to go a long way towards killing the whole school to which *Don Rodrigue* belonged.

CHAPTER XI

'CARMEN'

THE libretto of *Carmen* has been criticized for diametrically opposite reasons. To most contemporaries it was so shocking that it ought never to have been staged; later writers have damned it as a timid watering down of Mérimée's novel. Both criticisms fail for the same reason: they neglect the angle that most matters—the dramatic. Considered thus, *Carmen* has one of the half-dozen best libretti in operatic history. The story is so familiar as not to need summarizing here; it is more profitable to glance at the alterations—nearly every one a dramatic improvement—made by Meilhac and Halévy to Mérimée's original.

The adaptation of a novel to the stage is a risky undertaking; the two forms demand such different treatment. With a masterpiece like Mérimée's *Carmen*, which depends largely on style, the task is even harder. In order to gain the fullest effect from his tale of fascination and crime Mérimée brings it very close to the reader; his two principal means to this end are the novelist's device of putting the story into the mouth of one of the characters (José, who tells it to Mérimée himself on the eve of his execution) [1] and the low tone and classical detachment of his descriptions. Both methods were closed to the librettists (though something like the second can be and is supplied by the composer); they have to find other means of striking the balance. They drew Micaela as a foil to Carmen, acting on a hint of Mérimée's, and developed Escamillo (Lucas in the novel, a shadowy figure who never speaks) as a foil to José. If the full flavour of the Carmen-José situation is to be brought home to a theatre audience, it is essential for some such character as Micaela to appear on the stage: as Ellen Terry once observed, before you can be eccentric you must know where the circle is. The novelist has many ways of appealing to his audience;

[1] Just as Des Grieux tells the story of *Manon Lescaut*, another work in which (as Ernest Newman pointed out) the hero is the centre of interest though the title is that of the heroine.

the dramatist only one—by showing on the stage what he wants them to grasp; to point a contrast he must show both sides. The essence of Mérimée's *Carmen* is the transformation of José from the simple and honourable soldier to the murderous brigand; to appreciate this in the theatre we must see the former as well as the latter. Hence Micaela is (*a*) a standard by which to measure Carmen, (*b*) a symbol of José's character and psychological environment before he met Carmen.[1] So far from being a sin against Mérimée, she is an ally.

The necessary compression of the events related by Mérimée is carried out with remarkable skill. The librettists' second act is a synthesis of several incidents in the novel, in which neither Lucas nor the smugglers appear till later and the duel with Zuniga [2] takes place on a different occasion. Equally adroit are the means used to convey Mérimée's conception of the characters. The habanera, which concentrates in a few lines a great deal of Mérimée's Carmen; the seguidilla, which develops the character of José and Carmen and carries the action forward at the same time; the flower song; the card scene; the superbly dramatic finale of Act III; the little scene just before the catastrophe when Frasquita and Mercedes warn Carmen that José is lurking in the crowd: all these were the invention of Meilhac, Halévy and Bizet. The final duet is little altered, much of Mérimée's dialogue being preserved—except in one particular; in the novel it occurs (most movingly) in a lonely spot in the mountains and ends with José burying Carmen's body in a wood in accordance with her wish, before riding to Seville to give himself up. The change of scene to the bullring, where Escamillo's audible triumph coincides with José's last desperate appeal and the murder, was a master-stroke.

The libretto has been criticized for diluting Mérimée's characters, particularly José. There is a grain of truth in this. José's Basque pride is lost (Mérimée described him as looking like Milton's Satan), but all the essentials of his moral disintegration are there. In Mérimée he commits at least three murders, killing not only Carmen but her

[1] This point is carried rather far in a Russian adaptation by Lipskerov, *Carmencita and the Soldier*, in which the part of Micaela is taken by three singers representing the voice of true love in José's heart.

[2] Not so called by Mérimée. The librettists took the name from an authority cited in a footnote.

husband García le Borgne (one of the vilest scoundrels in literature) and the lieutenant (in the scene corresponding to the duel in Act II). The omission of these horrors is a gain to the opera. Mérimée, depicting the gradual collapse of an honest nature, carries the story over a period of many months between José's release from prison and the catastrophe. The librettists had much less space in which to show the same process. Having of necessity worked the duel with Zuniga into Act II, they could not allow José to kill him without making his deterioration in this act too rapid and weakening a great deal that follows, including the final murder. The inclusion of the inessential García would have made Act III too episodic, and the gradual decline of José from connivance at Carmen's escape, through desertion, armed resistance to an officer and smuggling to murder is far more effective than a string of duels and homicides. The softening down of Carmen, too, is more apparent than real. In Mérimée she is a thief and a perpetual liar; in the opera we have little of this, but those sides of her character that are essential to the tragedy—her unscrupulousness, courage, love of freedom and endless fascination—are preserved and exploited. Mérimée's novel has virtually only two characters. The librettists presented the central conflict at full strength (breaking conventions right and left in the process [1]) and, by setting it in a background of characters whom they invented or developed, displayed it to the best possible dramatic advantage.

Yet if anyone wanted to soften down Mérimée, it was not Bizet but Meilhac and Halévy. It was Bizet—following a principle he had evolved in his Rome days, that a composer should find his subjects for himself—who sent them to the novel in the first place; and when, fearful of the public reaction, they suggested modifying the original, he 'ferociously' [2] resisted them. There is extant, by a happy chance, a manuscript of the words of the habanera,[3] which prove to have been

[1] Vuillermoz's attempt to deny this reveals an astonishing ignorance of the history of *opéra-comique.*

[2] This is the librettists' word: Soubies and Malherbe, *Histoire de l'Opéra-Comique*, vol. ii.

[3] *See* plate No. 8. Edgar Istel, to whom we owe the fullest, most accurate and most sympathetic study of the opera, was the first to grasp its significance, though it was known to Weissmann and Landormy.

the work of Bizet himself. Halévy's suggested verses are much milder in tone and more remote from Mérimée, and a note in his writing states that his first inclination was to supply even 'tenderer' verses for Carmen's first song. The Yradier habanera was not the first version, which was in 3–4 time with a refrain in 6–8 and was actually rehearsed.[1] Fritz Oeser published the refrain, as sung by the chorus after Carmen has thrown the flower, in the appendix to his score; [2] we can be thankful that Bizet rejected this trivial and rhythmically impoverished little tune.

Another point at which Bizet improved the libretto, adding concrete detail and sharpening the characterization, is Carmen's solo in the card scene.[3] It is the merest accident that Halévy's first drafts of these passages have survived; we cannot tell how much else in the libretto may be due to Bizet. But we can, in the autograph and in the 1875 conducting score and parts discovered by Oeser, catch further glimpses of the composer at work. He subjected words and music to constant revision at every stage: before the score was copied, several times during the extended rehearsals, and in at least one respect after performance. These changes vary from small points of detail to radical transformation affecting the whole balance of the opera. The facts are too complex for full discussion here; [4] but the matter cannot be ignored, since attempts to restore an 'authentic' *Carmen*, first by Arthur Hammond and Maurits Sillem in productions by the Carl Rosa, Sadler's Wells and Covent Garden companies and later by Oeser in his edition, have created almost inextricable confusion.

Bizet's first version was much longer than the traditional score. Besides spoken dialogue, it made extensive use of *mélodrame* in the first

[1] According to Guiraud, Bizet rewrote the piece thirteen times before Galli-Marié was satisfied with it; perhaps this should be taken with a pinch of salt. Bizet did rewrite passages at the request of singers; Laparra quotes an example from the seguidilla, altered at the request of Lhérie, the original José. Lhérie said that Bizet showed a touching compliance in such matters.

[2] Alkor Edition, Kassel (1964), p. 805.

[3] For a comparison of the two versions, *see* Curtiss, p. 385.

[4] See my articles 'The True *Carmen*?' (*Musical Times,* Nov. 1965) and 'The Corruption of *Carmen*; the Perils of Pseudo-Musicology' (*Musical Newsletter*, Oct. 1973); also Appendix F, p. 293.

two acts, notably at the changing of the guard, when Carmen defies Zuniga after her arrest (the only *mélodrame* to survive, considerably shortened, in the 1875 score), during the approach of Escamillo's procession, and between the stanzas of José's offstage 'Dragon d'Alcala' song, which had a different melody with light orchestral accompaniment. Bizet made one major and many minor alterations before the score and parts were copied. Originally he had introduced two retrospective references to the scene in which Carmen foretells her death in the cards: between the two appearances of José's 'Dût-il m'en coûter la vie' in the third finale, and after he has stabbed her in the fourth. (These passages were included in the 1961 Sadler's Wells and 1967 Covent Garden productions, when they struck a note of facile conventionality; Oeser rightly rejected them.) Among other details abandoned at this early stage was the ineffective return of Escamillo's refrain with chromatic accompaniment for a single cello at the end of Act III.

Apart from the new habanera, one substantial piece was composed during rehearsals: an ironical *scène et pantomime* for Morales and chorus, commenting on a young wife's deception of her elderly husband, immediately before the changing of the guard in Act I. This was inserted in 1874 for the baritone Duvernoy (Bizet took great trouble, producing no fewer than three versions) and sung in the first thirty performances of the opera; it was cut, possibly with Bizet's consent, on 25th May 1875 [1] and omitted from all subsequent scores until Oeser printed the three versions in his appendix. The other rehearsal changes fall into two overlapping groups: cuts and modifications due to Bizet's second thoughts. Of the many cuts only the most substantial can be mentioned. The arrival and departure of the guard in Act I (page 25 of the current Choudens vocal score [2]) were linked by a *mélodrame* for solo violin and cello with string accompaniment in the form of a canon at the octave; the layout recalls Bizet's orchestral version of *Petit mari, petite femme*:

[1] Michel Poupet discovered this from an examination of the Opéra-Comique *livre de bord*.

[2] Except where stated all page references are to this score.

Among the episodes substantially shortened were the departure of the old guard, the cigarette girls' chorus (which lost part of its introduction and 34 bars with male chorus towards the end), the scene in which Carmen throws the flower and runs off, the quarrel ensemble, the *mélodrame* where Carmen's insolent humming provokes Zuniga, and the finale, which at one time had a sixteen-bar link with the seguidilla. Bizet modified the words of the latter, changing the calamitous first line 'J'irai dimanche en voiture', for which the rhyme was 'Manger une friture', to 'Près des ramparts de Séville'. Some of the suppressed passages are striking, notably the *mélodrame* quoted above and the extra bars in the cigarette girls' chorus and the quarrel scene (pp. 84–7), where Carmen entered not at the end of the chorus but in the middle, accompanied by a combination of her motive, several times repeated, with an early form of the A major tune heard in the orchestra when José picks up the flower (p. 56):

The quarrel, in which the soldiers as well as the women sang, was then resumed. One consequence of the new habanera was the exquisite nine-bar chromatic passage in its distinctive rhythm immediately before Carmen trips José in the finale (p. 107). This replaced several earlier attempts, culminating in the bald statement (in the rhythm of the rejected habanera):

In Act II there were cuts in the approach and departure of Escamillo's procession, which were much more leisurely, in the duet, where Carmen repeated José's lines beginning 'Je souffre de partir' (p. 186) in a tone of bitter mockery and a different key (B major instead of E flat), and in the finale. Act III opened with an empty stage and the smugglers assembling during the march. The duel scene was seventy-nine bars longer and the dramatic action different. In the fuller version Escamillo infuriates José by refusing to take the fight seriously; he has José at his mercy but spares him, observing that his job is to kill bulls, not men. It is in the second round that he slips and falls and is saved by the entry of Carmen. The complete passage is in the 1875 vocal score but not the autograph or later scores, until Oeser restored it from the conducting copy. The finale was much more diffuse, especially in its treatment of Escamillo's offstage refrain at the end. So was the later part of Act IV (from p. 339), which suffered half a dozen cuts, the most important of them at the moment of the murder (p. 361, last bar). José was directed to stab Carmen on the words 'Eh bien! damnée!' This was followed by a return of the fanfare and chorus 'Victoire!' over a descending chromatic scale, during which Carmen 'tombe appuyée sur son bras gauche'. After removing the reference to the card scene Bizet further shortened the passage (in which José sang 'Ah! ma Carmen adorée!' to the same phrase and in the same key as in the last bars of the opera) until he reached the masterly brevity of the traditional score, with the *fortissimo* triumph of 'Toréador, en garde!' coming right on top of 'damnée'.

He may have meant to convey something of that wonderful sentence of Mérimée: 'Je crois voir encore son grand œil noir me regarder fixement; puis il devint trouble et se ferma'—especially as the chorus at once breaks into the Toreador's refrain, 'Et songe bien en combattant qu'un œil noir te regarde'. There were several successive contractions in the closing bars of the opera, which originally ended in D major with a coda based on the Carmen-fate motive.[1]

Apart from the Morales pantomime, the complete duel and a longer instrumental coda to the first chorus of Act IV (apparently removed when Guiraud adapted the chorus to introduce the ballet), none of the suppressed passages reached print before Oeser's edition. That is to say, they were cancelled by Bizet or with his consent before the publication of the first vocal score, which he arranged and of which some of his corrected proofs survive, in March 1875, within a few days of the first night. Why? Hammond and Sillem, and later Oeser, assumed that he acted under duress and against his better judgment. Oeser blames the stupidity of the producer, the inexperience of the chorus, inadequate stage equipment, the hostility of du Locle, and the general bafflement caused by an unfamiliar and shocking subject. All this is pure guesswork; there is a far more probable explanation. While several of the omissions are of excellent quality, and a case can be made for restoring some of them as an experiment, they add considerably to the length of the opera. Act I, even as shortened, lasted for fifty-eight minutes on the first night, and the whole opera for nearly four and a half hours including intervals. Act IV did not begin till after midnight. Bizet had the strongest practical reasons for making cuts, as modern productions of fuller versions have demonstrated.

Nor is this all. Most of the contractions were by any standard artistic improvements. Bizet's aim was dramatic concentration and clarity; he tended to simplify the music by paring away inessentials, so that it strikes with the force of a sledge-hammer. He thus gives the impression of saving even more time than in fact he does. This is particularly evident in the finales, three of which he wrote no fewer than

[1] The 1875 Vienna score ended with a grand apotheosis of Escamillo's refrain. It is not clear who was responsible for this.

four times, always making them shorter. Oeser's text of the third and fourth finales, spatchcocked from several rejected versions, lets down the tension like a punctured balloon and involves both psychological and musical absurdities. The changes, taken as a whole, offer the most convincing demonstration of Bizet's dramatic genius and self-criticism at work. The same considerations may have governed the suppression in 1875 (not, as often stated, at Carvalho's 1883 revival) of the Morales pantomime and the longer duel. The former, though charming, holds up the action almost before it has begun, and the latter, while it throws light on the characters, has by far the feeblest music in the opera. Unfortunately the conductor who wishes to restore any of the cuts and has recourse to the Oeser score will find himself in a quicksand. For Oeser has systematically removed hundreds of corrections and improvements, many of crucial importance, introduced by Bizet as the result of experience in rehearsal, and attributed them to Guiraud, the conductor or some other interfering hand. The results are catastrophic; *see* Appendix F, pages 294–5.

Carmen has very seldom been performed as Bizet intended; and it has repeatedly been misjudged, not only by the public but by persons who ought to know better, on versions that are not authentic. One French critic, Gaudier, damns Bizet for the recitative before Micaela's Act III air, which he never wrote. The recitatives found in every edition of the score since 1875 [1] were composed by Guiraud after Bizet's death and inserted without apology by Choudens. Guiraud, sometimes using Bizet's themes, committed no solecisms; but in converting *Carmen* from *opéra-comique* to grand opera he seriously distorted it. The dialogue, which was much longer, not only introduced a good deal of Mérimée, but in many places eased the action and aided the evolution of character. The appearance of Micaela and Escamillo in Act III, which in the Guiraud version seems a typical piece of operatic coincidence, is well motivated in the original, Micaela having paid a guide a large sum to take her to the smugglers' haunt and Escamillo being engaged in collecting wild bulls for his next fight (perhaps as a pretext for tracking down Carmen). The loss of the dialogue in Act I

[1] Oeser prints both recitatives and dialogue.

deprives us of a typical piece of Carmen mendacity (the only one in the opera) and makes nonsense of Zuniga's request to José for information about the cigar factory, the point of which is that he has just been posted to Seville. The scene leading to the seguidilla, admirably managed in the dialogue, is mutilated in the recitative; and the same applies to several scenes in Act II, especially that immediately following José's entry, which is pure Mérimée. The effect is to propel the action forward in a series of jerks instead of by smooth transitions, and to take the stuffing out of many minor characters, especially Zuniga, Lillas Pastia and the smugglers. Guiraud also spoiled the *mélodrame* in which Carmen defies Zuniga by adding extraneous recitatives: only Carmen should sing here. These may appear small points, but their cumulative effect is considerable: an opera that depends so much on correctness of dramatic expression should not be subjected to distortion of this kind. Had Bizet himself composed recitatives for Vienna, there is no knowing what other changes he might not have made.

The restoration of the spoken dialogue is an artistic necessity. Until recently all English performances included the recitatives. They were ejected by the Carl Rosa company in 1947, followed on 2nd November 1953 by Covent Garden and on 27th September 1961 by Sadler's Wells. All three ventures were ill-fated. The Carl Rosa company has ceased to exist; Covent Garden developed cold feet and restored the recitatives; Sadler's Wells restored a great deal else that Bizet excluded. Later (11th May 1967) Covent Garden launched a bastard version combining Guiraud's recitatives with passages that even Oeser rejected, and then (4th July 1973) plumped for the Oeser score, a betrayal of Bizet for which it received a well-merited castigation from virtually the entire British press. The Sadler's Wells company, after moving to the Coliseum, retrieved its honour by mounting perhaps the finest modern production of *Carmen* (6th May 1970), with dialogue and one or two of the more acceptable cuts restored. The first American production with dialogue, by Herbert Graf at Central City, Colorado, in July 1953, destroyed itself by nonsensical insertions in the last act; one of the latest, at the New York Metropolitan, gave the Oeser text curiously amended by Leonard Bernstein, who corrected a few errors but introduced others of his own.

Since 1965 many German opera houses have adopted the Oeser score, no doubt because it was there. In France, ironically, the position has been almost reversed. For many years the Opéra-Comique performed a shortened version of the dialogue with the one Guiraud recitative that tripped up Gaudier. However, on 10th November 1959, with the solemnity of an act of national policy, *Carmen* was translated to the Opéra[1] in a bloated and spectacular production involving an enormous cast, human and animal (horses, donkeys, dogs and a monkey), most of Guiraud's recitatives and the attendance of President de Gaulle.

Carmen is above all great theatre. While it has little to lose from musical judgment alone, the two elements working in harness produce a result far beyond the sum of the parts. Hence individual items lose more than usual by subtraction from their context. Escamillo's *couplets*, the habanera and José's flower song, though they keep their freshness to a remarkable degree, are most memorable as a revelation of character. Escamillo's music, especially the famous *couplets*[2] and the duet in Act IV, 'Si tu m'aimes', has been damned as trite; but the triteness lies in the character, not the music. Escamillo is flashy and superficial, the successful sportsman whom neither bull nor woman can resist (and how well he knows it!); his *couplets* would perhaps be less abused if every singer obeyed Bizet's instructions and sang the refrain *piano avec fatuité*, ending *pianissimo*. Micaela is mild and conventional, and her Gounodesque music—the greatest possible contrast to Carmen's—though the least original part of the score, is wholly appropriate. The supreme vindication of the music of both these

[1] By an odd coincidence there is an undated letter from Meilhac to Geneviève Bizet announcing that the Opéra wishes to take over *Carmen* as it had taken over *Faust*, and implying that he had no objection.

[2] Bizet is said to have remarked after composing this piece: 'Well, they asked for ordure, and they've got it.' The critic who takes this as a serious self-criticism must be very hard up for ammunition. It has been stated that the *couplets* were inserted during rehearsal at the request of Halévy or du Locle. The autograph proves this to be untrue. Halévy, however, claimed to have suggested the idea at an earlier stage, 'speaking as a man of the theatre', and implied that here again words as well as music were written by Bizet.

characters comes in the finale of Act III, where it is fused with the professional gusto of the smugglers, the scorn of Carmen and José's jealousy into one of the finest dramatic *ensembles* in any opera. The ten-bar orchestral epilogue in which, as Istel well remarked, the conflicting emotions of each character are somehow revealed, is almost without a rival for pregnancy of dramatic statement. Similarly in Act IV, when the bullfighting music proclaiming Escamillo's triumph over an animal breaks in on the personal tragedy played out by Carmen and José on the stage, the effect is overwhelming: not because the bullfighting music is great in itself, but because it contributes to a superb theatrical situation. *Carmen* is rich in dramatic irony, a quality never so potent as when expressed through the suggestive powers of music; on page after page of the score we are struck by the extraordinary appropriateness of the detail both to the unfolding of character and to the progress of events. Nor is the situation ever static; the tension is subtly relaxed or tightened by turns. What appear to be set numbers in the old style, like the quintet in Act II, are as effective in carrying on the action as original conceptions like the seguidilla, whose combination of song, dance, *mélodrame* and recitative (typical of Spanish folk-music) was quite new in *opéra-comique*. Even pieces which seem at first glance out of touch with their surroundings —the *entr'acte* to Act III or Micaela's air 'Je dis que rien ne m'épouvante' [1]—are seen as essential points of repose before a renewed quickening of the drama.

Bizet's insight into dramatic truth is not confined to giving each character music that would be nonsensical in the mouth of any other. In José he has created a hero [2] whose far-reaching development

[1] The likelihood that both were written for other works—the *entr'acte* for *L'Arlésienne*, the air for *La Coupe du Roi de Thulé* or *Grisélidis*—is of course irrelevant. Landormy's attack on the beautiful *entr'acte* is one of the quaintest eccentricities of French criticism. According to Pigot the chorus 'Quant au douanier' also came from *L'Arlésienne*, where it began 'Pour récolter le vermillon'. This is evidently the chorus of which Daudet in 1872 sent Bizet two versions beginning 'Pour cueillir le vermillon' (quoted by Curtiss, pp. 461–2).

[2] Shaliapin is reported to have said that once only in his life he regretted

can be illustrated from the music alone. In Act I he is the simple countryman, albeit in dragoon's uniform: he and his music are in tune with Micaela:

Perhaps the turning-point is marked by the passionate tune in A major [1] just after Carmen has thrown the flower—a rhythmic cousin of the duke's wooing theme in *La Jolie Fille de Perth*—which returns in a wonderful *diminuendo* when José leads her, a defiant prisoner, out of the factory after the stabbing scene. The *entr'acte* before Act II, an anticipation of his first utterance after his release from prison, already shows the difference that experience has made: there is a touch of bravado, of a self-confidence more bumptious than balanced. It is his method of compensating for the disturbance Carmen has created in his heart. In the flower song we see how much more profound is this passion than his love of Micaela ever was; and the significance of the modulation [2] in the last bars that so startled Bizet's contemporaries surely lies in José's intuitive knowledge that his emotions have grown beyond his control; it is an appeal, at once desperate and pathetic, to Carmen's pity. In Act III he is a vagabond: a smuggler with a conscience, without the rude vigour of the rest of the gang, a man in the grip of a woman he knows he cannot trust but whom he cannot bring himself to leave. He is like an animal in a cage, and a cage of

---

that he was not a tenor—after his first reading of *Carmen*, 'a score in which the whole of life seems to vibrate'.

[1] Bizet greatly improved the melody during rehearsal, altering three of the first five notes and two more later. Sillem and Oeser restored the original (*see* example on p. 217) and spoiled the passage, which depends on the changed pattern and sudden release of emotion in the second and third bars. The structure of the duke's wooing theme (*see* p. 180) is similar.

[2] It is strictly not a modulation at all, but a bar and a half of alien harmony at the approach of an apparently conventional cadence. It anticipates a favourite practice of Debussy.

his own making; when she opens the door to drive him out he refuses to go. Maddened by jealousy, conscience and despair, with Micaela begging him to return to his dying mother and Escamillo vaunting his power over Carmen before his eyes, he bursts out in the emotional climax of the whole opera:[1]

The repetition of this passage a few moments later in G instead of G flat is one of those electrifying strokes that only the certainty of genius would risk.

In Act IV José is different again. He is still the slave of his feelings, but hysteria has given way to the desperation of the cornered animal, and the last pangs of conscience have been dispelled. He will make one more appeal; if Carmen still refuses, he knows what to do. His music has a grim quality, a hardness of heart alien to the simple dragoon of Act I but wholly convincing here, and Bizet reinforces it by anticipating the device so often used (and abused) by Puccini of writing for voice and bass in octaves with the harmony in between:

José is a character easily swayed. It is notable that whereas music associated with Carmen, Escamillo and even Micaela recurs later in the action, no phrase sung by José is repeated—except one: the music of his words to Carmen in the finale of Act III 'Tu me dis de la suivre!' is identical with that of 'Un baiser de ma mère' in Act I.

[1] The fact that Bizet was using material from *La Coupe du Roi de Thulé* in no way invalidates this claim, though it throws interesting light on his creative procedure. Landormy's attitude to the passage is amusing and typical. He criticizes the harmony and the dramatic handling: José ought to shrug his shoulders at Carmen's infidelity with Escamillo, which is insufficient to provoke such jealousy.

This is probably a subconscious reminiscence, but it is curiously moving and appropriate, for Carmen is telling him to go back to his mother.

José is the central figure of *Carmen*. It is his fate rather than Carmen's that interests us. But she is not only a very vital character; she is a new type of heroine, and she represents a new kind of love. Hitherto the heroines of nineteenth-century opera—and still more of *opéra-comique*—had belonged, almost to a woman, to the spotless soprano school. The majority were negative; they tended to suffer rather than act; despite (or because of) their scrupulous moral rectitude they were the football of men and fortune. They were a convention that had fallen behind the times and needed renewing; and much the same applied to the leading tenors. The 'villains', on the other hand, male and female, often initiated more of the action, attained a greater vitality and stole the audience's sympathy. In *Carmen* the heroine and the villain are combined in one person. Villain heroes had been seen before—Don Juan, for instance—but this invasion of one of the tenderest illusions of the old *opéra-comique*, that the heroine at least must be pure, was new and shocking,[1] especially as the authors had rejected a perfectly suitable heroine (and a soprano instead of a mezzo) in Micaela. Nor had a love like Carmen's been fully defined on the operatic stage. Violetta had been a prostitute, but at least we had not seen her exercising her trade. Carmen on the other hand not only seduced José, but set about it on the stage, and only too successfully: when the 'true' love of Micaela is thrown in the balance the scales sink down heavily on the wrong side. This of course is psychologically and dramatically right, but it gave great offence in 1875. The final murder, too, was unheard of in *opéra-comique*: indeed de Leuven, the director who wanted a plate dropped to enliven *Djamileh*, resigned because he could not persuade Bizet to provide a happy ending.

Carmen's love has the intensity and the capriciousness of flame, and it is all in her music. She acts on men like a plague: José, Zuniga,

[1] Violetta had been shocking enough, but her portrait was considerably softened by Alfred's 'true' love (not to mention the moral homilies of Germont senior, before which she is made to bow), and she is given something like an apotheosis at the end. Nor of course was *La Traviata* an *opéra-comique*.

Escamillo, all go down with it. With José, the most innocent and therefore the most vulnerable, it proves mortal, and in listening to the music that Bizet puts in the mouth of both we know that the end is inevitable. There is nothing sordid about Carmen; the many imitations perpetrated later, especially in Italy, have obscured Bizet's restraint here. He cannot be blamed if his successors exceeded the bounds of art; the *verismo* of Carmen never crosses this frontier. Her character receives a complete musical representation; we see not only her effect on others, but her own qualities—fearlessness, gaiety, freedom, fatalism (in the superb passage when she reads the cards), and an occasional glimpse of tenderness. One of Bizet's subtlest touches is the little phrase, marked *Très retenu*, in the middle of the whirling quintet:

Je suis a · mou · reu · · se!

which suggests that Carmen's love for José is, if only for the moment, something very different from her later dalliance with Escamillo (compare 'Si tu m'aimes').[1]

Bizet's great advance with *Carmen* was dramatic; musically he breaks less new ground. This is not to decry him; he broadens and consolidates the progress made in *Djamileh* and *L'Arlésienne*, while doing away with the weaknesses of his earlier operas. Even the Gounodesque elements are more enterprising than their model: there is more vitality in Micaela's music than in that of any Gounod heroine—a fact overlooked by those who wish Micaela to talk the same language as Carmen. The harmonic idiom of the exotic parts, especially the *chanson bohème* with its perpetual semitone clashes, is often striking; and it is easy to imagine the shudders that passages like the following (from the opening chorus of Act III) sent down French spines in 1875:

[1] Mina Curtiss has suggested that Carmen was a realization of Bizet's unconscious longing for the freedom denied him by the failure of his marriage. It may be so; but there are equal grounds for suspecting his own emotions in José. In any case both types occur in his music before his marriage (*see* p. 185).

The style of *Carmen* is essentially that of the two previous theatre works on a greater scale and put to a more powerful dramatic purpose. But its posthumous conversion to grand opera should not blind us to the fact that it is *opéra-comique*. That does not mean comic opera; it is the opera of everyday life, which includes comedy and tragedy. Bizet's renovation of the *genre* is discussed in Chapter XII; let it be noted here that though he seems to hold out one hand to Verdi and Puccini, the other points back past Auber and Rossini to his first and greatest love, Mozart. The quintet in Act II ranks with the *ensembles* of *The Marriage of Figaro* and *The Barber of Seville* among the finest blossomings of the old *opera buffa* stock. Like the composers of those works Bizet had the not too common gift of musical humour; the scene of Zuniga's capture by the smugglers is exquisitely humorous, and the bassoon counterpoint with which it is embellished never topples into farce.

On the Spanish element much unnecessary ink has been spilt. One critic [1] has devoted a whole book to the question how much

[1] Raoul Laparra, *Bizet et l'Espagne*. His conclusion is that *Carmen* would have been a better opera had Bizet lived among Spanish gypsies. As Chantavoine tersely remarked (*Le Ménestrel*, 21st October 1938), a Carmen expressing herself in such literal terms would have ceased to be a living individual and become 'un mannequin géographique'.

of *Carmen* is genuinely Spanish, and how much better the rest would be if it attained an equal level of Hispanicism. This is to misconceive Bizet's whole purpose. It is not the business of a composer whose scene is set in a foreign country to imitate the music of that country. This could only result in pastiche, for the native can obviously do it better than the foreigner. All Bizet had to do was to conjure up a Spanish background for French listeners; being a Frenchman he could not do better than write French music. He never went to Spain (when it was suggested he said it would be tiresome and unnecessary [1]); yet in one or two places he created, apparently by instinct, music so deeply imbued with the Spanish spirit that listeners have been misled into supposing that this was one of his principal aims and condemning the rest of the score accordingly. The facts of his borrowing from alien sources are as follows.

The habanera, as is well known, is an adaptation of a song called *El Arreglito ou la Promesse de mariage* by the Spanish-American composer Sebastián Yradier (1809–65), who wrote many pieces popular in the *salons* of the day. Apparently [2] Bizet had heard it sung as a folk-song and based his habanera on what he remembered, ignorant of its true authorship; when this was pointed out he added the note in the vocal score 'Imitated from a Spanish song, the property of the publishers of *Le Ménestrel*'—i.e. Heugel, who had issued it in Yradier's *Fleurs d'Espagne* (1864). This was not its first appearance; it is advertised on the front page of *Le Ménestrel* for 11th January 1863. Yradier was one of those composers whose adaptations of folk-song fall half way between the original and art music, but he is known to have composed at least one Mexican 'folk-song'. In any case the provenance of the piece would not be Spain at all, but Cuba: the habanera, akin to the tango, is a product of Negro music, and an orgiastic dance, not a song. Its erotic connotation seems to have been grasped intuitively by Bizet. The significant point, however, is the manner in which he improved on his original. Although Yradier's basic scheme—verse in D minor, refrain in D major—is the same, and the melody of both is

[1] Compare Debussy, who never went farther into Spain than San Sebastian: yet according to Falla he could be completely Andalusian in feeling.

[2] *Le Ménestrel*, 2nd January 1887.

in some sort preserved, Bizet transformed it from a drawing-room piece into a potent instrument of characterization. Yradier's song is long-winded and lop-sided; it is full of weak ritornelli and has a rambling second half on new material. Bizet did away with all this, improved the melody by prolonging its chromaticism and adding the triplet in the fourth bar, and above all by varying the threefold repetition in the refrain; and he substituted a vital harmonic interest for Yradier's stiff and awkward accompaniment. This is Yradier's version of the melody and refrain:

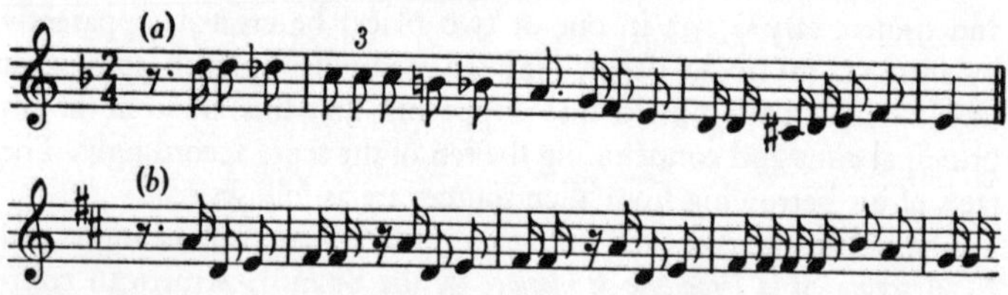

The brilliant *entr'acte* before the last act tells a similar story. It is based on a *polo* (a wild Andalusian song) from a *tonadilla* or short dramatic dialogue called *El criado fingido* by Manuel García, the father of a line of famous singers. García first sang this in Madrid in 1804, when he was an unknown minstrel of obscure (possibly gypsy) origin; his compositions bear about the same relation to Spanish folk-song as Yradier's to Spanish-American—that is to say he took elements of genuine folk idiom and embroidered them for his own purposes. His *polo* was printed in a volume called *Échos d'Espagne*,[1] brought out in 1872 by P. Lacome and J. Puig y Alsubide. Thanks to the autograph-hunting propensities of an employee of the Conservatoire library, a slip is preserved bearing the words: 'I request a list of the Spanish songs in the possession of the library.—BIZET.' According to Tiersot the only volume available was *Échos d'Espagne*; and it seems likely that this collection of Spanish songs and dances (some genuine, some bogus) was the sole documentary source for the

[1] Where however it is wrongly attributed to another *tonadilla*, *El poeta calculista*, written a year later. This contains a similar *polo*; it is possible that both had the same folk origin. *See* Julien Tiersot's article in *The Musical Quarterly*, October 1927.

Spanish elements in *Carmen*.[1] But for García's *polo*, all the pieces are anonymous. Again Bizet transformed his original from a rambling recitation to a taut masterpiece. García's two main themes are:

Bizet follows him in emphasizing and concluding on the dominant: this is a characteristic of *cante jondo* (literally 'deep song'), the folk melody of southern Spain that reflects the centuries of Moorish domination.[2] The influence of the guitar, an instrument introduced by the Moors and always used for the accompaniment of *cante jondo*, is apparent here and in other parts of the opera, such as the *chanson bohème* of Act II, where Bizet is not using Spanish material but working independently within the framework of its idiom. This is a creative process, not an imitation, and it produces music that is far more vital than many a pious resuscitation of folk material. Other features redolent of *cante flamenco* (Spanish gypsy music, a later derivative of *cante jondo*) are the treatment of the accompaniment to the *chanson bohème* in successive fifths, the irregular descending scale in the bass of the introduction to the same piece and the augmented seconds of the Carmen motive.

Istel proved that Bizet used one more Spanish tune in *Carmen*. This is the snatch of melody sung by Carmen when she defies Zuniga in Act I. The words ('Coupe-moi, brûle-moi', etc.) are taken from a translation by Mérimée of a work by Pushkin, *Les Bohémiens*; [3] the tune:

[1] In fact Bizet's library contained a copy of *Échos d'Espagne* (and also five songs by Yradier, but not *El Arreglito*). His widow's statement that he had only *Fleurs d'Espagne* is an obvious slip.

[2] Compare the lament in *Djamileh*.

[3] A variant is quoted by Liszt, *Des Bohémiens et de leur musique en Hongrie*.

a satirical song on female hair styles, comes from Ciudad Real, south of Madrid. The change of rhythm from 3–4 to 6–8 is typical of Bizet's neat modification. This may be the tune that Sarasate, a colleague of Bizet's at the Conservatoire, is supposed to have contributed to *Carmen*. But although these foreign bodies, whether they be Spanish, South American, Moorish or gypsy, do help to create that haunting and picturesque atmosphere which no amount of repetition seems to stale, they form a very small ingredient in the whole. This is a French, not a Spanish, opera, as any Spaniard will confirm; and Laparra goes much too far in calling García's *polo* the egg from which the whole of *Carmen* sprang.[1] The chief significance of the alien elements lies in the complete transformation they undergo in their passage through Bizet's imagination: they emerge as much his own as the rest of the score.

Bizet's use of the motto theme in *Carmen* is simple but supremely effective, thanks partly to its distinctive intervals and partly to the economy with which he manages it. Its appearances are never mechanical; it always carries a load of dramatic irony. Like the Yorick motive in *La Coupe du Roi de Thulé* it has what may be called objective and subjective forms depending on the character whose emotions are uppermost:

Pushkin's play is the source of a number of operas, including Rakhmaninov's *Aleko*, where the same words appear.

[1] He even tries to show that the leading motive is thematically derived from it.

The prelude form is quoted second, for there can be no doubt that Istel is right in maintaining that (*a*) is, as it were, the root position. The prelude was composed after the rest of the opera, and it is manifestly designed to conjure up the atmosphere of Act IV rather than Act I. Thus (*a*) represents Carmen herself, fickle, laughing, elusive, while (*b*) stands for her fatal influence on José. In Act I (*a*) predominates; it occurs on four [1] different occasions to (*b*)'s solitary appearance when Carmen throws the flower in José's face. In Act II (*a*) appears only in the suppressed *mélodrame* between the stanzas of 'Dragon d'Alcala', but (*b*) is used very effectively on the English horn just before the flower song. In Act III we hear (*a*) when Carmen foretells her fate in the cards [2] and (*b*) at the climax of the finale, when José leaves her and her new lover with the threat of his return. In Act IV we have (*a*) muttered by the violins at José's entrance (not (*b*) because it is Carmen's fate that is foreshadowed here; we are meant to recall the card scene) and (*b*) at the climax of the duet and when José gives himself up after the murder. Bizet's theme in its two forms is admirably adapted to its purpose and is never run to death: he had learned restraint since *Les Pêcheurs de perles*. And if contrast were needed, it is supplied by the scoring. There is a world of difference between (*a*) on the flute and on the cellos and basses (before and after Carmen reads the cards), and (*b*) on the English horn (Act II) and the full orchestra (Act IV).

The variety of aspects under which Bizet will present a theme without subjecting it to symphonic treatment in the Wagnerian manner is astonishing. The delightful tune of the duet 'Là-bas, là-bas, dans la montagne' in Act II is made to evoke anything from wistful nostalgia to a rousing paean in honour of 'la chose enivrante, la liberté!' Even the habanera and the refrain of Escamillo's *couplets*

[1] Originally five, including Carmen's entry during the quarrel (*see* p. 217).

[2] Perhaps also in the duet for José and Escamillo at the latter's words 'C'est une Zingara, mon cher' (p. 288). If this is not a coincidence, it almost qualifies as a third version of the theme.

undergo such transformations, the former generating profound suspense in D flat over sustained chords on the strings just before Carmen's escape in Act I,[1] and the latter (in the same key) with its clinging organ-like harmonies painting a vivid picture of the self-satisfied Escamillo leaving the smugglers' den.[2] The amount of contrapuntal ingenuity to which this bold-as-brass tune is subjected almost redeems it for the most refined ears. One of the great moments of the opera is the orchestral counter-theme added to it during the murder of Carmen: crude and naïve on paper, this is overwhelming in the theatre. Another such felicity is the combination of the recall theme (two cornets) with Carmen's dance in Act II; it is so simple and so fluent as almost to escape attention:[3]

[1] The suspense here is purely musical. We know exactly what is going to happen (even if we do not know the story, Carmen has just told us), yet the moment never loses its thrill.

[2] This passage was originally scored for cellos only in four parts.

[3] Bound up with the autograph is a faint pencil sketch in which the themes are tried out in combination.

Bizet's counterpoint usually serves a dramatic purpose. The fugue that accompanies the bustle of Carmen's escape in Act I stands as an action piece beside the battle fugue in Verdi's *Macbeth*. Nor did Bizet the miniaturist die with *L'Arlésienne*: the twenty bars for solo clarinet and bassoon in the *entr'acte* to Act II are exquisite, and the finely drawn lines of the next *entr'acte* rise to the height of lyrical intensity. With this we may couple his almost Schubertian unexpectedness in modulation. He needed less space in which to take the remotest tonal corners than almost any composer before him. Often—as in the seguidilla—his modulations seem on paper so reckless as to disintegrate the fabric of the music, yet in performance he always triumphs. It is the same with his transitions. With all his impetuosity he had an impeccable and very French sense of style in the finish of a piece or its junction with its successor.[1] It is this combination of passion and restraint that gives the opera its chief musical distinction.

It would be easy to expend a whole chapter on the scoring of *Carmen*, which sets the crown on Bizet's claim as one of the supreme masters of the orchestra. He was far in advance of his French contemporaries. Richard Strauss told Georg Szell that if he had to give advice to young composers he would say: 'If you want to learn how to orchestrate, don't study Wagner's scores, study the score of *Carmen*. . . . What wonderful economy,' he said, 'and how every note and every rest is in its proper place.'[2] It is interesting to compare Bizet's method with Wagner's. Both used the orchestra, not in the traditional stage manner as a skeleton to support the voice (for long Verdi's chief resource), but to create a world of sound in which the characters have their being. But whereas Wagner, with a different purpose in view, often produces an impression of stress and turmoil in which the voices have to struggle to be heard, Bizet's aim was always clarity and cooperation. Wagner's orchestra might be likened to the elements

[1] See for instance the departure of Escamillo in Act II and the smugglers in Act III, or the link between the flower song and 'Là-bas, là-bas, dans la montagne', always ruined in the theatre by applause. Bizet may have planned his codas as transitions to the spoken dialogue. Méhul had done something similar in *Mélidore et Phrosyne*, an opera of which Bizet possessed a full score.

[2] *The Gramophone*, Feb. 1971, p. 1291.

against which the voices strive; Bizet's supplies the air they breathe. His scoring has something of the sharp outline and virility of Berlioz (whose famous treatise he admired and recommended to his pupils), combined with the grace and economy of Mozart. It is remarkably supple; its specific gravity varies with the dramatic situation, from the blatancy of the bullfighting music to the mountain air and flute-coloured serenity of the *entr'acte* to Act III, from the rustling of the muted strings in the cigarette girls' chorus, which Nietzsche likened to a breath from the garden of Epicurus, to the electric expectancy of the last *entr'acte*. Although the extremes of noise and delicacy are both employed, the listener is seldom conscious of any overloading or undue thinning of the texture: problems of balance seem to have been solved almost before they were posed. What could be more imaginative or more economical than the short passage in Act IV when Frasquita and Mercedes warn Carmen that José is in the crowd? The simple tune for the flutes in thirds with the bassoons in contrary motion against it has a Mozartian charm that might seem absurdly out of place: yet in conjunction with a single cornet,[1] which has but two notes throughout the scene (thirty-one bars), it suggests incomparably the hidden danger, the sign as yet no larger than a man's hand that Carmen's basking in Escamillo's triumph is to be short-lived. Played on the piano the passage sounds almost commonplace.

All through the opera Bizet uses the wind instruments with great subtlety, variety and sureness of effect. The shrill chorus of the street urchins marching behind the soldiers as they change the guard is introduced by two piccolos, cornet and plucked strings. A single low D on solo clarinet (page 287 of Peters full score) paints Carmen's amazed anger when José says he must answer the recall to barracks. As Carmen foretells her death in the cards, the gradual piling up of the heavy brass suggests the full weight of destiny poised to destroy a single human life. (This passage is followed by one of Bizet's most breath-taking transitions, a little phrase of six quavers on second violins and cellos in octaves leading back to the cheerful ditty in which Frasquita and Mercedes began to foretell their own happy futures.) The colour of the *entr'acte* to Act IV is unique, with its blend

[1] In the Peters and Oeser full scores the cornets are, quite without authority, replaced by trumpets.

of the picturesque and the sinister in the sinuous tune for solo piccolo and clarinet two octaves apart. Of all the wind instruments it is the flute on which Bizet lavishes most care. Its low notes, remote and often ineffective, are exploited as well as the more familiar upper register. In the seguidilla, besides leading off with the main theme,[1] the first flute, beginning on its bottom D, indulges in a grotesque little canon with Carmen herself as she plays the harlot with José. A few moments earlier, again at the bottom of its compass, it has been echoing her contemptuous laughter at her captors. At the end of the duet 'Là-bas, là-bas, dans la montagne' it lingers nostalgically in the distance (*ppp*) over a sustained chord (*pppp*) on four horns—to be followed by another lovely transition passage for violins in four parts and violas. It is difficult not to mention once more that masterpiece of rich yet delicate scoring, the *entr'acte* to Act III, in which all the woodwind soloists, including the English horn (which makes only two other appearances in the opera), combine with the harp and some very attractive string writing to weave a spell of rare magic. Bizet gives comparatively few opportunities to solo strings, but the ironic commentary by the solo violin in the duet 'Je suis Escamillo', when that worthy is telling José (who does not know him) that Carmen's affections have already left her soldier-friend, should not escape notice.

Carmen is one of the comparatively few operas that are at once a treasure for musicians [2] and a sure success with the public. It owes this position to a rare equilibrium between the musician and the dramatist in Bizet. Just as his musicianship ensured a stylistic balance between *élan* and finish, so in his handling of the drama he could give

[1] These eight introductory bars, and the two opening bars of the duet 'Je vais danser' in Act II, also for flute, were afterthoughts added in the margin of the autograph.

[2] The list of its admirers among other composers is unusually comprehensive, including such opposites as Brahms and Wagner, Gounod and Wolf, Tchaikovsky and Busoni, Debussy and Saint-Saëns, Puccini and Stravinsky, Stanford and Delius, Grieg and Prokofiev. *See* John W. Klein, 'Bizet's Admirers and Detractors', in *Music & Letters*, October 1938. We might add Queen Victoria, Bismarck (who saw the opera twenty-seven times), John Galsworthy and James Joyce.

the fullest expression to the passions of the characters (and in *Carmen* they tear at the roots of human nature) while standing apart and allowing their fate to move us. He writes as it were from inside and outside at the same time; he does not distort or load the dice; he makes no extraneous assault on the emotions, as Puccini does. He thus conveys the same impression as Mérimée of reality heightened by art, of a perilous proximity to everyday life [1] combined with a timeless detachment from it. It was this freedom from moral preoccupation (so unlike Wagner, and so rare in the nineteenth century) that impressed Nietzsche, the maligned author of some of the most sensible criticism of *Carmen*, when he was seeking a personal antidote to Wagner. His opposition of Bizet to Wagner is by no means the nonsense it has been called, for the two stand at opposite poles: in Wagner's music-dramas the most interesting character is Wagner himself, whereas Bizet's object was to present his characters in the round and withdraw his own personality into the background (he did this so successfully that he has been accused of having no personality at all). Wagner wrote symphonic music in dramatic form, but the symphonic interest predominates. Bizet brought the more orthodox operatic tradition to a climax by making music and drama reinforce one another at every turn instead of standing in each other's light. All his powers are subordinated to this end, and they enable him to achieve that synthesis of two wilful and not easily reconcilable arts to which opera aspires but very seldom attains. Bizet may not rank with the greatest composers—though he might have reached this position had he lived—but in *Carmen* he achieved one of the finest musico-dramatic creations of any age.

[1] It is possible that Mérimée's story was based on personal experience. A *soi-disant* descendant of Carmen even appeared in 1907. She claimed to be the child of Carmen's daughter and a British artilleryman at Gibraltar.

CHAPTER XII

DEVELOPMENT AND MUSICAL PERSONALITY

BIZET'S development as an artist presents a curious problem, on which his biographers have shed little light. Until the discovery of the Symphony it was generally held (despite other evidence to the contrary) that he developed very slowly, taking a good twelve years to free himself from the cramping influences around him. But the Symphony cannot be explained on this hypothesis. It bears alien influences, of course, but possesses a maturity astonishing in a boy of seventeen; above all, it is completely free from doubts and hesitations. It goes straight to the mark. How did it come about that a composer who wrote this at seventeen could fall so adrift in after years and only fulfil its promise in the last few years of his life? What eclipsed the spontaneity of his earliest and latest work?

The answer is to be found in the letters written from Rome in the winter of 1858–9. They supply two interrelated reasons, one mainly artistic, the other psychological. At the age of twenty Bizet began to be assailed by the doubts that afflict all young artists. Delmas printed an interesting letter to a painter written in December 1858:

> Like you I am afraid, and like you I begin many things with ardour and get discouraged the moment I finish them, when I see I have not done what I wanted to do. Yet I have taken a big step forward since leaving Paris: at the Conservatoire I was a good pupil; here I am beginning to think myself an artist, I go forward alone, but what howlers, what failures! Truly happy is he who avoids breaking his neck amid the obscurities of art. Yet I have a living light to guide me, I have a goal, I know what is good and what is beautiful; there are moments when I think I am getting there, and then a big cloud descends on me and I have to start groping again.... Happy the men who, like Raphael, Mozart, Correggio, Rossini, have received from heaven the artistic gift in all its purity and perfection; happy also those who, like Michelangelo and Beethoven, have by the power of their *reason* and their genius come to discover the last word in greatness and beauty. It would really be wonderful to put one's name even

in the margin of the golden book of intelligence! Quiet! If anyone heard us they wouldn't understand, they would take our ambition for conceited folly; let us await the future in silence and say only this: whatever happens, we shall always be among the privileged, for we love and understand beauty. Yes, I certainly thank God every day for having made me like this. . . . I see many who don't think as I do. They haven't my artistic worries and doubts, but they haven't my joys either, and I pity them.

On the last day of the year he developed this in a letter to Hector Gruyer:

There are two sorts of genius: natural genius and rational genius. While immensely admiring the second, I shall not conceal from you that the first has all my sympathies. Yes, I dare to prefer Raphael to Michelangelo, Mozart to Beethoven, and Rossini to Meyerbeer. . . . It is solely a matter of taste, one type of ideas has a greater attraction for me than the other. When I see the 'Last Judgment', when I hear the Eroica Sympathy or the fourth act of *Les Huguenots*, I am moved, surprised, I have not enough eyes, ears or intelligence to admire with. But when I see the 'School of Athens', the 'Dispute of the Holy Sacrament', the 'Virgin of Foligno', when I hear the *Marriage of Figaro* or the second act of *William Tell*, I am completely happy. I experience a sense of perfect well-being and satisfaction, I forget everything. Oh, how lucky one is to be thus favoured!

He was always trying to find an underlying correspondence between the arts.

All the arts touch, or rather there is only one art. Whether one expresses one's ideas on canvas, in marble or in the theatre is of little importance: the idea is always the same. I am more than ever convinced that Mozart and Rossini are the two greatest musicians. While admiring Beethoven and Meyerbeer with all my faculties, I feel my nature brings me to love art that is pure and fluent rather than dramatic passion. It is the same in painting —Raphael is the same man as Mozart; Meyerbeer feels as Michelangelo felt.

We may smile at Bizet's examples (nearly everyone at that date overrated Meyerbeer), but the broad distinction between the two types of genius is familiar to all students of the arts, especially of music; and there is no doubt that Bizet was right in feeling that his true place was with Mozart and Rossini. This was the Bizet of the Symphony and *Don Procopio*, and of *L'Arlésienne* and *Carmen*, the Bizet who so often finds as if by instinct the touch that redeems some old formula from the commonplace and gives it a new bloom. But it was not the only Bizet: about the same time he began to feel that he was letting his music come too easily. 'Happily I have made great progress,' he wrote in October:

I can *rewrite*, and I am profiting by it. You know that in Paris, when I composed anything, I could never begin it again; here, on the contrary, I am delighted to do so. Another sign of progress: it seems to me that all my facility and musical *triture* is no longer any use to me; I can do nothing without an idea. . . . I have enormous trouble in composing.

Another letter in much the same terms has been quoted in Chapter II. This greater self-consciousness has been taken as a sign of advance; but in a composer of Bizet's type this by no means follows. For him self-consciousness is the supreme danger. If any ulterior aim interposes itself between his response to a stimulus and its realization, the result is apt to be spoiled. Like Carmen's love, natural genius will not be tamed; it must be free. Even Mozart, the prince of instinctive composers, found his muse constrained when he had to accommodate it to the King of Prussia's cello. With Bizet the results were more serious. In his middle works, beginning with *Vasco de Gama*—the next thing he wrote after that winter—though much is gained, the freshness is partly lost. We are conscious of effort, of a forcing of the inspiration into channels for which nature never intended it, in particular of an attempt to achieve the heroic. He proposed in 1859 to write 'something tragic and purely German', and this remained his ambition for many years. In March 1867 he was ashamed to confess to Lacombe his natural susceptibility to Italian music:

I am German by conviction, heart and soul, but I sometimes get lost in artistic houses of ill fame. And I confess to you under my breath, I find infinite pleasure there. I love Italian music as one loves a courtesan. . . . Like you, I put Beethoven at the head of the greatest and most excellent. The choral Symphony is for me the culminating point of our art. Dante, Michelangelo, Shakespeare, Homer, Beethoven, Moses! Neither Mozart with his heavenly form, nor Weber with his powerful and colossal originality, nor Meyerbeer with his mighty dramatic genius, can in my opinion dispute the palm with the Titan, the Prometheus of music.

Beethoven has ousted Mozart, Raphael has yielded to Michelangelo. At the same time comes a renewed emphasis on absolute music: he advises Lacombe not to write for the stage till he knows what he wants to do, but 'one must write symphonies'. He is suspicious of music that sounds like improvisation: only Chopin succeeded in that, and he is a bad model. Rational genius is now supreme; natural genius, it seems, is an illicit love. But who is Bizet's example in the cult of German music? Not a German at all, but Charles Gounod; and a less suitable model he could not have found. For Gounod was not only a less original composer than the Germans (Weber, Mendelssohn, Schumann) who also influenced Bizet at this period; he had taken the same wrong turning as Bizet. It was a case of the blind leading the blind. Instead of developing his charming lyrical gift, he had in *Faust* tackled a subject far too big for him and in *La Reine de Saba* set himself to outdo Meyerbeer; and his attempts to write heroic and religious music were calamitous. Bizet imitated him with distressing faithfulness, especially in *Ivan IV*. He did work through this cult of the monumental, which swamped the less vital Gounod, but not till the end of the sixties; it reared its head even later in *Patrie* and *Don Rodrigue*; and we may perhaps be thankful that *Geneviève de Paris* never saw the light. The whole process began in Rome when Bizet discovered the need for an 'idea' and set out to compose German music.

The second reason for his decline explains why he succumbed to the first. He lacked the self-knowledge to understand, and the strength of character to correct, his deviations from the course marked out for him by nature. This was not due to any lack of creative vitality, or to want of trying, still less to deliberate stifling of his gifts. The letters show clearly where the fault lay. Somewhere deep within him, in regions it is now impossible to explore (it may or may not be connected with too easy success in childhood), there lay a basic lack of self-confidence which was for ever inhibiting surrender to his creative impulses. 'You accuse me of having too little stability in my ideas,' he wrote to his parents, 'and appearances support you.' His vacillation between one operatic project and another might be set down to youth's propensity for false starts, did it not persist throughout his life. Bizet in less than twenty years must have left more operas unfinished than almost any composer who ever lived. What appeared a splendid idea one day was condemned as hopeless the next. The symptom of the trouble was fear. 'I am afraid of my return,' he wrote in the letter of October 1858 quoted above,

> I am afraid of contact with the directors and the makers of stage pieces, whom I do not dignify with the name of poets. I am afraid of the singers; I am afraid, in a word, of that silent ill will which says nothing disagreeable to your face but obstinately prevents your going ahead.

The only way he could see of killing this fear was to prove to himself that he was a success. We have seen how this need for self-esteem (and hence for the esteem of others) not only led him to pursue false gods and deprive the world of much that it had a right to expect, but brought very little material reward. A letter of March 1859 in which he discusses the recent failures of French operatic composers is revealing. He finds Massé deficient in style and breadth of conception and sees a want of experience in Félicien David, but the chief lack—and he applies this even to Gounod—is

> the sole means a composer has of making himself understood by the public today: the *motif*, wrongly called the idea. One can be a great artist without having the *motif*—it is then necessary to renounce money and popular success—but one can also be a superior artist and possess this precious gift, witness Rossini. Rossini is the greatest of all [*sc.* contemporaries] because like Mozart he has all the qualities: loftiness, style and last of all —the *motif*.

Bizet goes on to claim that he has found the *motif* in comic opera (in *Don Procopio*); next year he will look for it in grand opera, which is much more difficult. He couples this with one of those asseverations that seem designed to encourage himself as much as his mother. 'I know what I am doing and what I am worth, and when I say "I have arrived" there will be many other people of the same opinion.' Whatever Bizet meant by the *motif*, he was clearly running a risk in the emphasis he laid on the need for being understood by the public. The composer with something to say must train his public (difficult as this was in nineteenth-century France), not follow it; and if a large measure of incomprehensibility has attained a certain snob-value in recent years, it remains a fault on the right side.

However grave this defect in Bizet's moral make-up, it is very far from being the cynical betrayal of his art that certain critics have denounced. Works like *L'Arlésienne* and *Carmen* are not written by mistake, as Landormy seems to suppose. Moreover, nearly all the pronouncements quoted against Bizet date from his twenty-second year or earlier, an age when any amount of brash theorizing and self-justification is surely forgivable. There is nothing cynical about his reflections in 1871 on the public attitude towards talent and ideas as exemplified by the experience of Auber and Berlioz; [1] and recently discovered letters of that period furnish clear evidence that his standpoint and his character had matured considerably since his Rome years [2]—a development not without a bearing on *L'Arlésienne* and *Carmen*. In any case it is neither profitable nor becoming for the essentially barren race of critics to take up a lofty moral tone towards creative artists. Bizet needed sympathy, and if we are to understand him his memory still needs it. He was sadly ill-equipped to deal with failure. 'In order to succeed today you have to be either dead or German,' he wrote to Gallet; and to Galabert: 'To be a musician today you must have an assured independent income or else a real talent in diplomacy.' Bizet had none of these assets, and although death did give a boost to his reputation, this was followed by an extreme reaction that has scarcely yet been corrected.

What, then, is his position in the history of music? His contributions to the progress of opera were considerable, but they have been obscured by two facts: they are clearer in the dramatic than the musical sphere, and they have not been followed up. In 1869 he set himself to revolutionize *opéra-comique*. The form had become nearly as fossilized as grand opera. Originally a reaction against the inflated heroics of the larger institution, it had ceased to represent real-life characters and descended to the reproduction of types. With the dubious exception of *Mignon*, no French *opéra-comique* between *Fra Diavolo* (1830) and *Carmen* has kept the stage. By giving the form a blood transfusion from real life, including its tragic elements, Bizet killed the stale *buffo* and sentimental types. He went some way towards

[1] *See* p. 90. [2] *See* pp. 92–4.

finishing off the old grand opera as well: one of the clearest results of *Carmen* was that the two kinds of opera ceased to diverge and gave place to a single intermediate form. In the operas of Massenet the old distinctions, including that of spoken dialogue, lost their validity. At the same time Bizet helped to break the tyranny of the singer, which by the suppression of dramatic unity was threatening—as it had done a century earlier in the age of Metastasio—to kill opera as an art (especially in Italy and France) and turn it into a concert in fancy dress. He thus brought the contest between drama and music which is the history of opera to a fresh climax. Then, all too soon, he died. He founded no school, and none of his successors had the power to carry on where he left off. In Italy Puccini developed the *verismo* side of *Carmen* till it became threadbare. In France the slender talent of Massenet inclined more and more to Gounod rather than Bizet, and the one composer with enough vitality to extend the *genre*, Emmanuel Chabrier, allowed his senses to be seduced by the odour of Bayreuth. For in the years following Bizet's death France went Wagner-mad. *Carmen*, damned as Wagnerian in 1875, passed suddenly from the spearpoint of advance into the cul-de-sac of reaction, and was condemned for the lack of those very qualities that had been found so dangerous ten years before. Doubtless Bizet would have advanced beyond *Carmen* by that time, especially in the harmonic sphere; but he was no longer alive to hold his position in the race. After the Wagner furore the last chance of a Bizet school of opera had vanished.

One result of this reaction was that French critics, judging *Carmen* by Wagnerian standards, found it tame and tentative. But though Bizet was not a revolutionary like Wagner or Liszt, he was an innovator in his own way, the typical French method of beginning from the inside and working outwards. He used old devices to open up new lines of advance; and it is possible to consider this a more progressive process than the use of new devices to say what has often been said before—the operatic method of Richard Strauss. Bizet's innovations were just sufficient to serve his own purposes; it would be churlish to demand more. The composers who lay up a stock of technical material for their successors, like Liszt, are seldom gifted with first-rate creative power; perhaps it is their method of compensating for the defect. The artist with something to say is generally too busy to experiment in a vacuum.

Bizet was not entirely without influence on his successors. Chabrier certainly and Ravel probably owed him something. But he left the clearest mark on a composer of a very different temperament—Tchaikovsky. What may be called the Frédéri-José element, which we have seen was implicit in Bizet as early as the unpublished *Romance sans paroles* and first became explicit in *La Coupe du Roi de Thulé*, exercised a growing fascination over Tchaikovsky towards the end of his life. Perhaps he saw in the passion-torn José something of himself; at any rate his later work, especially the first movement of the B minor Symphony, is full of echoes of Bizet's tragic heroes. Compare the melody, texture and harmony of its second subject with this from José's flower song:

There is no space to add to what has been said on the musical development of Bizet's style and his mastery of the orchestra. But his wonderful melodic gift has sometimes received less than justice. It was indeed related to Gounod through what may be termed the female line, but there was far more to it than that. Gounod's melody at its best, as in the opening theme of the *Mireille* overture, is charming, but it is subject to the same limitations as Mendelssohn's, being apt when lively to fall into an amiable jogtrot, when tender into sentimentality. Bizet's has greater energy, variety and flexibility. The length and the compass of many of his tunes are alike remarkable. The main melody of the *entr'acte* to Act III of *Carmen* and 'L'Innocent's' theme from *L'Arlésienne* have a range of two octaves and extend for ten and a half and sixteen bars respectively of unbroken melody in slow time; the *Maestoso* march when Paddock enters with the cup in Act I of *La Coupe du Roi de Thulé* is even longer, running to nineteen bars; all three are beautifully balanced and articulated to escape a too regular symmetry. He had an easy command of the two extremes of movement, by steps and leaps, and often happily combined them; in Carmen's seguidilla, where there is also great freedom of modulation, the effect is extraordinarily individual. He was a master of the paragraph, and by judicious control over rhythm and the rise and fall of the melody produced whole numbers that seem to spring forth complete from the first bar to the last. From the earliest days he had shown skill in extending a melody a little longer than the ear expects, and his approach to a cadence often has a character of its own. When he combined these qualities in a single piece, as in José's flower song or the *Arlésienne* Adagietto, he produced gems of a singular perfection—quite apart from their dramatic connotations.

Rhythmically the influence of Gounod was more dangerous, but even at the worst period it was never exclusive. Some credit should probably go to Félicien David for the quasi-oriental rhythms which, though monotonous in themselves, helped to liberate Bizet from the four-squareness of Gounod. They enabled him to give continuity to a piece by treating them in the manner of an elementary passacaglia. This process reached its climax in the Ghazel and Almée of *Djamileh*. But the chief counter-agent to Gounod was Verdi, whose rhythmic energy (in his early work) seemed to be concentrated on the propulsion of the melody, leaving a subordinate function to the accompaniment. With Gounod the tendency was all the other way, a weak melody often reposing on a rich accompaniment; and Bizet did need some thrust to overcome the paralytic grip of the four-bar sequence, especially in the heroic parts of his middle-period operas. Later he could write square melodies, such as the tenors' welcome to the cigarette girls ('La cloche a sonné') in Act I of *Carmen*, that retain their freshness. The much-abused refrain of Escamillo's *couplets* need only be compared with the thrice-repeated rhythm of the soldiers' chorus in *Faust* for the saving grace of its rhythmic variety to be appreciated. French music has not been fertile in melodic invention, having contented itself for the most part with two or three types of tune. Bizet ranks with the still more individual Berlioz among its few outstanding melodists.

His work at all periods bears certain well-marked fingerprints. His very personal use of chromatic harmony over a pedal (by no means reserved for the conventional suggestion of the bucolic) has already been noted. There is a family resemblance, rhythmic and melodic, between the bolero in *Vasco de Gama*, the opening chorus of *Djamileh* and one of the themes of the F sharp minor chorus in *L'Arlésienne*, all designed to evoke an exotic atmosphere. José's 'Dût-il m'en coûter la vie' is several times foreshadowed, as well as being directly anticipated in *La Coupe du Roi de Thulé*. The opening phrase of the *Roma* scherzo is prominent in the first finale of *Don Procopio*, the Glover motive and Mab's *couplets* (Act I) in *La Jolie Fille de Perth*, the gaming chorus in *Djamileh* and the card scene in

Carmen; in each context except the last it suggests a cheerful bustling. The most prominent of all the fingerprints derives from a phrase in the slow movement of Mozart's clarinet Quintet:

This struck many an echo from Bizet (as it did from Mendelssohn, e.g. in the slow movement of the D minor piano Concerto). It is prominent in the duet for Leila and Zurga in *Les Pêcheurs de perles*, *Le Golfe de Baïa,* the song *Vieille Chanson,* the *Sérénade* for piano, the trio that precedes the Ghazel in *Djamileh* and most of all at Escamillo's 'Si tu m'aimes' in Act IV of *Carmen*. The resemblances are of course fortuitous and only serve to reveal certain grooves along which Bizet's mind worked in the process of creation.

There is often a link of another kind between his works. Like Bach, Handel, Berlioz and others, he had a habit of re-using earlier material. There are more than thirty instances of this process, which has little significance in itself; but it is notable how seldom the old matter adorns its new surroundings. The alien passages in *Les Pêcheurs de perles* are among the weakest in the opera, and some charming things in *Don Procopio* are damaged by translation elsewhere. Only twice—in *Trompette et tambour* and José's 'Dût-il m'en coûter la vie'—did Bizet markedly improve on his first versions; perhaps we should add the flower song, though the original in *Grisélidis* is no more than a sketch. The sources of the other insertions in *Carmen* do not survive. In his earlier work he seems to have taken up old material uncritically as it came to hand instead of passing it anew through his imagination.

He wrote his best work very rapidly. The early Symphony was finished in a month, *L'Arlésienne* in not more than two, and probably less; whereas the laboured *Roma* took him years. His method of composition was to immerse himself in his subject and write down little or nothing till the music was nearly complete in his head. With a composer of his instinctive type the success of this method depends a good deal on the quality of the original stimulus: a libretto that was inadequate, especially in construction and presentation of character (like *La Jolie Fille de Perth*), would tend to produce an uneven response. Not that he accepted his libretti without criticism: in every instance of which we have information he made considerable modifications in the text,[1] sometimes rewriting whole scenes himself. But he lacked the fertility of musical invention that could turn a triviality like the book of *Così fan tutte* into a masterpiece. Nor was he open to a great range of stimuli. Religion drew from him the sorry *Te Deum*; patriotism had no better result. He was most susceptible to certain fundamental emotions, especially sexual passion and jealousy. If his imagination was stirred he interpreted the clash of character with an intensity and objectivity of vision rare in any age and almost unknown among his contemporaries with the exception of Verdi. Here is the compensation for his lack of a strong directive personality or moral preoccupation. He could sink himself in his characters. To very few is it given to enter into the natures of such diverse human beings as it was to Bizet. In his best work the characters never shout and thump a tub; whenever this happens, it is Bizet ventriloquizing and trying to supply at a conscious level what his libretto failed to inspire.

Bizet had it in him to be the greatest musical dramatist of his age. Where Wagner's characters were legendary, Meyerbeer's historical, Gounod's classical and Verdi's at first those of romantic melodrama, Bizet's in his two greatest works were of his own century and of the common people. He steered a course equally remote from the disguised symphonist Wagner and the calculating eclectic Meyerbeer. There are two kinds of effect in the theatre—effect for effect's sake and effect to reinforce the impact of the drama. The former, which was Meyerbeer's method, calls attention only to itself; the latter, which was Bizet's, is willing to conceal itself if it contributes to the whole. Meyerbeer, who introduced a ballet of bathing belles in *Les Huguenots*, would hardly have been content with less than a Highland Rally, complete with a caber-tossing demonstration by Henry Smith, in *La Jolie Fille de Perth*. It is Verdi to whom Bizet stands closest—Verdi who was thirty-nine when he uttered the irresistible crudities of *Il*

[1] See in particular his correspondence with Galabert about *La Coupe du Roi de Thulé* and with Gallet about *Don Rodrigue*.

Trovatore and over seventy before he reached the height of his powers. It is well to remember that had Verdi died at thirty-six, as Bizet did, we should scarcely have known his name.

Chantavoine draws an interesting parallel between Bizet and a composer who died at almost the same age, Mozart. He emphasizes the similar equilibrium between novelty and tradition and between the theatrical and symphonic (orchestral) elements, adding that '*Carmen* is perhaps the only work of the lyric theatre in which the balance of *Don Giovanni* is reborn'. As we have seen, Bizet himself felt this affinity. Both composers have puzzled the moralizing type of critic, who has complained of a lack of creative anguish and found little apparent correspondence between the men and their art. This of course is a perilous criterion, which accounts for the periodical depreciation, especially in England, of the natural genius in favour of the rational, more self-conscious type of artist.

Equally to the point is Chantavoine's comparison between Bizet's common sense, free from arrogance and vanity, the painful fastidiousness of Debussy and the sceptical intelligence that ultimately sterilized Dukas's creative gift. For however often Bizet proclaimed that his heart was Italian or German, however remote from France his operatic travels (not a single one of his operas, finished or unfinished—with the sole exception of the Provençal *Calendal*—has its scene in France), he remains essentially French, the supreme musical realization, as Romain Rolland says, of one pole of the French genius. He is the counterweight, perhaps the complement, of Debussy, the clear sunshine of the Mediterranean as opposed to the twilight and the moonlight, exuberance and enthusiasm against delicate understatement. Perhaps there is less difference between the two extremes than is apparent to an outsider; perhaps every Frenchman has something of both. Certainly Debussy and Fauré, who had little superficially in common with Bizet, both ranked his genius at its true value. And they would have endorsed as wholly French the advice Bizet gave to his pupil Galabert: 'Without form, no style; without style, no art.'

APPENDIX A

CALENDAR

(Figures in brackets denote the age reached by the person mentioned during the year in question.)

Year	*Age*	*Life*	*Contemporary Musicians*
1838		Georges Bizet (registered Alexandre César Léopold) born, Oct. 25, in Paris, son of Adolphe Amand Bizet (28), a teacher of singing.	Bruch born, Jan. 6; Castillon born, Dec. 13. Adam aged 35; Alkan 25; Auber 56; Balakirev 2; Balfe 30; Benedict 34; Berlioz 35; Borodin 4; Brahms 5; Bruckner 15; Cherubini 78; Chopin 28; Cornelius 15; Cui 3; David (Félicien) 28; Dargomizhsky 25; Delibes 2; Donizetti 41; Flotow 26; Franck 16; Gade 21; Gevaert 10; Glinka 35; Gounod 20; Guilmant 1; Halévy 47; Heller 23; Liszt 27; Lortzing 35; Mendelssohn 29; Mercadante 43; Meyerbeer 47; Nicolai 28; Offenbach 19; Reyer 15; Rossini 46; Rubinstein 8; Saint-Saëns 3; Schumann 28; Smetana 14; Spohr 54; Spontini 64; Strauss (J. ii) 13; Thomas (A.) 27; Verdi 25; Wagner 25.
1839	1		Mussorgsky born, March 21; Paer (68) dies, May 3.
1840	2	Baptized (Georges) at church of Notre-Dame-de-Lorette, March 16.	Götz born, Dec. 17; Svendsen born, Sept. 3; Tchaikovsky born, May 7.
1841	3		Chabrier born, Jan. 18; Dvořák born, Sept. 8; Pedrell born, Feb. 19.
1842	4	Learns his notes from his mother at the same time as his letters.	Boito born, Feb. 24; Cherubini (82) dies, March 15; Massenet born, May 12; Sullivan born, May 13.

Appendix A—Calendar

Year	*Age*	*Life*	*Contemporary Musicians*
1843	5		Grieg born, June 15; Sgambati born, May 28.
1844	6		Rimsky-Korsakov born, March 18.
1845	7		Fauré born, May 12; Widor born, Feb. 22.
1846	8	Shows signs of remarkable aural memory. Receives elementary musical instruction from his father (36).	
1847	9	Interviewed by Meifred (56) with a view to entering the Conservatoire though under age. Sent to Marmontel's (31) piano class through the influence of his uncle Delsarte (36).	Mackenzie born, Aug. 22; Mendelssohn (38) dies, Nov. 4.
1848	10	Admitted to Conservatoire, Oct. 9.	Donizetti (51) dies, April 8; Duparc born, Jan. 21; Parry born, Feb. 27.
1849	11	Wins first prize for solfeggio. Receives private lessons in fugue and counterpoint from Zimmerman (64), whose place is sometimes taken by Gounod (31).	Chopin (39) dies, Oct. 17; Nicolai (39) dies, May 11.
1850	12	Earliest known compositions, 2 Vocalises, Feb.	
1851	13	Wins second prize for piano at first attempt.	d'Indy born, March 27; Lortzing (48) dies, Jan. 21; Spontini (77) dies, Jan. 14.
1852	14	Shares first prize for piano with Savary. Joins Benoist's (58) organ class.	Stanford born, Sept. 30.
1853	15	On Zimmerman's (68) death joins Halévy's (54) composition class.	Messager born, Dec. 30.
1854	16	Wins second prizes for organ and fugue. Composes *Grande*	Humperdinck born, Sept. 1; Janáček born, July 3

Year	Age	Life	Contemporary Musicians
		Valse de Concert and 1st *Nocturne* for piano, Sept. First published work (2 songs) issued, together with a song by his father (44).	
1855	17	Wins first prizes for organ and fugue. Recommended by Halévy to director of Opéra-Comique as 'young composer, pianist and accompanist', Sept. Composes Symphony in C major (begun Oct. 29, finished Nov.).	Chausson born, Jan. 21; Liadov born, May 11.
1856	18	Awarded second Prix de Rome for cantata *David*.	Martucci born, Jan. 6; Schumann (46) dies, July 29; Sinding born, Jan. 11; Taneiev born, Nov. 25.
1857	19	Ties with Lecocq (25) for prize offered by Offenbach for setting of one-act operetta *Le Docteur Miracle*. Bizet's operetta produced at Bouffes-Parisiens, April 9. Awarded first Prix de Rome for cantata *Clovis et Clotilde*, performed at Institut with great success, Oct. 3. Leaves for Rome with fellow-pensioners, Dec. 21.	Bruneau born, March 1; Elgar born, June 2; Glinka (54) dies, Feb. 15.
1858	20	After leisurely journey and much sight-seeing reaches Florence, Jan. 12, where he hears Verdi's *I Lombardi*. Arrives in Rome, Jan. 27, and achieves immediate success as pianist. Composes *Te Deum* for Rodrigues prize, Feb.–May. Makes friends with writer Edmond About (30). Fortnight's holiday in Alban	Hüe born, May 6; Leoncavallo born, March 8; Puccini born, June 22; Smyth (Ethel) born, April 23.

Year	*Age*	*Life*	*Contemporary Musicians*
		Hills, May – June. *Don Procopio* begun, summer.	
1859	21	*Don Procopio* finished, March. Prolonged holiday, May 15–late Oct., during which he visits Cape Circe, Terracina, Naples and Pompeii and plans many compositions never finished. Serious attack of throat trouble at Naples. Begins a second Symphony, Oct., but abandons it and destroys MS., Dec. Receives permission to spend extra year in Rome instead of Germany. Begins Ode Symphony *Vasco de Gama*, Dec.	Chevillard born, Oct. 14; Spohr (75) dies, Oct. 22.
1860	22	*Vasco de Gama* finished, March. Begins and abandons *opéra-comique L'Amour peintre* and cantata *Carmen saeculare*, Jan.–April. Joined by his friend Ernest Guiraud (23). Short tour in mountains, June. Portrait painted by Giacomotti, July. Leaves Rome with Guiraud, late July. Plans symphony *Roma*. On reaching Venice hears of his mother's (45) serious illness and hurries home, Sept.	Albéniz born, May 28; Charpentier born, June 25; Mahler born, July 7; Wolf born, March 13.
1861	23	His piano-playing impresses Liszt, May 26. Composes (or finishes) *Scherzo et Marche funèbre* for orchestra and overture *La Chasse d'Ossian*. His mother (46) dies, 8 Sept.	Bréville born, Feb. 21; Chaminade born, Aug. 8; Loeffler born, Jan. 30; MacDowell born, Dec. 18.
1862	24	Composes *opéra-comique La Guzla de l'Émir*. Assists Gounod (44) with production	Debussy born, Aug. 22; Delius born, Jan. 29; Halévy (63) dies, March 17.

Year	Age	Life	Contemporary Musicians
		of *La Reine de Saba*, Feb. Son by Marie Reiter born, June. Visits Baden for music festival with Berlioz (59), Reyer (39) and Gounod, Aug. Probably begins first version of opera *Ivan IV*.	
1863	25	Scherzo performed by Pasdeloup at Cirque Napoléon, Jan. 11; repeated on 18th. *Vasco de Gama* performed by Société Nationale des Beaux-Arts, Feb. 8. Withdraws *La Guzla de l'Émir* from rehearsal at Opéra-Comique on being offered libretto of *Les Pêcheurs de perles*, April. Opera completed early Aug.; first performed at Théâtre-Lyrique, Sept. 30, and meets with mixed reception. B.'s father (53) buys land for summer residence at Le Vésinet, Oct. 3.	Mascagni born, Dec. 7; Pierné born, Aug. 16.
1864	26	Does much hack work for publishers and theatre directors, which probably undermines his health. Accompanies rehearsals cf Berlioz's *L'Enfance du Christ*, April. Begins second version of *Ivan IV*, commissioned by Carvalho for Théâtre-Lyrique.	Meyerbeer (73) dies, May 2; Ropartz born, June 15; Strauss (R.) born, June 11.
1865	27	Production of *Ivan IV* repeatedly postponed. Score offered to Opéra, which refuses it, Dec. *Chants du Rhin* and probably other piano works written. Meets Edmond Galabert, who becomes his pupil (June), and Comtesse de	Dukas born, Oct. 1; Glazunov born, Aug. 10; Magnard born, June 9; Sibelius born, Dec. 8.

Year	*Age*	*Life*	*Contemporary Musicians*
		Chabrillan (Céleste Mogador) (41).	
1866	28	Working on *Roma*, June–July. *La Jolie Fille de Perth* begun July, finished Dec. Also composes many songs and makes innumerable arrangements of dance-music and operas for publishers; complains of overwork.	Busoni born, April 1; Satie born, May 17.
1867	29	Paul Lacombe (30) becomes his pupil (by correspondence). Hears and severely criticizes Verdi's (54) *Don Carlos*, March. Visit to Bordeaux March. Writes cantata and hymn for competitions in connection with Grand Exhibition, *c.* May. Publishes critical article in *La Revue Nationale et Étrangère*, Aug. 3, but withdraws a second article when editor wishes to tamper with it. Becomes engaged to Geneviève Halévy (18), Oct., but engagement broken off in same month. Contributes an act to composite operetta *Malbrough s'en va-t-en guerre*, produced Athénée, Dec. 13. *La Jolie Fille de Perth* produced at Théâtre-Lyrique after long delays, Dec. 26.	Granados born, July 29; Koechlin born, Nov. 27.
1868	30	Visits Brussels and Antwerp, April. Makes first attempt to complete Halévy's *Noé*, finishes *Roma*, Aug., and composes songs and piano music, including *Variations chromatiques*, July. Serious attacks of quinsy	Bantock born, Aug. 7; Rossini (76) dies, Nov. 13.

Year	Age	Life	Contemporary Musicians
		July and Aug., accompanied by spiritual crisis, during which he begins to set *La Coupe du Roi de Thulé* for Opéra competition, Aug.–Oct.	
1869	31	Finishes *La Coupe du Roi de Thulé* and submits it, but takes pains to conceal his participation. Invited by du Locle to change the *genre* of *opéra-comique*. *Roma* performed by Pasdeloup (without scherzo) under title *Fantaisie symphonique, Souvenirs de Rome*, Feb. 28. Marries Geneviève Halévy (20), June 3. Completes *Noé* at second attempt, Nov.	Berlioz (66) dies, March 8; Dargomizhsky (56) dies, Jan. 17; Pfitzner born, May 5; Roussel born, April 5.
1870	32	Working at *Clarissa Harlowe* and *Grisélidis*. Holiday at Barbizon interrupted by outbreak of Franco-Prussian War, July 19. B. joins National Guard and remains in Paris throughout siege.	Balfe (62) dies, Oct. 20; Mercandante (75) dies, Dec. 17; Novák born, Dec. 5; Schmitt born, Sept. 28.
1871	33	Visit to Bordeaux, where his wife has nervous breakdown, Feb. Leaves Paris for Le Vésinet after insurrection of Commune, March 18. Resumes work on *Clarissa Harlowe* and *Grisélidis*, but latter rejected by Opéra-Comique, on ground of expense. *Djamileh* offered instead; music composed late summer. *Roma* revised and *Jeux d'enfants* written, Sept.? Resigned appointment as chorus-master at Opéra, Oct.	Auber (89) dies, May 12.

Year	Age	Life	Contemporary Musicians
1872	34	*Djamileh* produced at Opéra-Comique, May 22; a failure. B.'s son Jacques born, July 10. Incidental music to *L'Arlésienne* composed rapidly during summer and produced at Vaudeville, Oct. 1. Another failure, but orchestral suite performed with immediate success by Pasdeloup (53), Nov. 10.	Skriabin born, Jan. 4; Vaughan Williams born, Oct. 12.
1873	35	B. acts for Gounod (55), then in London, in revival of *Roméo et Juliette* at Opéra-Comique, Jan. 20. *Petite Suite d'orchestre* from *Jeux d'enfants* performed at first Colonne concert, March 2. *Carmen* begun (spring), but dropped owing to difficulties with Opéra-Comique. *Don Rodrigue* composed during summer, but abandoned when Opéra burned down, Oct. 28.	Rakhmaninov born, April 1; Reger born, March 19; Séverac born, July 20.
1874	36	Overture *Patrie* performed by Pasdeloup (55), Feb. 15. Completes *Carmen*. Rehearsals begun, Oct. During winter B. attends Franck's (52) organ class.	Cornelius (50) dies, Oct. 26; Holst born, Sept. 21; Schoenberg born, Sept. 13; Suk born, Jan. 4.
1875		Appointment as chevalier of Legion of Honour announced, March 3. *Carmen* produced at Opéra-Comique, March 3. B. is taken seriously ill, late March. Slow recovery leads to relapse, May, and Bizet dies at Bougival nr Paris, June 3.	Coleridge-Taylor born, Aug. 15; Ravel born, March 7; Roger-Ducasse born, April 18.

APPEN-

CATALOGUE

(*Autographs * Bibliothèque Nationale, Paris;* †

I. DRA-

	Title	Author of Words	Date of Composition
1.	Opéra-comique, 'La Maison du docteur' (1 act)	Henry Boisseaux	*c.* 1855
2.	Operetta, 'Le Docteur Miracle' (1 act)	Léon Battu and Ludovic Halévy	1856
3.	Opera, 'Parisina'	Felice Romani	1858
4.	Opéra-comique (1 act) [title unknown]	Edmond About	1858
5.	Opera buffa, 'Don Procopio' (2 acts)	Carlo Cambiaggio	1858-9
6.	Opera, 'Esmeralda'	Victor Hugo	1859
7.	Opera, 'Le Tonnelier de Nuremberg' (3 acts)	E. T. A. Hoffmann (based on)	1859
8.	Opera, 'Don Quichotte'	Cervantes (based on)	1859
9.	Opéra-comique, 'L'Amour peintre'	Bizet, based on Molière	1860
10.	Operetta, 'La Prêtresse' (1 act)	Philippe Gille	?
11.	Opéra-comique, 'La Guzla de l'Émir' (1 act)	Jules Barbier and Michel Carré	1862
12.	Opera, 'Ivan IV' (5 acts)	François Hippolyte Leroy and Henri Trianon	?1862-3, revised 1864-5
13.	Opera, 'Les Pêcheurs de perles' (3 acts)	Michel Carré and E. Cormon	1863
14.	Opera, 'Nicolas Flamel'	Ernest Dubreuil	? 1865
15.	Opera, 'La Jolie Fille de Perth' (4 acts)	J. H. Vernoy de Saint-Georges and Jules Adenis	1866
16.	Operetta, 'Malbrough s'en va-t-en guerre' (4 acts)	Paul Siraudin and William Busnach	1867
17.	Opera [title unknown]	Arthur Leroy and Thomas Sauvage	1868

DIX B

OF WORKS

Stiftelsen Musikkulturens Främjande, Stockholm.)

MATIC

First known Performance	*First Publication*	*Remarks*
? None	None	* (Vocal score only)
9 Apr. 1857	Editions françaises de musique 1962	*
None	None	Projected; perhaps not begun
None	None	Projected; probably not begun
10 Mar. 1906	Choudens 1905 (vocal score; full score 1906)	* Differing in essentials from published scores
None	None	Projected; probably not begun
None	None	Projected; probably not begun
None	None	Projected; probably not begun
None	None	Unfinished; probably destroyed
? None	None	Autograph sketch survives
None	None	Probably destroyed
1946	Choudens 1951 (vocal score)	* (Act V unfinished); published score unreliable
30 Sept. 1863	Choudens 1863 (vocal score only; full score much later)	1863 score differs in essentials from all later scores until 1975
None	None	Projected; partly sketched at piano
26 Dec. 1867	Choudens 1868 (vocal score only; full score *c.* 1891)	* 1868 score differs in essentials from all later scores
13 Dec. 1867	None	Act I only by Bizet; probably destroyed
None	None	Projected

I. Dramatic

	Title	Author of Words	Date of Composition
18.	Opera, 'La Coupe du Roi de Thulé' (3 acts)	Louis Gallet and Édouard Blau	1868–9
19.	Opera, 'Les Templiers' (5 acts)	Léon Halévy and Saint-Georges	1868
20.	Opera, 'Noé' (3 acts)	J. H. Vernoy de Saint-Georges	1868–9
21.	Opera, 'Vercingétorix'	Émile Délérot	1869
22.	Opera on Caucasian subject	?	?
23.	Opéra-comique, 'Calendal' (4 acts)	Paul Ferrier	1870
24.	Opera, 'Rama' (4 acts)	Eugène Crépet	*c.* 1870
25.	Opéra-comique, 'Clarissa Harlowe' (3 acts)	Philippe Gille and Adolphe Jaime the younger	1870–1
26.	Opéra-comique, 'Grisélidis' (3 acts)	Victorien Sardou	1870–1
27.	Opéra-comique, 'Djamileh' (1 act)	Louis Gallet	1871
28.	Incidental music, 'L'Arlésienne'	Alphonse Daudet	1872
29.	Operetta, 'Sol-si-ré-pif-pan (1 act)	William Busnach	1872
30.	Opera, 'Don Rodrigue' (5 acts)	Louis Gallet and Édouard Blau	1873
31.	Opéra-comique, 'Carmen' (4 acts)	Henri Meilhac and Ludovic Halévy	1873–4

II. Orches-

32.	Overture in A minor–major	...	*c.* 1855
33.	Symphony in C major	...	1855
34.	Symphony	...	1859
35.	Scherzo and 'Marche funèbre' (F minor)	...	1860–1

[1] *See* Nos. 38, 88, 100, 102,

—continued

First known Performance	*First Publication*	*Remarks*
12 July 1955 (excerpts)	None [1]	* (Incomplete)
None	None	Unfinished; ? not begun
5 Apr 1885	Choudens 1885 (vocal score only)	Completion of F. Halévy's opera
None	None	Projected
None	None	Removed from canon. See p. viii
None	None	Projected; perhaps not begun
None	None	Projected
None	None	* (Sketches)
None	None	* (Sketches)
22 May 1872	Choudens 1872 (vocal score) 1892 (full score)	†
1 Oct. 1872	Choudens 1872 (vocal score; full score later)	* See also No. 40
16 Nov. 1872	None	Probably destroyed. *See* p. 71
None	None	* (Unfinished)
3 Mar. 1875	Choudens 1875 (vocal score) ? 1877 (full score)	* 1875 vocal score contains passages omitted in all later scores before 1964

TRAL

26 Oct. 1938	Universal 1972	*
26 Feb. 1935	Universal 1935	*
None	None	Two versions begun; destroyed Dec. 1859
Nov. 1861	None	* (Marche) Scherzo used in No. 37

104, 105, 108, 131, 132

II. Orchestral

	Title	*Author of Words*	*Date of Composition*
36.	Overture, 'La Chasse d'Ossian'	...	1861
37.	Symphony in C major ('Roma')	...	1860–8, revised 1871
38.	'Marche funèbre' (B minor)	...	1868–9
39.	Petite Suite	...	1871
40.	Suite, 'L'Arlésienne'	...	1872
41.	Overture, 'Patrie'	...	1873

III. Key-

42.	Four Preludes (C major, A minor, G major, E minor)	...	Very early
43.	'Valse' in C major	...	Very early
44.	'Thème brillant' in C major	...	Very early
45.	First 'Caprice original' in C sharp minor	...	*c.* 1851
46.	'Romance sans paroles' in C major	...	Very early
47.	Second 'Caprice original' in C major	...	*c.* 1851
48.	'Grande Valse de concert' in E flat major	...	1854
49.	'Nocturne' in F major	...	1854
50.	'Trois Esquisses musicales' (originally for harmonium)	...	? 1858
51.	'Chasse fantastique'	...	? 1865
52.	'Chants du Rhin' (6 pieces)	Based on poems by Méry	1865
53.	'Marine'	...	? 1868
54.	'Variations chromatiques de concert'	...	1868

—continued

First known Performance	*First Publication*	*Remarks*
? None	None	Lost
28 Feb. 1869	Choudens 1880	Includes Scherzo from No. 35, also No. 89
12 Dec. 1880	Choudens 1881	Originally Prelude to No. 18
2 Mar. 1873	Durand 1882	* Arrangement of 5 pieces from No. 56. One more ('Les Quatre Coins') unpublished
10 Nov. 1872	Choudens ? 1876	Arrangement of 4 pieces from No. 28. Second Suite by Guiraud (3 pieces from No. 28, 1 from No. 15)
15 Feb. 1874	Choudens 1874	

BOARD

...	None	*
...	None	*
...	None	*
27 Oct. 1938	None	* † (slightly revised)
...	None	*
...	None	* † (slightly revised)
27 Oct. 1938	None	*
27 Oct. 1938	None	*
...	Regnier-Canaux 1858	Shortened piano arrangement by I. Philipp (1905)
...	Heugel 1865	
...	Heugel 1865	Orch. Maurice le Boucher
...	Hartmann 1868	* Originally entitled 'La Chanson du matelot, souvenir d'Ischia'
...	Hartmann 1868	* Orch. Felix Weingartner (1933)

III. Key-board

	Title	Author of Words	Date of Composition
55.	'Nocturne' in D major	...	1868
56.	'Jeux d'enfants' (12 pieces for piano duet)	...	1871
57.	'Promenade au clair de lune'	Suggested by Verlaine	c. 1871
58.	'Causerie sentimentale'	? Suggested by Verlaine	c. 1871
58a.	'Troisième danse	...	c. 1871
59.	Finale of 'Roma' for 2 pianos (8 hands)	...	1871

Also a great many arrangements, including

IV. Miscellaneous

60.	Various fugues and exercises	...	1850–4
61.	Fugue in 4 parts (A major, subject by Halévy)	...	early
62.	Fugue in 4 parts (A minor, subject by Auber)	...	1854
63.	Fugue in 4 parts (F minor, subject by Auber)	...	1855
64.	Fugue in 4 parts (G major)	...	1856
65.	Fugue in 4 parts (E minor, subject by A. Thomas)	...	1857
66.	Fugue in 2 parts	...	1866
67.	Duet, bassoon and cello (C minor)	...	1874

V.

68.	'L'âme triste est pareille au doux ciel'	Lamartine	Very early

—continued

First known Performance	*First Publication*	*Remarks*	
	Hartmann 1868	*	
...	Durand 1872	* See No. 39	
18 June 1975	None	†	Nos. 3, 5 and 6 of a set of pieces perhaps all based on Verlaine's 'Fêtes galantes'
18 June 1975	None	Aut. survives	
...	None	†	
23 Dec. 1871	None	* ('Final de la Ière Symphonie')	

some of his own songs and dramatic pieces.

Instrumental Works

None	None	* With corrections and comments by F. Halévy
None	None	†
None	None	** (2 copies) 2nd Prize, 1854
None	None	* † 1st Prize, 1855
None	None	* Prix de Rome
None	None	* Prix de Rome
None	None	Written for Galabert. ? Lost
...	Musica Rara, 1970	† Test piece for Conservatoire

Songs

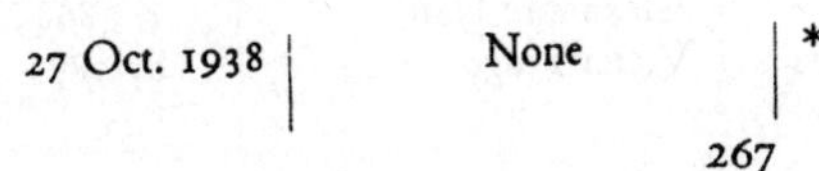

27 Oct. 1938	None	*

V. Songs

	Title	Author of Words	Date of Composition
69.	'Petite Marguerite'	Olivier Rolland	? 1854
70.	'La Rose et l'abeille'	Olivier Rolland	? 1854
70a.	'La Foi, l'Espérance et la Charité'	Rousseau de Lagrave	*c.* 1854
71.	'Vieille Chanson'	Millevoye	1865
72.	'Adieux de l'hôtesse arabe'	Victor Hugo	1866
73.	'Après l'Hiver'	Victor Hugo	1866
74.	'Douce Mer'	Lamartine	1866
75.	'Chanson d'avril'	Louis Bouilhet	? 1866
76.	'À une Fleur'	Alfred de Musset	1866
77.	'Adieux à Suzon'	Alfred de Musset	1866
78.	'Sonnet'	Ronsard	1866
79.	'Guitare'	Victor Hugo	1866
80.	'Rose d'amour'	Millevoye	1866
81.	'Le Grillon'	Lamartine	1866
82.	'Pastorale'	Regnard	1868
83.	'Rêve de la bien-aimée'	Louis de Courmont	1868
84.	'Ma vie a son secret'	Félix Arvers	1868
85.	'Berceuse'	Marceline Desbordes-Valmore	1868
86.	'La Chanson du fou'	Victor Hugo	1868
87.	'La Coccinelle'	Victor Hugo	1868
88.	'La Sirène'	Catulle Mendès	1868
89.	'Le Doute'	Paul Ferrier	by 1868
90.	'L'Esprit Saint'	?	?
91.	'Absence'	Théophile Gautier	?
92.	'Chant d'amour'	Lamartine	?
93.	'Tarantelle'	Édouard Pailleron	?
94.	'Vous ne priez pas'	Casimir Delavigne	?
95.	'Le Colibri'	Alexandre Flan	*c.* 1868
96.	Serenade, 'Oh, quand je dors'	Victor Hugo	by 1873

—continued

First known Performance	*First Publication*	*Remarks*
...	Cendrier 1854	Reissued by Choudens in 1888 as 'En Avril' and 'Rive d'amour', with new words by Armand Silvestre
...	Cendrier 1854	
...	privately *c.* 1854	
...	Choudens 1865	†
...	Choudens 1867	
...	Choudens 1867	Text combines two different poems
...	Choudens 1867	
...	Choudens 1867	
...	Heugel 1866	Published together as 'Feuilles d'album'
...	Heugel 1866	
...	Heugel 1866	
...	Heugel 1866	
...	Heugel 1866	
...	Heugel 1866	
...	Hartmann 1868	Aut. Royal Academy of Music, London
...	Hartmann 1868	Aut. Royal Academy of Music, London
23 Dec. 1871	Hartmann 1868	* Words altered by Bizet
...	Hartmann 1868	*
...	Hartmann 1868	*
...	Hartmann 1868	*† (earlier version)
...	Choudens 1886	Dramatic fragment from No. 18
...	Choudens 1886	? Dramatic fragment. Used in No. 37
...	Hartmann 1869	* Published with separate harmonium part, and later as one of the *Motets et Hymnes*
...	Choudens 1872	
...	Choudens 1872	
...	Hartmann 1869	* Originally set to Italian words
7 Mar. 1874	Choudens 1873	* Original title 'L'Âme du Purgatoire'
27 Oct. 1938	None	*
21 Feb. 1965	None	* Rejected from 'Vingt Mélodies', 1873

V. Songs

	Title	Author of Words	Date of Composition
97.	'Vœu'	Victor Hugo	c. 1868
98.	'Voyage'	Philippe Gille	?
99.	'Aubade'	Paul Ferrier	?
100.	'La Nuit'	Paul Ferrier	1868
101.	'Conte'	Paul Ferrier	?
102.	'Aimons, rêvons!'	Paul Ferrier	? 1868
103.	'La Chanson de la rose'	Jules Barbier	?
104.	'Le Gascon'	Catulle Mendès	? 1868
105.	'N'oublions pas!'	Jules Barbier	1868
106.	'Si vous aimez!'	Philippe Gille	?
107.	'Pastel'	Philippe Gille	?
108.	'L'Abandonnée'	Catulle Mendès	? 1868

Excerpts from the published dramatic

VI. Miscellaneous

109.	Vocalise for tenor in C major	...	1850
110.	Vocalise for two sopranos in F major (Barcarolle)	...	1850
111.	'Chœur d'étudiants,' male chorus and orchestra	Scribe	Early
112.	'Valse' in G major, mixed chorus and orchestra	?	1855
113.	Cantata, 'L'Ange et Tobie'	Léon Halévy	c. 1855–7
114.	Cantata, 'Héloïse de Montfort'	Émile Deschamps	c. 1855–7
115.	Cantata, 'Le Chevalier enchanté'	Marquis de Pastoret	c. 1855–7
116.	Cantata, 'Herminie'	Vinaty	c. 1855–7
117.	Cantata, 'Le Retour de Virginie'	Rollet	c. 1855–7
118.	Cantata, 'David'	Gaston d'Albano	1856
119.	'Le Golfe de Baïa', soprano or tenor, chorus and piano	Lamartine	1856

—Continued

First known Performance	*First Publication*	*Remarks*	
27 Oct. 1938	None	*	
...	Choudens 1886	Used in No. 130	Most, if not all, of these are excerpts from unfinished dramatic works fitted with fresh words after Bizet's death
...	Choudens 1886		
...	Choudens 1886	Used in No. 132 From No. 18	
...	Choudens 1886		
...	Choudens 1886	Used in No. 131 ? From No. 18	
...	Choudens 1886		
...	Choudens 1886	? From No. 18	
...	Choudens 1886	From No. 18	
...	Choudens 1886		
...	Choudens 1886		
...	Choudens 1886	? From No. 18	

works are excluded from the above list.

VOCAL WORKS

...	None	*
...	None	*
...	None	*
...	None	*
None	None	* Unfinished
None	None	* Unfinished
None	None	* Unfinished
None	None	* Unfinished
None	None	*
...	None	2nd Prix de Rome. ? Lost
...	Choudens 1880	* Prix de Rome. Used in No. 12. A version for piano solo also exists

VI. Miscellaneous

	Title	*Author of Words*	*Date of Composition*
120.	'La Chanson du rouet', solo voice, chorus and piano	Leconte de Lisle	1857
121.	Cantata, 'Clovis et Clotilde'	Amédée Burion	1857
122.	'Te Deum,' soli, chorus and orchestra	...	1858
123.	Ode Symphony, 'Ulysse et Circé'	Based on Homer	1859
124.	Ode Symphony, 'Vasco de Game'	Louis Delâtre, altered by Bizet	1859–60
125.	Cantata, 'Carmen saeculare'	Horace	1860
126.	'Saint-Jean de Pathmos,' part-song for male voices	Victor Hugo	? 1866
127.	'Chants des Pyrénées'	Traditional	? 1867
128.	Cantata, 'Les Noces de Prométhée'	Romain Cornut the younger	1867
129.	Hymn	?	1867
130.	Duo, 'Le Retour'	Jules Barbier	?
131.	Duo, 'Rêvons'	Jules Barbier	? 1868
132.	Duettino, 'Les Nymphes des bois'	Jules Barbier	1868
133.	Cantique, 'La Mort s'avance', mixed chorus and orchestra	Abbé Pellegrin	1869
134.	'Ave Maria'	Charles Grandmougin	?
135.	Duo, 'La Fuite'	Théophile Gautier	1870
136.	Dramatic Legend, 'Geneviève de Paris'	Louis Gallet	1875

Except 'L'Esprit Saint' (see no. 90) the four *Motets et Hymnes* are arrangements

For a list of the principal works by other composers transcribed

VOCAL WORKS—*continued*

First known Performance	*First Publication*	*Remarks*
...	Choudens 1880	* Prix de Rome. Published with new words by Édouard Blau
3 Oct. 1857	None	* 1st Prix de Rome
Mar. 1970	Simrock 1971	*
None	None	Projected; probably not begun
8 Feb. 1863	Choudens 1880	*
None	None	Unfinished; ? destroyed
...	Choudens 1874	
	Flaxland 1867	Accompaniments to 6 'Mélodies Populaires'
None	None	Written for competition. Lost
None	None	Written for competition. Lost
...	Choudens 1887	See No. 98 } Posthumous dramatic fragments fitted with fresh words
...	Choudens 1887	See No. 102
		? From No. 18
...	Choudens 1887	See No. 100
		From No. 18
...	None (parts engraved by Hartmann)	*
...	None	? Lost
...	Choudens 1872	Autograph in Library of Congress, Washington
None	None	Projected; libretto survives (*)

not made by Bizet.

by Bizet, *see* Mina Curtiss, *Bizet and his World*, pp. 468–9.

APPENDIX C

PERSONALIA

About, Edmond François Valentin (1828–85), French writer, born in Lorraine. Studied archaeology in Athens. Wrote novels and political pamphlets, one of which cost him a week's imprisonment from the Germans after the war of 1870.

Adam, Adolphe Charles (1803–56), French composer. Prolific writer of ballet and *opéra-comique*. Professor of composition at the Paris Conservatoire from 1849.

Aubryet, Xavier (1827–?), minor French music critic. Published a volume *Les Jugements nouveaux* in 1860.

Banville, Théodore de (1823–91), French lyric poet. Also a literary and musical critic.

Bellaigue, Camille (1858–1930), French music critic. A prolific author of musical biographies, including an early Life of Verdi. Attached to the *Revue des Deux Mondes* from 1885.

Benoist, François (1791–1878), French organist and composer, professor of organ at the Paris Conservatoire 1819–72. Prix de Rome 1815; composed operas, ballets and a mass.

Benoît, Camille (1851–1923), French composer, pupil of César Franck. Curator of the Louvre museum from 1895.

Béranger, Pierre Jean de (1780–1857), French poet. Wrote many popular songs, the satirical tone of which brought him government persecution and imprisonment.

Blaze de Bury, Baron Henri (1813–88), French writer on music, mostly under the name of F. de Lagenevais. Succeeded Scudo as music critic of of the *Revue des Deux Mondes* 1864.

Bouhy, Jacques Joseph André (1848–1929), Belgian baritone singer. Studied at Liège and Paris, where he first appeared at the Opéra in 1872. The first Escamillo in *Carmen*. Director of the New York Conservatoire 1885–9.

Bülow, Hans Guido von (1830–94), German pianist and conductor, first husband of Cosima Wagner (*née* Liszt).

Calvé, Emma (real name *Rose Emma Calvet*) (1858–1942), French soprano singer. One of the most successful interpreters of Carmen.

Carafa. See note, p. 18.

Carvalho, Léon. See note, p. 48.

Carvalho, Marie Caroline Félix (*née Miolan*) (1827–95), French soprano singer. Married the impresario Léon Carvalho in 1853. Created the heroines in most of Gounod's successful operas.

Castro, Guilhem da (1569–1631), Spanish dramatist. Corneille owed much to his play on the Cid.

Clapisson, Antoine Louis (1808–66), French composer and violinist. A successful composer of *opéra-comique*, he was elected to the Academy in preference to Berlioz.

Clément, Félix (1822–85), French composer and writer on music. Compiler of compendious encyclopaedias on church music and opera.

Colonne, Édouard (really *Judas*) (1838–1910), French conductor and violinist. Founder of Concerts Colonne 1873. The first to popularize Berlioz.

Combarieu, Jules Léon Jean (1859–1916), French musicologist. Founder of the *Revue Musicale* and author of an important history of music.

Comettant, Jean Pierre Oscar (1819–98), French pianist and music critic, for many years on the staff of *Le Siècle*.

Daudet, Alphonse (1840–97), French novelist and dramatist, renowned for his studies of Provençal peasant life.

David, Félicien César (1810–76), French composer. Travelled in the east and introduced mild orientalism to western music in his symphonic ode *Le Désert* (1844).

Delaborde, Élie Miriam (1839–1913), French pianist and composer, pupil of Alkan and Moscheles, professor at the Paris Conservatoire 1873. The war of 1870 drove him to London with his hundred and twenty-one parrots and cockatoos.

Delmas, Marc Marie Jean Baptiste (1885–1931), French composer and writer on music. Prix de Rome 1919.

Delsarte, François Alexandre Nicolas Chéri. See p. 2.

Dubois, François Clément Théodore (1837–1924), French composer. Prix de Rome 1861. Organist at the Madeleine 1877, director of Paris Conservatoire 1896–1905.

Escudier, Léon (1821–81), French music critic and publisher. With his brother Marie he wrote a *Dictionnaire de Musique* (1844) and published many of Verdi's works.

Faure, Jean Baptiste (1830–1911), French baritone singer. Leading baritone at the Paris Opéra for many years from 1861.

Galli-Marié, Marie Célestine Laurence (1840–1905), French mezzo-soprano singer. First appeared at Strasbourg in 1859. The original Carmen.

García, Manuel del Popolo Vicente (1775–1832), Spanish tenor singer and composer. Author of many rudimentary operas based on folksong, in which he himself appeared. His three children were all famous singers.

Gasperini, A. de (*c.* 1825–68), French music critic. Wrote for *Nation, Liberté* and *Figaro* (1861–7).

Gauthier-Villars, Henry (1859–1931), French author and music critic, advocate of Wagner in France. Published many of his books under the pseudonym Willy. Put his name to E. Vuillermoz's life of Bizet.

Gautier, Théophile (1811–72), French poet and novelist. For a time dramatic and musical critic of *La Presse* and *Le Moniteur Universel.*

Gille, Philippe Émile François, French writer (1830–1901). Literary critic of *Le Figaro.* Author of libretti for Offenbach, Delibes, Massenet and others.

Gouvy, Louis Théodore (1819–98), German-French composer. Of French parentage and education, he lived mostly in Germany, where he found himself more appreciated. Composer of seven symphonies.

Grisar, Albert (1808–69), Belgian composer. Abandoned a business career at Liverpool for successful light opera in Paris.

Guiraud, Ernest (1837–92), French composer, born at New Orleans. Prix de Rome, 1859. Professor of composition at the Paris Conservatoire from 1876.

Habeneck, François Antoine (1781–1849), French violinist and conductor, of German descent. Founder of Société des Concerts du Conservatoire, conductor at the Paris Opéra 1824–47. The first conductor to cultivate Beethoven in France.

Halévy (really *Lévy*), *Jacques François Fromental Élie* (1799–1862), French composer of Jewish extraction. Prix de Rome 1819. Composed many operas in various styles. Professor at the Paris Conservatoire from 1827.

Halévy, Léon (1802–83), archaeologist and dramatist, brother of the above. Wrote librettos for his brother and others.

Halévy, Ludovic (1834–1908), dramatist, son of the above. Author (in collaboration with Henry Meilhac) of many librettos for Offenbach.

Heller, Stephen (1814–88), Hungarian pianist and composer, resident in Paris from 1838.

Hérold, Louis Joseph Ferdinand (1791–1833), French composer. Prix de Rome 1812. Wrote numerous light operas (many in collaboration) and died of consumption.

Heugel, Jacques Léopold (1815–83), French music publisher and founder of the musical periodical *Le Ménestrel* (1833).

Hoffmann, Ernst Theodor Wilhelm (1776–1822), German novelist and amateur composer of operas. Changed his third name to Amadeus in homage to Mozart. The hero of Offenbach's *Contes d'Hoffmann.*

Imbert, Hugues (1842–1905), French writer on music. Attempted to popularize Brahms in France.

Appendix C—Personalia

Isouard, Niccolo (1775–1818), Maltese composer. Abandoned the study of artillery for music and wrote numerous light operas in Paris.

Istel, Edgar (1880–1948), German musicologist and composer. Wrote on various aspects of opera.

Jonas, Émile (1827–1905), French composer. Professor of solfège at the Paris Conservatoire 1847–65, bandmaster and copious composer of operettas.

Joncières, Victorin de (real name *Félix Ludger Rossignol*) (1839–1903), French composer and critic, originally a painter. Opera composer, an early French admirer of Wagner and music critic of *La Liberté* from 1871.

Jouvin, Benoît Jean Baptiste (known as *Bénédict*) (1820–?), French music critic. On staff of *Le Figaro* from 1856. Wrote books on Auber and Hérold.

Jullien, Jean Lucien Adolphe (1845–1932), French critic. A passionate champion of Wagner, Berlioz and other composers then regarded as modern. Music critic of the *Journal des Débats* for over fifty years

Lacombe, Paul (1837–1927), French composer. Correspondence pupil of Bizet.

Lamoureux, Charles (1834–99), French violinist and conductor. His Concerts Lamoureux (1881) popularized Wagner with the French public.

Landormy, Paul Charles René (1869–1943), French critic. Author of many books on history of music.

Laparra, Raoul (1876–1943), French composer and writer on music. Wrote operas in a Spanish idiom.

Lecocq, Alexandre Charles (1832–1918), French composer. A prosperous composer of operettas in the Offenbach manner.

Legouvé, Ernest (1807–1903), French dramatist. Collaborated with Scribe in *Adrienne Lecouvreur* (1849).

Litolff, Henry Charles (1818–91), Anglo-Alsatian composer mostly resident in Paris. He owned a successful music-publishing business at Brunswick.

Malherbe, Charles Théodore (1853–1911), French musicologist. Librarian at the Opéra from 1898. A famous collector of musical autographs.

Mapleson, James Henry (1830–1901), English impresario. He sang opera in Italy, managed a number of London opera-houses, called himself a colonel and published a book of chatty reminiscences (*The Mapleson Memoirs* 1888).

Maréchal, Charles Henri (1842–1924), French composer. Prix de Rome 1870. Inspector of musical education 1896. Wrote mostly for the stage.

Marmontel, Antoine François (1816–98), French pianist and teacher. Professor of piano at the Paris Conservatoire from 1848.

Massé, Félix Marie (known as *Victor*) (1822–84), French composer. Prix de Rome 1844. Professor of composition at the Paris Conservatoire from 1866. A facile composer of operas and operettas.

Mendès, Catulle (1841–1909), French poet, journalist and dramatist, author of several librettos.

Mercadante, Giuseppe Saverio Raffaele (1795–1870), Italian composer, mostly of operas and masses. Director of the Naples Conservatoire from 1840.

Mérimée, Prosper (1803–70), French novelist and author of archaeological and historical dissertations.

Méry, Joseph (1798–1865), French poet.

Mistral, Frédéri (1830–1914), Provençal poet, author of several epics in the Provençal language. Nobel prize 1904.

Mogador, Céleste (real name *Vénard*, afterwards *Comtesse Moreton de Chabrillan*) (1824–1909), French actress, circus-rider, author and courtesan. Published plays, novels, poems and memoirs.

Mottl, Felix (1856–1911), Austrian conductor and composer, worked under Wagner and (1881–1903) at Carlsruhe, where he revived many unfamiliar works.

Nilsson, Christine (1843–1921), Swedish soprano singer. Appeared first in Paris 1864, London 1867.

Paer, Ferdinando (1771–1839), Italian composer. Wrote operas for Venice, Vienna and Dresden and finally settled in Paris.

Paladilhe, Émile (1844–1926), French composer. Prix de Rome 1860.

Pasdeloup, Jules Étienne (1819–87), French conductor. Founded the Société des Jeunes Artistes du Conservatoire (1851) and the Concerts Pasdeloup (1861), at which he introduced many unfamiliar works.

Perrin, Émile César Victor (1814–85), French impresario. Successful manager at various times of the Opéra-Comique, Opéra and Théâtre Français in Paris.

Pougin, François Auguste Arthur Eugène Paroisse- (1834–1921), French musicologist. A prolific author, biographer and contributor to periodicals.

Reber, Napoléon Henri (1807–80), French composer. Professor of harmony (1851) and composition (1862) at the Paris Conservatoire.

Reyer (originally *Rey*), *Louis Ernest Étienne* (1823–1909), French composer. Wrote operas on oriental and Nibelungian subjects and succeeded Berlioz as music critic of the *Journal des Débats*.

Roqueplan (really *Rocoplan*), *Louis Victor Nestor* (1804–70), French journalist and impresario. Director of the Paris Opéra (1847–54), Opéra-Comique (1857–60) and other theatres. Dramatic critic of *Le Constitutionnel*.

Roze, Marie Hippolyte (*née Ponsin*) (1846–1926), French soprano singer. Appeared first at the Opéra-Comique in 1865. For some years a member of the Carl Rosa Company in England.

Saint-Georges, Jules Henri Vernoy, Marquis de (1801–75), French novelist and librettist. Wrote a hundred and twenty librettos for Donizetti, Auber, Adam, Halévy, etc.

Saint-Victor, Paul de (1825–81), French literary and musical critic. A formalist of the old school.

Sarasate y Navascues, Pablo Martín Melitón (1844–1908), Spanish violinist and composer, studied at Paris Conservatoire.

Sarcey, Francisque (1827–99), French journalist and dramatic critic.

Sardou, Victorien (1831–1908), French dramatist. Many of his melodramatic plays were found suitable for conversion into opera librettos.

Scribe, Eugène (1791–1861), French dramatist and librettist. A prolific manufacturer of opera and *opéra-comique* librettos, especially for the school of Meyerbeer, Halévy, Auber, etc.

Scudo, Pierre (originally *Pietro*) (1806–64), Italian critic who lived in Paris and wrote in French. After failing as a singer he took to criticism and became music critic of the *Revue des Deux Mondes*.

Séré, Octave (pseudonym of *Jean Poueigh*) (1876–1958), French critic and composer, pupil of Fauré and Lenepveu.

Soubies, Albert (1846–1918), French musicologist. Wrote many historical works, especially on opera.

Tarbé, Eugène, French critic, son of a female amateur composer. Some time music critic of *Le Figaro*. Founder and director (1869–77) of *Le Gaulois*.

Thalberg, Sigismond (1812–71), Austrian pianist and composer, natural son of a count and a baroness. Toured with great success as a *salon* virtuoso.

Tiersot, Jean Baptiste Élisée Julien (1857–1936), French musicologist and composer, pupil of Massenet and Franck. Librarian at the Paris Conservatoire from 1910 and President of Société Française de Musicologie.

Trélat, Marie (*née Molinos*) (1837–1914), French mezzo-soprano singer and singing-teacher. Her *salon* gave opportunities to many young musicians.

Vidal, François (1832–?), Provençal poet and author of a work on the tambourine and pipe (galoubet) of Provence.

Weber, Johannès (1818–1902), French critic. Secretary to Meyerbeer in Paris. Music critic of *Le Temps*, 1861–95.

Weissmann, Adolf (1873–1929), German music critic, author of many biographical studies and historical works.

Wilder, Jérôme Albert Victor (*van*) (1835–82), Belgian critic and poet. Made French translations of many great works, including *Messiah* and Wagner's later operas.

Yradier, Sebastián (1809–65), Spanish composer. Was singing-master to Empress Eugénie in Paris and lived for some years in Cuba. Wrote popular Spanish songs based on folk melodies.

Zimmerman, Pierre Joseph Guillaume (1785–1853), French pianist, teacher and composer. Professor of piano at the Paris Conservatoire from 1820. He was Gounod's father-in-law.

APPENDIX D

BIBLIOGRAPHY

(NOTE.—*Only a few of the most important periodical references are listed below. A great number of other books and periodicals have been used in the compilation of this book.*)

Bellaigue, Camille, 'Georges Bizet, sa vie et son œuvre.' (Paris, 1891.)

Berlioz, Hector, 'Les Musiciens et la musique.' (Paris, 1903.)

Berton, Pierre, 'Souvenirs de la vie de théâtre.' (Paris, 1913.)

Bizet, Georges, 'Lettres à un ami, 1865–72,' ed. Edmond Galabert. (Paris, 1909.)

—— 'Lettres. Impressions de Rome, 1857–60. La Commune, 1871,' ed. Louis Ganderax. (Paris, 1908.)

—— 'Exposition Georges Bizet au Théâtre National de l'Opéra,' illustrated catalogue. (Paris, 1938.)

—— 'Georges Bizet,' inauguration of monument. (Paris, privately, 1876.)

Brancour, René, 'La Vie et l'œuvre de Georges Bizet.' (Paris, 1913.)

Bruk, Mira, 'Bizet.' (Moscow, 1938.)

Burgess, Francis, 'Carmen.' (London, 1905.)

Chanet, Howard, 'Bizet's Suppressed Symphony', in *The Musical Quarterly*, October 1958.

Changeur, Jean-Paul, six articles on 'Ivan IV' in *La Vie Bordelaise*, 12th October–16th November 1951.

Chantavoine, Jean, 'Quelques Inédits de Georges Bizet,' in *Le Ménestrel*, 4th August–22nd September 1933.

—— 'Le Centenaire de Georges Bizet,' in *Le Ménestrel*, 21st–28th October 1938.

Charlot, André and Jean, 'À propos de la Millième de Carmen,' in *L'Art du Théâtre*, January 1905.

Chevalley, H., 'Carmen, textlich und musikalisch erläutet'. (Berlin, 1907.)

Cooper, Martin, 'Georges Bizet.' (London, 1938.)

—— 'Carmen.' (London, 1947.)

—— 'Georges Bizet,' in *The Heritage of Music*, Vol. III. (London, 1951.)

Curtiss, Mina, 'Bizet and his World.' (New York and London, 1958.)

—— 'Bizet, Offenbach and Rossini,' in *The Musical Quarterly*, July 1954.

—— 'Unpublished Letters by Georges Bizet,' in *The Musical Quarterly*, July 1950.

Dean, Winton, 'Bizet's Ivan IV,' in *Fanfare for Ernest Newman.* (London, 1955.)
—— 'Bizet's Self-Borrowings,' in *Music & Letters,* July 1960.
—— 'Carmen.' (London, 1949.)
—— 'Introduction to the Music of Bizet.' (London, 1950.)
—— 'An Unfinished Opera by Bizet,' in *Music & Letters,* October 1947.
—— 'The True Carmen?' in *The Musical Times,* November 1965.
—— 'The Corruption of *Carmen*: The Perils of Pseudo-Musicology,' in *Musical Newsletter,* October 1973.
Delmas, Marc, 'Georges Bizet.' (Paris, 1930.)
Galabert, Edmond, 'Georges Bizet. Souvenirs et Correspondance.' (Paris, 1877.)
Gallet, Louis, 'Notes d'un librettiste.' (Paris, 1891.)
Gatti, Guido M., 'Giorgio Bizet.' (Turin, 1914.)
Gaudier, Charles, 'Carmen de Bizet.' (Paris, 1922.)
Gauthier-Villars, Henry, 'Bizet.' (Paris, 1911.) In fact by Émile Vuillermoz.
Gerver, Frans, 'Georges Bizet.' (Brussels, 1945.)
Grélinger, Charles, 'Bizet.' (Paris, n.d., *c.* 1915.)
Halévy, Ludovic, 'La Millième Représentation de Carmen,' in *Le Théâtre,* January 1905.
Hühne, Fritz, 'Die Oper Carmen als ein Typus musikalischer Poetik.' (Greifswald, 1915.)
Imbert, Hugues, 'Portraits et études. Lettres inédites de Georges Bizet.' (Paris, 1894.)
—— 'Georges Bizet.' (Paris, 1899.)
—— 'Médaillons contemporains.' (Paris, 1903.)
Imsan, Dora, 'Carmen, Charakter-Entwicklung für die Bühne.' (Darmstadt, 1917.)
Istel, Edgar, 'Bizet und Carmen.' (Stuttgart, 1927.)
Jullien, Adolphe, 'Musiciens d'aujourd'hui.' (Paris, 1892.)
Kremlev, J. U., 'Georges Bizet.' (Leningrad, 1935.)
Lalo, Pierre, 'De Rameau à Ravel: portraits et souvenirs.' (Paris, 1947.)
Landormy, Paul, 'Bizet.' (Paris, 1924; reissued 1950.)
Laparra, Raoul, 'Bizet et l'Espagne.' (Paris, 1935.)
Malherbe, Henry, 'Georges Bizet.' (Paris, 1921.)
—— 'Carmen.' (Paris, 1951.)
Maréchal, Henri, 'Paris: Souvenirs d'un musicien.' (Paris, 1907.)
Marmontel, Antoine, 'Symphonistes et virtuoses.' (Paris, 1881.)
Mastrigli, Leopoldo, 'Giorgio Bizet: la sua vita e le sue opere.' (Rome, 1888.)
Moser, Françoise, 'Vie et aventures de Céleste Mogador.' (Paris, 1935.)

Muller, Monique, 'L'Œuvre pianistique originale de Georges Bizet'.(University of Neuchâtel thesis, Yverdon, 1976.)
Musica, special Bizet number, June 1912.
Nietzsche, Friedrich, 'Randglossen zu Bizets Carmen,' ed. Hugo Daffner. (Ratisbon, 1912.)
Northcott, Richard, 'Bizet and Carmen.' (London, 1916.)
Noske, Frits, 'La Mélodie française de Berlioz à Duparc.' (Paris, 1954.)
Parker, D. C., 'Georges Bizet, his Life and Works.' (London, 1926; 2nd ed., 1951.)
Pigot, Charles, 'George Bizet et son œuvre.' (Paris, 1886; 2nd ed. with additions, 1911.)
Poupet, Michel, 'Les Infidélités des *Pêcheurs de Perles*,' in *Revue de Musicologie*, 1965, no. 2.
Rabe, Julius, 'Georges Bizet.' (Stockholm, 1925.)
Revue de Musicologie, special Bizet number, November 1938.
Revue de Paris, 15th December 1899. (Gounod's correspondence with Bizet.)
Reyer, Ernest, 'Quarante ans de musique.' (Paris, 1910.)
Robert, Frédéric, 'Georges Bizet.' (Paris, 1965.)
Saint-Saëns, Camille, 'Portraits et souvenirs.' (Paris, 1900.)
Séré, Octave, 'Musiciens français d'aujourd'hui.' (Paris, 1915.)
Servières, Georges, 'Georges Bizet d'après les souvenirs de Pierre Berton,' in *Le Guide musical*, 8th–22nd March 1914.
Soubies, Albert, 'Histoire du Théâtre-Lyrique, 1851–70.' (Paris, 1899.)
Soubies, Albert, and *Malherbe, Charles*, 'Histoire de l'Opéra-Comique.' (Paris, 1892.)
Stefan-Gruenfeldt, Paul, 'Georges Bizet.' (Zürich, 1952.)
Tiersot, Julien, 'Un Demi-siècle de musique française, 1870–1917.' (Paris, 1918.)
—— 'Bizet and Spanish Music,' in *The Musical Quarterly*, October 1927.
Voss, Paul, 'Georges Bizet.' (Leipzig, 1899.)
Vuillermoz, Émile. See Gauthier-Villars.
Weissmann, Adolf, 'Bizet.' (Berlin, 1907.)
Westrup, Jack, 'Bizet's *La Jolie Fille de Perth*' in *Essays Presented to Egon Wellesz*. (Oxford, 1966.)
Wilder, Victor, obituary notice in *Le Ménestrel*, 4th–18th July 1875.

APPENDIX E

BIZET'S ARTICLE IN 'LA REVUE NATIONALE ET ÉTRANGÈRE', 3RD AUGUST 1867

No doubt you have sometimes come across people, very intelligent and enlightened people at that, who seriously maintain the following somewhat paradoxical opinion: 'In order to give a sound estimate of a work of art, the first necessity is not to be an artist oneself.' There follow, in confirmation of this strange aphorism, a string of more or less specious reasons which may be roughly summed up as follows: 'Eclecticism, from which impartiality springs, is the critical virtue above all others; an artist with a strong personality cannot be eclectic; therefore art criticism should be confined to diplomats, doctors, financiers, writers—every honest citizen in fact who can read or write, provided he is not painter nor sculptor nor architect nor musician.' This ingenious system is of course not extended beyond the realm of art; its most ardent partisans would consider it ridiculous if you suggested a sculptor to look after their children's health or a musical composer to look after their business. I agree that every educated and enlightened man of feeling has the power, and therefore the right, to praise or blame any artistic production whatever; but that the creative artist, continually busy both with the highest ideas and the specialities of his art, should not be allowed to judge the work of his peers, under whatever pretext of propriety or good fellowship, seems to me completely illogical and supremely unjust. Holding this conviction, and following the example of Berlioz and Reyer, I have, though myself a composer, accepted the post of musical critic to the *Revue Nationale*, which has kindly been entrusted to my inexperience and goodwill.

Being a very modest amateur in all that concerns literature, I have never till today taken up the pen except to converse with my friends. This is my first 'copy', my journalistic début. A timid and blushing schoolgirl in her white ballroom dress is less nervous at her first waltz than I am at the prospect of seeing myself printed alive. I come therefore bravely to ask the indulgence of the public—that public, kindly and terrible by turns, that is so severe on the hoarseness of Monsieur X, so indulgent towards the huskiness of Mademoiselle Z. So you realize, my dear reader, that you will find in my column not the powerful imagery of Paul de Saint-Victor, nor the sparkling wit of Nestor Roqueplan, nor the enchanting style of Théophile Gautier, nor the formal elegance and conciseness of B. Jouvin, nor the congenial ardour of Gasperini, nor the quick sensitivity of Xavier Aubryet, nor the caustic vigour of Ernest Reyer, nor . . . But some ill-natured fellow interrupts me and cries: 'Then what *shall* we find, you humbug?' You will find, sir, not the talents of the masters I have just mentioned, but two of their most essential qualities with which I hope you will be satisfied: (i) a profound study of the art of music and all that appertains to it, (ii) a good faith which neither my friendships nor my enmities will be able to weaken. I will tell the truth, nothing but the truth, and so far as possible the whole truth. I belong to no clique, and I have no comrades; I have only friends, and they will cease to be my friends the day they no longer respect my freedom of judgment and complete independence. Confining myself to the examination of purely artistic matters, I shall study the works themselves without bothering about the labels they bear. Respect and justice for all, that is my slogan. Neither incense nor insults, that is my line of conduct.

Since I have begun a profession of faith, I will go on and plunge straight into my subject. For some years now the cult of system has made disturbing progress in art and art criticism. From it springs that barren warfare, those arid discussions which bewilder, sap and consume the boldest, strongest and most fertile movements. From it also come those divisions, subdivisions, classifications, definitions, sometimes ambiguous and often quite wrong, but always valueless and dangerous. Quibbling takes the place of progress, wrangling supersedes creation. Composers are growing rare, while parties and sects multiply without limit. Art is reduced to abject poverty, while technology flourishes in abundance. Judge of it yourselves: we have French music, German music, Italian music, and by way of accessory Russian music, Hungarian music, Polish music and so on, without counting Arab music, Japanese music and Tunisian music, all three much in favour since the opening of the Universal Exhibition. We have also the music of the future, the music of the present and the music of the past; then there is philosophical and ideological music, recently discovered by a very talented journalist, to whom in passing I am happy to express my high esteem and lively sympathy. We have, too, melodic music, harmonic music, learned music (the most dangerous of all) and finally a state-patented brand of cannon music.[1] But I forget: tomorrow we shall have needle music and screw music, force-pump music and double force-pump music—this last above all! What balder-

[1] An allusion to Rossini's *Hymne à Napoléon III et à son vaillant peuple,* performed 1st July 1867, in which the composer asked for cannon fire—and much else.

dash it all is! For me there are only two kinds of music—good and bad. Béranger defined art like this: 'Art is art, and that's all there is to it.' For those who have ears to hear, these few words contain a far more useful lesson than the weightiest tomes on aesthetics. Must we run down Molière in order to love Shakespeare? Is not genius of all countries and all times? Are not the tragedies of Aeschylus more 'of the future' than those of Racine? Beauty does not grow old. Truth does not die. A poet, painter or musician devotes the utmost of his brain and soul to the conception and execution of a work; he thinks, doubts, grows enthusiastic, despairs, rejoices and suffers in turn; and when, more anxious and afraid than a criminal, he comes to us and says 'Look, and judge', instead of letting ourselves be moved we ask him for his passport, we ask ourselves about his opinions, his relations and his artistic antecedents. That is not the business of criticism; it is police work. The artist has neither name nor nationality. He is inspired or he is not; he has genius or talent or he has not. If he has, we must adopt him, cherish him, acclaim him; if he has not, we must respect him, condole with him—and forget him. Mention Rossini, Auber, Gounod, Wagner, Berlioz, Félicien David, Pitanchu—whoever you like. Make me laugh or cry; show me love, hate, fanaticism, crime; charm me, dazzle me, carry me away: I shall never do you the stupid injustice of classifying and labelling you like an insect in a show-case. Let us be unaffected and genuine, not demanding from a great artist the qualities he lacks, but learning to appreciate those he possesses. When a passionate, violent, even brutal personality like Verdi endows our art with a work that is vigorously alive and compounded of gold, mud, blood and gall, do not let us go up to him and say coldly: 'But my dear sir, this lacks taste, it is not gentlemanly.' *Gentlemanly!* Are Michelangelo, Dante, Homer, Shakespeare, Beethoven, Cervantes and Rabelais *gentlemanly*? Must genius be dressed up with rice-powder and almond icing? Let us rather order our zouaves to storm the battlements in white ties and silk breeches! Pardon my anger. But if you knew all I have read and heard in the last five or six years, all the grief and misery I have shared! Believe me, prejudiced criticism is a cruel, terrible, mortal weapon. I was the pupil and friend of Halévy; more than once I had his confidences on this subject. Neither his high position nor his incontestable reputation could console him for the unjust and odious attacks of which he was the victim. I do not want to doubt the good faith of Monsieur X. I believe he was blinded and led astray by passion and prejudice, but I could never forgive him the extreme pain he caused to the famous and revered master whose memory I cherish. If the bitter critic wants to learn the art of being at the same time severe and polite, friendly and sincere, let him study the articles of Messieurs Tarbé des Sablons and Gaston de Saint-Valry. I recommend these models of courtesy and good taste; these gentlemen at least know the respect due from every critic to conscientious and sincere workers. But I fear my advice is too good to be listened to.

One further word. I have a horror of pedantry and false erudition. Certain critics of the third and fourth rank use and abuse a so-called technical jargon which is as unintelligible to themselves as to the public. I shall take care to avoid this absurd error. You will find here no information about octaves, fifths, tritones, false fifths, dissonances, consonances, preparations, resolutions, suspensions, inversions, cadences broken, interrupted or avoided, canons in cancrizans or other refinements. I will refer those who love this pleasing language to the learned articles of Monsieur de L——,[1] where they will learn, among other matters of earth-shaking interest, that Nicolo wrote *Les Rendezvous bourgeois* in non-invertible counterpoint; that we must listen to Mendelssohn's scoring with the most scrupulous attention, the composer of *A Midsummer Night's Dream* having treated the second bassoon part as melodically as that of the first violin. They will also discover there an admirable dissertation on Meyerbeer's celebrated unison, including a most curious parallel between the round from *Les Porcherons* and the introduction to the fifth act of *L'Africaine*; the minor tenth is there treated as a major tenth with charming confidence and adorable candour. Anxious to share his enlightenment not only with the public but also with composers (thus incidentally showing a fine upright character), Monsieur de L. is prodigal of advice as novel as it is ingenious on the use of brass instruments in general and the trombones in particular. I do not dare quote from memory, being afraid of spoiling certain felicities of style, but I strongly urge the reader to be assiduous in following Monsieur de L.'s courses. They are edifying, instructive—and fun.

The musical programme, so slow-moving in ordinary times, has been brought to a complete standstill by that millionaire-fairy known as the Universal Exhibition. The cashiers of our lyric theatres are asking for help: composers without work, please note! *Don Carlos* and *L'Africaine* at the Opéra; *Mignon* and *L'Étoile du Nord* at the Opéra-Comique; *Roméo et Juliette* and *Faust* at the Théâtre-Lyrique; *L'Oca del Cairo* at the Fantaisies-Parisiennes; *La Grande Duchesse de Gérolstein* at the Variétés—such is the musical balance-sheet at present. Meyerbeer, Mozart, Gounod, Ambroise Thomas, Verdi, Offenbach: two of them dead, two French and two

---

[1] Probably Achille de Lauzières, Marquis de Thémines, music critic of *La Patrie* and an unsuccessful composer. He was one of those most scandalized by *Carmen* in 1875.

foreigners—these are the lucky ones today. All things considered, the choice is excellent, and the art of music is worthily represented. Let us give our approval and applause.

[There follows a catalogue of stage works in production or preparation, including Bizet's own *Jolie Fille de Perth*. The announcement of a probable production of *Lohengrin* at the Théâtre-Lyrique is accompanied by three exclamation marks, and Bizet notes: 'M. de Leuven has at last commissioned a one-act piece from Monsieur Conte, winner of the Grand Prix de Rome in 1855! This date has a dreary eloquence!']

Before all these works are admitted to the honour of performance, there will be a deal of impatience, disappointment and despair. I tell you in all truth, composers are the pariahs and the martyrs of modern society. Like the gladiators of old, they cry as they fall: *Salve, popule! te morituri salutant!* [*sic*]. Music! What a splendid art, but a dreary profession! Still, let us wait in patience, and above all let us hope!

APPENDIX F

THE CULT OF THE MASTERS IN FRANCE

I HAVE borrowed this title from Jean Chantavoine (1877–1952), the one French musicologist who has bestowed more than a casual glance on Bizet. He applied it ironically, in a late article,[1] to the complete lack of interest in Bizet's unpublished works displayed by publishers, conductors, radio stations and musicians of every kind. In fact the position is worse than Chantavoine supposed, since even the published operas (except *Djamileh* and, since 1975, *Les Pêcheurs de perles*) are available only in texts so corrupt that they grievously misrepresent the composer. All the printed full scores and current vocal scores include—alongside many other errors, and without a word of explanation—music that has no connection with Bizet.

After her husband's death Geneviève Bizet devoted her life to her *salon* and her health. She seems to have attached no importance to his autographs (apart from *Carmen* and *L'Arlésienne*) and gave many of them away as souvenirs. Nor did she worry how his works were performed. In 1919 Saint-Saëns protested energetically and in vain to her and Straus, her second husband, against the defilement of *Carmen* by a 'useless scandalous ballet'. In his opinion the firm of Choudens were responsible for this 'hideous blemish', as they were for countless other sins against Bizet's memory. In the twelve years after his death they issued a number of works for the first time—*Vasco de Gama*, *Noé*, *Roma*, the mistitled *Marche funèbre*, a volume of songs, and various small vocal pieces—and later added *Don Procopio* and eventually *Ivan IV*. They also printed full scores of the principal operas. In nearly every publication the text has been grossly tampered with; this can often be demonstrated even where the autograph has disappeared, as is the case with most of the first group above.

The grimmest fate befell the finest work, the autograph full score of *La Coupe du Roi de Thulé*. Bizet used material from this in *Grisélidis*, *Djamileh* and *Carmen*, but does not seem to have mutilated it. After his death many sections were removed, arranged for voice and piano, supplied with new and often inappropriate words, and published either separately or in the so-called *Seize Mélodies* without any indication of their origin. Choudens or the arranger (probably Guiraud) never returned the autographs, which have vanished. The condition of the surviving fragments suggests that further pages were at some time removed, destroyed or simply mislaid.

---

[1] *La Vie Musicale*, Dec. 1951/Jan. 1952.

Appendix F—The Cult of the Masters in France

Geneviève Bizet bequeathed the autographs of *Carmen* and *L'Arlésienne* to the Paris Conservatoire. Many further Bizet autographs arrived there by various routes, from Charles Malherbe, Camille Bellaigue and Reynaldo Hahn among others. After the death of Émile Straus in 1929 his nephew and heir René Sibilat offered the Conservatoire all the manuscript music that seemed worth preserving. Chantavoine and Henri Rabaud visited his house and removed a substantial pile in a taxi. In 1933 Chantavoine described many of the Conservatoire autographs, with quotations, in an interesting series of articles in *Le Ménestrel.* His attempts to interest a French conductor or publisher in the Symphony were fruitless; none of them would look at it. The French radio turned an equally deaf ear to *Ivan IV.*

When, about 1950, Mina Curtiss acquired the surviving papers of Bizet and Halévy from Sibilat's widow, a further batch of autographs turned up. These included two early fugues, the sketches for *Grisélidis,* two more fragments from *La Coupe du Roi de Thulé,* and Bizet's arrangements of *Les Quatre Coins* for orchestra and the finale of *Roma* for two pianos (eight hands), besides manuscript librettos of *Geneviève de Paris* and Act III of *La Jolie Fille de Perth,* both annotated by the composer, and some corrected proofs of the 1875 vocal score of *Carmen.* Mrs Curtiss subsequently presented these, together with the rest of the papers, to the Bibliothèque Nationale.

There are three printed scores of *Don Procopio,* a vocal score published in 1905 before performance and a full score (not on general sale) and a second vocal score issued after the Monte Carlo production in the following year. All three are seriously misleading; none distinguishes the genuine Bizet from the fake, of which there is a great deal, including the *entr'acte* and the recitatives. The second and third scores include two airs for Don Procopio based on *Le Gascon* and *Aubade* from *Seize Mélodies.* The arrangement is very clumsy, the words being quite unsuited to the music, which is interrupted and watered down by patches of feeble recitative. According to Vuillermoz both pieces were composed for *Clarissa Harlowe*; he gives no authority, and no airs from this opera are known to survive. In his additional numbers Charles Malherbe added two cornets, side-drum, bass drum, triangle and cymbals to Bizet's sufficiently ample orchestra.

The autograph score of *Ivan IV,* with the orchestration of the last act incomplete, reached the Conservatoire from Sibilat in 1929. It was described in detail by Chantavoine in 1933 and shown at the Bizet Centenary Exhibition at the Opéra in 1938. During the war a private concert performance with piano accompaniment took place at the Théâtre des Capucines. The Germans then microfilmed the manuscript, supplied a new libretto called *König Turpin* with the action transferred to the sixth-century Merovingian court, and planned a production at Dresden. The end of the war put a stop to this, and the first performance took place at Mühringen Castle near Tübingen in 1946 under the title *Ivan le Terrible*.

The prospect of a publication by Schott of Mainz at last roused Choudens to the existence of the opera. A legal action followed, as a result of which the German score was suppressed, the opera was produced at Bordeaux on 12th October 1951 in a version 'revised' by Henri Busser, and a vocal score published by Choudens. In this score the opera has been reduced from five acts to four (by running Bizet's first two acts into one), heavily cut, and altered in many details, verbal and musical. It includes several episodes (the *Prélude dramatique* printed in the appendix, the love duet for Marie and Ivan on pages 224–8, adapted from the song *Rêve de la bien-aimée*, the recall of this on pages 333–4, and the first seventeen bars on page 320) and one character (Sophia) that do not occur in Bizet's opera at all. Busser's preface says not a word about any of this and gives an account of the opera's history that is inaccurate in almost every verifiable particular.

The textual history of *Les Pêcheurs de perles* is no more edifying. There are at least three widely different Choudens vocal scores, none of which agrees with the full score, and more than one version of the libretto. Further refinements have been added in revivals at the Opéra-Comique and Sadler's Wells and doubtless elsewhere. Yet the only authentic edition, the 1863 vocal score (the autograph has disappeared), remained neglected until the re-issue of 1975. The most radical changes concern the last scene, which has suffered repeated and wholesale upheavals involving words, music and action. It was perhaps not satisfactory as Bizet left it; other hands have made it impossible.

In 1863 the opera ended with the theme of the duet 'Au fond du temple saint' sung by the lovers in the distance out at sea (not to the words in the current score), and Zurga survived. In the revivals of 1886 and 1889, perpetuated in the second vocal score (probably 1885), the whole scene was rewritten to produce a grand Meyerbeerian holocaust, Zurga being burned on the pyre prepared for Leila and Nadir. This involved the repetition of the chorus 'Dès que le soleil' with Nadir's farewell to Leila transferred bodily to Zurga (it is cut altogether in later scores); and the opera ended not with the duet theme but with this chorus—as it still does in modern editions of the libretto. It was for this version that the lamentable trio 'O lumière sainte', which holds up the action at the most unsuitable moment, was composed by Godard. In Bizet's score these words are sung as a duet by Leila and Nadir before Nourabad's denunciation and are therefore dramatically more defensible. The music, based on one of the weaker movements in *Ivan IV*, was translated into a *Regina Coeli* in which Bizet had no hand. Adolphe Jullien reviewed the Godard version in April 1889 with characteristic acerbity, and failed to notice any difference from what he had heard in 1863.

The current vocal score, said to date from the 1893 Opéra-Comique revival, abolishes the repeat of the chorus and restores Bizet's end, but places the lovers uncomfortably upon a rock on stage. It retains Godard's trio and further tinkers with the words and the story. Zurga is now stabbed in the back by an Indian. In the full score this service is performed by Nourabad, who snatches a dagger from one of the chiefs. At the Opéra-Comique Zurga commits suicide. Sadler's Wells in 1954 contrived both to burn Zurga and to end with the duet, an unsatisfactory compromise. Not one of these versions is an improvement on 1863. The Welsh National Opera demonstrated this beyond doubt in 1973 by reverting to Bizet's last act with the missing portions orchestrated by Arthur Hammond. Several other passages in Bizet's score—some of them admittedly very poor, like the original F major second half of 'Au fond du temple saint'—have been suppressed or altered in all the posthumous scores except that of 1975.

The text of *La Jolie Fille de Perth*, too, has undergone a species of creeping corruption. Only the 1868 vocal score has Bizet's authority and his recitatives. Sir Jack Westrup[1] described many but not all of the subsequent ramifications. The first puzzle concerns Mab's air 'Catherine est coquette', which is in the 1868 vocal score but neither the autograph nor the first printed libretto. Westrup's suggestion that the vocal score was engraved from Bizet's draft and the air subsequently removed before performance is invalidated by the fact that Bizet always composed directly into full score, arranging the vocal score (or delegating its arrangement) later. Moreover there are clear signs that the autograph has been patched at this point; most of the linking recitative that replaced the air is written on an inserted page. Whether the air was actually sung we cannot be certain.[2] Reyer mentioned it in his review of the opera, but he could have read it in the vocal score.

In 1883 the opera was produced at Weimar and Vienna, and in 1885 at Parma. Early in the former year Choudens brought out a vocal score with German and Italian text only, but a large number of musical and verbal cuts and other changes, including new recitatives in Acts I and III by Antony Choudens. The chorus of the Watch (one of the finest things in the

---

[1] 'Bizet's *La Jolie Fille de Perth*' in *Essays presented to Egon Wellesz* (Oxford, 1966).

[2] It was scored by Ivor Keys and included in his revival at Birmingham in May 1970.

opera) and three pieces in Act III, the opening chorus with its two subsequent repetitions (though the material was still heard in the orchestra at the rise of the curtain), the Duke's cavatina and an ensemble in B major near the beginning of the finale, vanished completely. Catherine's air 'Vive l'hiver' lost its quartet at the reprise; Glover's tipsy *chanson* in the first finale was reduced to an unaccompanied fragment of eight bars mostly sung offstage; eighteen bars with chorus parts disappeared at Mab's entry in Act II, and there were many cuts in the last scene, including the important recitative (fifteen bars) in which Mab conceives her plan to save Catherine. The St Valentine chorus was put up a semitone to A major, and the passage after it (but not that before it) adjusted accordingly. The initial chord of the foreshortened Act III finale was altered from Bizet's *piano* to *fortissimo*. A few of the shorter cuts are marked in the autograph, which seems to have been used as the conducting score in 1867–8, and may date from the original run. Others are singularly unimaginative; one of their objects was evidently to reduce the element of comedy.

In 1886 the Opéra-Comique announced a revival for the following season. This did not take place owing to the destruction of the theatre; but a libretto printed in 1888 (Calmann-Lévy) was almost certainly prepared for the occasion. It transformed the work into a traditional *opéra-comique* by substituting new spoken dialogue for the 1883 recitatives. These were not Bizet's, but they had incorporated some of his music. Their removal involved the total disappearance of Glover's motive (its single entry in an ensemble, the first finale, had gone in 1883) and the loss of one very effective return of the Duke's love theme. Most of the 1883 cuts were confirmed. The next vocal score, probably associated with the 1890 revival, restored the Choudens (not the Bizet) recitatives, but printed them in an appendix. Its most important new change was the replacement of Catherine's 'Vive l'hiver' by a 'rêverie' based on the song *Rêve de la bien-aimée*, which is certainly no improvement. The published full score, a hashed job photographed from a copyist's manuscript, is based on this version (hence its omission of the chorus of the Watch), though the St Valentine chorus is back in A flat. The orchestration of the 'rêverie' cannot be Bizet's.

The current (fourth) vocal score reduces a truncated torso to mindless incoherence. Besides restoring Antony Choudens's recitatives to the main text and miscalling the work an *opéra-comique*, it rewrites the libretto wholesale (rejecting many words written by Bizet, which are quite as good as the replacements) and bungles the stage directions so as to produce gross absurdities, for example at the Duke's first entry and during the seduction scene. The excision of an important minor character, the workman who rallies Smith on not attending the carnival in the finale of Act II and summons him to the duel in Act IV, spoils both those scenes and involves clumsy musical patching in the latter. Two trumpet signals are inserted to call Smith to the duel, Glover comes in to remove the fainting Catherine, and the two scenes of this act—one in the mountains, the other in the main square of Perth—are conflated into one. Guiraud's *entr'acte* is inserted before Act III, undermining the impact of the minuet in its proper place, and the design of Smith's serenade is wrecked. It appears in its *salon* form of two identical stanzas (it was published thus as a separate piece in 1868), with the clarinet cadenza (as Smith thinks he sees Catherine at her window) and the delicious F major section, the Aubade of the Beecham suite, both thrown out. This of course kills the return of the cadenza in the last scene, when Catherine does reply to the serenade. Three previous cuts, 'Vive l'hiver', the chorus of the Watch and the Duke's Act III cavatina, are restored, the first two in mutilated form and the third with dubbed words. The emasculation of the Watch chorus deprives it of its comic stage directions and indeed of its whole point, the collapse of the courage of Glover and his bold burgesses as soon as they hear a sound.

The 1875 vocal score of *Carmen* contains three passages (identified in Chapter XI, pages 216–19) that do not appear in the Choudens full score (ascribed on the evidence of plate number to 1877), in vocal scores of 1877, 1879 and later, or in the copy prepared for Vienna in the summer of 1875. After Bizet's death there was a partial and misguided attempt to make the autograph conform to his final wishes as expressed in the 1875 vocal score. Guiraud's recitatives were bound in, and other changes superimposed in his and other hands; most of Bizet's modifications during rehearsal had naturally been incorporated in the conducting score and parts, not in the autograph.

The Choudens full score, which contains Guiraud's recitatives and his extraneous ballet, is not an authoritative document. Some of its metronome marks are appreciably faster than those of the 1875 vocal score and are almost certainly wrong. The latter in many respects has more authority than the autograph, since the proofs were corrected by Bizet. Moreover he did make changes at this stage: his corrections on the twenty proof sheets that survive (they are not consecutive) include four altered and two inserted metronome marks. It is worth noting that Minnie Hauk, who sang Carmen constantly from early in 1878, said in her memoirs [1] that the *tempi* indicated in the full score for the *ensembles* in the second and third acts, and

[1] *Memories of a Singer* (London, 1925).

especially for the quintet, were too fast. Although she got some of her facts wrong (she thought that the score had been published before Bizet's death and that he had composed the recitatives), there may, as she suggested, have been an authentic tradition behind the slower *tempi* she received from Joseph Dupont, who coached her in the opera and conducted it at Brussels. The full score was the first to add higher (soprano) alternatives for Carmen; these are not by Bizet, who wrote the part for mezzo-soprano.

Oeser's discovery of the 1875 conducting score and orchestral parts enabled him to print fresh material (Alkor, 1964) and to establish approximate dates for the rehearsal changes; but he threw away this advantage by misinterpreting the evidence of the autograph and the 1875 vocal score. He virtually ignores the latter and the proofs; when he mentions its readings he attributes them to Guiraud. As a result hundreds of demonstrably authentic changes to words, notes, scoring, phrasing, accentuation, dynamics, tempo and metronome marks, stage directions, and occasionally to prominent themes, are consigned to limbo and many of them denounced as grave sins against the basic principles of Bizet's style and dramatic vision. Of dozens of wrong tempo marks, the most disastrous is the *Même mouvement* (i.e. *Allegro giocoso*, ♩ = 116 instead of *Moderato*, ♩ = 84) when the fate motive crashes in *fortissimo* just before the murder. The suspicion that Oeser has misunderstood both the composer and the opera is confirmed by his failure to grasp the central emotional relationships of the plot. Oeser—or perhaps Walter Felsenstein, to whose conception he pays tribute—is convinced that when in the quintet Carmen sings 'Je suis amoureuse à perdre l'esprit', she is thinking not of José, whom she has come to reward after his release from prison, but of Escamillo, whom she has just seen for the first time and coolly brushed off. To support this quaint thesis he systematically salts the stage directions with interpolations of his own: for example 'Carmen suit Escamillo longtemps des yeux' at Escamillo's first exit and 'Carmen, en extase, le suit des yeux', when he goes out in the Act III finale. When Carmen approaches José after the habanera Oeser makes him lift his eyes and stare at her, whereas in the libretto and Bizet's score 'il est toujours occupé de son épinglette'. That is the whole point; it is the refusal of José, unlike everyone else on stage, to take the slightest notice of Carmen that causes her to throw the flower and precipitate all that follows. This is made doubly clear in the words of the habanera. (Bizet composed the extended 38-bar development of the Carmen-fate motive for this scene. When he transferred it to the prelude, for obvious musical and dramatic reasons he shortened it here to 12 bars. Oeser restores it.) This *Kritische Neuausgabe nach den Quellen*, perhaps the most corrupt score of any major masterpiece published in modern times, is an arbitrary selection from almost every stage of Bizet's work; the editor adopts readings scrapped before the score was copied, others rejected later, and some that were never admitted at all, while frequently dismissing the definitive text with words of contempt and sometimes not even citing it. The third and fourth finales in particular reflect none of Bizet's versions and are full of extraneous stage directions that contradict both the libretto and the music.

APPENDIX G

BIZET'S MUSIC LIBRARY

BIZET's library of printed music, of which he kept a meticulous catalogue, now belongs to the Comtesse de Chambure. A substantial collection running to 241 different composers, it is the library of an opera composer and a pianist—though of the *salon* rather than the concert-hall. Bach's Forty-Eight and Handel's Suites and Fugues are heavily outweighed by the trivial and showy compilations of forgotten virtuosos. Most of the concertos are represented by the solo part only. Bizet had a fair amount of keyboard music by Dussek, Field, Weber, Chopin, Hummel and Moscheles, but his Liszt was confined to five full scores, including the Faust and Dante Symphonies and the Gran Missa Solennis.

He had almost the complete works of Beethoven and Schumann, a great deal of Mozart, Mendelssohn and Gounod, of Haydn only the keyboard trios and violin sonatas. There is little church music; Palestrina, Lalande and Marcello appear among older composers, Cherubini (three Masses) and Franck (*Ruth* and *Rédemption*) among the more modern. Of Schubert Bizet had forty songs and three opera overtures arranged for piano duet. There are sixty-seven full and eighty-one vocal scores of operas. The proportion of full scores is remarkably high, since few operas were published in this form in France after about 1830. The composers represented by three or more full scores are Auber, Gluck, Grétry, Lully, Méhul, Meyerbeer, Mozart (including *Idomeneo*), Rossini and Spontini. Berlioz's operas were not so published; but Bizet had the vocal scores and a full score of *L'Enfance du Christ*. He had four Wagner operas (up to *Lohengrin*) in vocal score and a full score of the *Meistersinger* overture. The most surprising feature is the total absence of Verdi—apart from an arrangement of the *Trovatore* 'Miserere' for piano, violin and organ by Bizet's enemy Jules Cohen.[1]

Bizet's books have long since been dispersed. Among the few survivors when the property came into the hands of Mrs Curtiss were a late eighteenth-century Voltaire, a collection of Wagner's librettos (1861) and presentation copies of several plays by Dumas *fils*.

---

[1] For further details see the selected list in Curtiss, Appendix IV (pp. 472–4). To this may be added fifty-one clavecin pieces by Couperin, Mendelssohn's G minor piano Concerto and a full score of Salieri's *Tarare*.

INDEX